W9-CUT-310

THE ART OF F. SCOTT FITZGERALD

SERGIO PEROSA

—

The Art
of
F. Scott
Fitzgerald

Translated by Charles Matz and the author

Ann Arbor Paperbacks
The University of Michigan Press

First edition as an Ann Arbor Paperback 1968
Copyright © by The University of Michigan 1965
All rights reserved
Published in the United States of America by
The University of Michigan Press and simultaneously
in Rexdale, Canada, by Ambassador Books Limited
United Kingdom agent: The Cresset Press
Manufactured in the United States of America

Originally published in 1961 by
Edizioni di Storia e Letteratura, Roma.

For permission to quote from writings of F. Scott Fitzgerald
grateful acknowledgment is made the following:

Charles Scribner's Sons:
The Letters of F. Scott Fitzgerald, edited by Andrew Turnbull (copyright © 1963 by Frances Scott Fitzgerald Lanahan), *Afternoon of an Author, The Beautiful and Damned,
The Great Gatsby, The Last Tycoon, Tender Is the Night,
This Side of Paradise,* and *The Stories of F. Scott Fitzgerald,* edited by Malcolm Cowley. Copyright 1920, 1922,
1925, 1933, 1934, 1941, 1951 Charles Scribner's Sons; renewal copyright 1948 Zelda Fitzgerald, 1950, 1953, ©
1961, 1962 Frances Scott Fitzgerald Lanahan. Copyright
1957 Frances Scott Fitzgerald Lanahan.

The Bodley Head Ltd.:
*All the Sad Young Men, The Beautiful and Damned,
Flappers and Philosophers, The Last Tycoon, The Great
Gatsby, Taps at Reveille, Tales of the Jazz Age, This
Side of Paradise, The Crack-up, Afternoon of an Author,
Tender Is the Night* (edited by Malcolm Cowley), *The
Letters of F. Scott Fitzgerald* (edited by Andrew Turn-
bull), *The Stories of F. Scott Fitzgerald* (edited by Malcolm
Cowley).

New Directions:
The Crack-up. Copyright 1945 by New Directions.

Harold Ober Associates Incorporated:
"The Pope at Confession," from *A Book of Princeton Verse,
II.* Princeton University Press, 1919.

to Alberta

FOREWORD TO THE ITALIAN EDITION

—not a legend but a reputation

The present study intends to examine the fiction of F. Scott Fitzgerald as a whole. Although necessary attention is given to the single novels and stories, the stress falls on the interdependent links that exist among them. Some stories, though perhaps of small artistic worth, are therefore considered because they demonstrate the continuity of motives, reveal the origins and the early elaborations of themes later developed in the novels, and offer a valuable counterpoint to the examination of the major works. Not all of them however are mere sketches or preparatory studies for the novels, and many are examined for their intrinsic value, as finished works that stand by themselves.

This study is strictly literary. The autobiographical aspect of Fitzgerald's fiction and its representative quality as related to the Jazz Age—two aspects on which there has been so much insistence until now—are therefore given second place and ignored as much as possible, so that an aesthetic evaluation of its intrinsic achievement can be attempted.

This study would not have been possible along its present lines without a Fulbright Fellowship which allowed me to study for a year the manuscript material and the works concerning Fitzgerald which are kept in a special section of the Manuscript Room of the Princeton University Library. For the few quotations for which no bibliographical reference is given, it is to this material that reference is made. For permission to consult the manuscripts and the unpublished material I am indebted to the late Harold Ober, who was Fitzgerald's literary agent for many years and then trustee of the Fitzgerald Estate. I wish also to thank Mr. Alexander Clark, who so willingly helped me in my researches while at Princeton, and Professors Willard Thorp and R. P. Blackmur, who helped me to clarify certain problems and gave me the assistance of their learning and critical perception.

Finally, I owe a debt of particular gratitude to Professors Benvenuto Cellini, Nemi D'Agostino, Carlo Izzo, and Agostino Lombardo, who were on varied and frequent occasions generous in their counsels, criticisms and valuable comments on my work. To Pro-

fessors Nemi D'Agostino and Agostino Lombardo I am also indebted, either directly or indirectly, for many ideas and suggestions
which were worked into my text and for which any precise reference
would be impossible; a general acknowledgment of their help can
do small justice to the degree of my indebtedness.

Venezia, Italy, 1961.

FOREWORD TO THE TRANSLATION

The text here given is a faithful translation of the Italian edition.
The temptation to revise it has been resisted. The recent additions
to the body of the Fitzgerald criticism have confirmed more points
than they have questioned and a thorough revision of the text would
have resulted in a different kind of book. Factual mistakes, however,
have been corrected; in two or three places some cuts have been
made (where the explanations seemed unnecessary for an American
or English reader), while elsewhere small additions have been made
to clarify certain statements. A few quotations which had been originally cut in the Italian edition for reasons of space have been reintegrated into the text; but the main argument of the book remains
as it was originally conceived and developed.

The notes have been thoroughly revised and brought up to
date. Some of them, which were specifically meant for the Italian
reader, have been obviously cut; others have been enlarged and
more have been added so as to take into account the latest critical
works on Fitzgerald. When it was possible, references have been
added to works by or on Fitzgerald which were published after
1961, and which I had formerly consulted in manuscript. The bibliography has been slightly shortened and brought up to date.

Harvard University, 1964.

Contents

A A   *Afternoon of an Author.* A Selection of Uncollected Stories and Essays, ed. by Arthur Mizener. Princeton University Library, 1957.

A S Y M   *All the Sad Young Men.* New York, Scribner's, 1926.

B D   *The Beautiful and Damned.* New York, Scribner's, 1950.

C U   *The Crack-up,* ed. by Edmund Wilson. New York, New Directions, 1945.

F., F.S.F.   Francis Scott Fitzgerald.

F P   *Flappers and Philosophers.* New York, Scribner's, 1920.

F S P   Arthur Mizener, *The Far Side of Paradise.* A Biography of F. Scott Fitzgerald. London, Eyre & Spottiswood, 1951.

L T , G G   *The Last Tycoon* and *The Great Gatsby,* ed. by Edmund Wilson. New York, Scribner's, 1951.

Letters   *The Letters of F. Scott Fitzgerald,* ed. by Andrew Turnbull. New York, Scribner's, 1963.

S E P   *The Saturday Evening Post.*

S S   *The Smart Set.*

Stories   *The Stories of F. Scott Fitzgerald,* ed. by Malcolm Cowley. New York, Scribner's, 1951.

T A R   *Taps at Reveille.* New York, Scribner's, 1935.

T J A   *Tales of the Jazz Age.* New York, Scribner's, 1922.

T S P   *This Side of Paradise.* New York, Scribner's, 1951.

T T N   *Tender Is the Night.* With the Author's Final Revisions, ed. by Malcolm Cowley. New York, Scribner's, 1956.

CHAPTER I

A Biographical Sketch

There never was a good biography
of a good novelist. There
couldn't be. He is too many
people, if he's any good.

CU, p. 177.

1

The life of F. Scott Fitzgerald was sharply divided in every sense. The years of youth, of his first maturity and his early success in the 1910's and 1920's contrast markedly with the years full of personal and public happenings that led to his premature death in 1940. These later years, full of disillusionment and suffering, though identified with human and artistic growth, were cut off at the very moment when Fitzgerald's career seemed about to bear its best fruits. But Fitzgerald's life was divided above all in a personal and human sense. It was divided between the pursuit of the artistic ideal and the continual, too frequent concessions to the taste of the moment or to the lure of easy success; it was divided between a rigorous application to the craft of fiction and the waste of precious energy in purely commercial literary activity. Fitzgerald was a victim, in so many ways, of the myth of success and money, the false gods, as Hemingway was to call them in *Green Hills of Africa*, on whose altars so many promising young writers were sacrificed. Fitzgerald was able, nevertheless, to save his better part and succeeded in reaching an awareness that his own greatness was in literary art. The tensions and sufferings of his mature period redeemed the limitless complacency of the first years and the shock of recognition bore fruit in his later writings.

Fitzgerald was born in St. Paul, Minnesota, on September 24, 1896. His father Edward worked for a small company, but counted among his forebearers a congressman at the time of Jefferson's administration. From the gentility of his Southern family Edward Fitzgerald preserved all the sensitivities and habits of a gentleman. He married Mary McQuillan, from an Irish family that had immigrated in 1850 ("straight potato-famine Irish," Fitzgerald once called them), but grown prosperous. She gave her son the eccentricity and restlessness of these antecedents, adding her own indiscriminate passion for literature as well as a rare quality of indulgence. In his parents' characters, Fitzgerald could already witness a primary division: between sensitivity and financial security, between genteel manners and practical ability. These contrasts were reflected in his own character and were to characterize motives and attitudes in his later novels. In his admiration for his father he was well aware of the impracticality; on the other hand, he realized that his mother's money had been too recently acquired to have been transformed into a certain style in living.[1] These are early warnings of later themes.

In 1898 his family moved to Buffalo, New York, where it remained, with varying fortunes—except for two years in Syracuse, from 1901 to 1903—until 1908, the year in which his father gave further proof of his ineptitude by being dismissed from his job. On an earlier visit to Maryland in 1903 Fitzgerald had become aware of ties with an aristocratic family past, but the new situation did nothing but show him the specter, later to become an obsession with him, of decadence.

Back in St. Paul, this specter haunted the youth as the family moved from one neighborhood to another, farther and farther away from the fashionable part of the city. During this time, he had entered St. Paul's Academy and had begun writing. He wrote a mystery story, played with the idea of drawing up a history of the United States, and kept a "Thoughtbook" on the characters and happenings of the city. He was unpopular in school, and yet he did publish a short story in the student paper (1909), followed by two more sketches on the Civil War, and a sports piece.[2] He had his first experience as a "playwright" putting together a short suspense drama, a comedy called *A Regular Fix,* and a western play, *The Girl from the Lazy J.*

In 1911 he went on to the Newman Academy, a good Catholic school in Hackensack, New Jersey; there he repeated the earlier mistakes: wasting time in a thousand activities, alternating between dreams of being a great athlete and of becoming a great writer.[3] Again he was unpopular because of his independence of spirit and his arrogance. He wrote two plays, *The Captured Shadow* and *The Coward,* which were given by local actors in St. Paul in the summers of 1912 and 1913. Attending a performance given by the Princeton University "Triangle Club," or perhaps, as he was to remark later, watching a football game in which the Princeton team "just lost the football championship" made him decide to continue his studies there. After failing the entrance examinations once, he was admitted in September 1913.

Entering Princeton meant leaving the Middle West, which was closed and conservative, for the East, which was rich and unprejudiced; it meant leaving the provincial city for an intellectually alive university campus: it meant, that is, confronting the reality of experience outside the shelter of the family circle. And, in fact, these years at Princeton were the most intense and determinant phase of Fitzgerald's development. They were years of exultation and depression, of intellectual awakening, as well as of misdirected energy. His athletic ambitions were shattered, he suffered repeated humiliations from companions richer than he; but at Princeton he found his way to literary achievement. Quickly, after an initial moment of ostracism, Fitzgerald became a member of the Triangle Club and of the editorial board of the *Daily Princetonian,* contributed to *The Nassau Lit.* and *The Tiger,* and was admitted to one of the best eating clubs, The Cottage. There is something impressive in the lucid perception with which the young outsider discovered the subtle secrets of the place, and in the iron will with which he pursued his social and cultural aims under a pretense of aristocratic detachment.

He wasted time on girls and on trips to nearby New York, but almost all doors now seemed open to him. He wrote librettos for the musicals that the Triangle Club produced,[4] he was about to become its president, and had hopes of getting the editorship of *The Tiger.* The most banal of reasons shattered all his hopes: low grades prevented him from taking part in extracurricular activities. An unexpected illness brought the final blow: in December 1915 he had to drop out of Princeton for the rest of the academic year. Fitzgerald never recovered from this trick of fate and regretted it even in later years.[5]

It was at Princeton, especially after his return there in the fall of 1916, that he came in touch for the first time with true culture. There he met Father Sigourney Fay (Monsignor D'Arcy in *This Side of Paradise*), formed ties of friendship with John Peale Bishop (Parke d'Invilliers in the same novel) and Edmund Wilson (his "intellectual conscience," as he was later to describe him). He heard of Tolstoi and Whitman, read Booth Tarkington and Shaw, H. G. Wells and Compton Mackenzie, Wilde and Pater, John Masefield and Rupert Brooke, to name only a few. It was an enriching experience: in that intellectual climate, as A. Mizener rightly states, he began "to write for the first time in his life with the mature intention of realizing and evaluating his experience." [6]

At Princeton he wrote the first drafts of *This Side of Paradise*, and by the end of 1917 the novel was already "completed," so that when he was commissioned as a second lieutenant in the army and reported at Fort Leavenworth, Kansas, his professor and friend Christian Gauss was entrusted with a manuscript. Gauss frankly refused to recommend it to a publisher. Not discouraged, Fitzgerald rewrote it quickly, and a few months later, when he was transferred to Camp Taylor, Kentucky, he sent a copy to John Peale Bishop and a copy to his "protector," Shane Leslie, to whom he had been recommended by Father Fay. This second copy, with the grammatical errors corrected, was sent to Scribner's, but it was soon returned with an encouraging letter and a polite request for certain revisions. A hurried and careless revision of the book brought only its final rejection.

Meanwhile, in July 1918, Fitzgerald met Zelda Sayre in Montgomery, Alabama, near the army camp where he was stationed in June. For both, it was love at first sight. As soon as he was discharged from the army in February 1919, Fitzgerald went to seek his fortune in New York, oblivious of his novel. He took a job with the Barron Collier Advertising Agency, with a small salary and meager prospects. Desperate to improve his position, he worked at night on his fiction. In three months he wrote nineteen short stories—and received one hundred twenty rejection slips.

Growing "nervous" in Montgomery, Alabama, Zelda Sayre broke their engagement (June 1919): like many young men, mauled in the big city struggle, and stabbed in the back by the *femme fatale*, Fitzgerald quit his job and went back to his hometown. In far-off St. Paul, offended and humiliated, he began to rewrite the novel that had been dragging along for years. "Emotion recollected in tranquillity"— as Wordsworth had said; now Fitzgerald himself found that writing was not only a way to recapture his love, but also, and more importantly, a way of affirming himself as a man. The new manuscript was sent to Scribner's and this time Maxwell Perkins overrode the other editorial advisers. The book was accepted in only thirteen days, on September 16.

From Alabama, Zelda Sayre reaffirmed a love which had really never died, and now Fitzgerald was in seventh heaven. What's more, he had found his vocation. Even before *This Side of Paradise* was successful both with the public (40,000 copies in less than a year) and the critics, he began to write a new novel (only the title, *The Demon Lover,* is now known), and to rewrite or revise old stories for *The Smart Set, Scribner's Magazine* and *The Saturday Evening Post.* His income would soon reach fantastic figures. Zelda came to New York for a gorgeous wedding (April 1920), and in a short time the couple became one of the city's attractions.

2

According to those who knew her, Zelda Fitzgerald was a fascinating and intelligent woman even in the darkest moments of her life. She played an important part in Fitzgerald's life. She was more ambitious for success and social prominence than for literary distinction. She was an admirer, but, if we trust Hemingway's opinion, a little jealous of her husband. She brought no tranquillity to his work. She almost certainly served to accentuate his tendency to waste himself in fruitless endeavors; she stimulated a certain fatuity of attitude in him and accentuated the split between a taste for popular success and the obligations imposed upon him by his literary talent. It was certainly not peace that Fitzgerald expected from her, but she speeded up notably the pace of his existence and the rhythm of his activity. Their life of parties and their expensive habits [7] provided him with matter for artistic elaboration, but also with acute financial problems. Fitzgerald was forced to market products of poor quality, and his life was further divided between activities and projects not easily reconciled. The artistic results were not always in proportion with the waste of energy they required.[8]

On this dangerous tightrope, swirled in the turmoil of his new life, he did publish a collection of short stories (*Flappers and Philosophers*), and in less than a year completed a new novel (*The Beautiful and Damned*). In 1921 the couple took their first trip to Europe. During this short visit Fitzgerald met Galsworthy in London and Joyce in Paris—and was particularly impressed by the latter.[9] Back in St. Paul for the birth of their daughter (October 1921), he enjoyed a period of peace and began to write a play. His new novel was published first serially, then in book form, and was followed in a few months by a second collection of stories with the misleading title *Tales of the Jazz Age*. From St. Paul the Fitzgeralds moved to Great Neck, New York. His play was a failure, but in the meantime he had undertaken, almost stealthily, a third novel. This work came in the end to a happy fruition—*The Great Gatsby* was to prove the best achievement of his better part—but even in this case, his literary ideal had to give way before the financial muse.

Fitzgerald was able to cope with his most pressing debts only at the cost of a desperate "drive to make money," which compelled him to the writing of numberless short stories of little or no value. With the illusion of reducing expenses, the family went to live in France in May 1924. Fitzgerald was able to finish his novel, but not to reduce his expenses.[10] Moreover, his serenity was shattered under the Riviera sun by Zelda's restlessness and by her affair with a French aviator. This was a new trial for Fitzgerald, but it was also a step toward maturity: "It has been a fine summer—I've been unhappy, but my work hasn't suffered from it. I am grown at last," he wrote to Maxwell Perkins.

He was not completely grown. While the novel (published in April 1925) was on its way to becoming a critical success, Fitzgerald went on to Rome—where he was involved in a night brawl and ended up in prison—and to Capri—where Zelda suddenly decided to take up painting and then to become a ballet dancer. Depressed by the poor sales of the book he returned to Paris and plunged himself in a life of "1000 parties and no work." In Paris, then the refuge of a whole generation of American writers, Fitzgerald might have intensified his cultural ties and improved his intellectual awareness. But he was once more separated from his dream, and he seemed to prefer the sunny Riviera, with its demimonde of rich expatriates. This world was material for his future literary work, but although he moved in the exclusive and refined circle of the Murphys, Fitzgerald too often gave the impression that he was happy to identify his own life with the lives of the questionable pleasure seekers, prodigal of money and whiskey.

In this extravagant and ambiguous setting Fitzgerald found a background for the exercise of the charm of his personality; but he had begun a new novel—*Tender Is the Night*—and the needs of artistic creation confronted him with more tormenting and pressing problems. He was trying to use new and difficult material, to reduce it to new formal patterns, and to bend it to new requirements. The themes and techniques of his early novels had been exhausted, and the struggle to recreate an artistic world that would renovate them coincided with the least happy period of his life.

His financial problems were temporarily resolved with the sale of the motion-picture rights of *The Great Gatsby*. While still in Europe he published a third collection of stories, *All the Sad Young Men* (1926)—the title betrays at least a different attitude toward his former subject matter. But Zelda was getting more and more restless, and Fitzgerald himself noticed a touch of hysteria in their continual round of parties. In addition, his commercial vein seemed dry (from February 1926 to June 1927 he wrote hardly one story). Tired and disillusioned, he and his wife returned to America to try Hollywood. There he gathered new material (in particular for the character of Rosemary in *Tender Is the Night*). But the murderous rhythm of work wore him out, the script he had written was refused, and two months later (March 1927) they left Hollywood and moved to Ellerslie, outside Wilmington, Delaware.

A dark and tormented period of wandering began, in the intervals of which Fitzgerald tried continually to give a definite form to his novel. At Zelda's wish he took her to Paris for ballet lessons in the summer of 1928, but they came back to Ellerslie more exasperated than ever. The following spring they were again in Paris and on the Riviera, where Fitzgerald began for the first time to drink heavily, to create disturbances, and to disappoint his friends. He was arrested once and even quarreled with his friend and colleague Hemingway.[11] A trip to Algeria precipitated the situation. Zelda had her first nervous breakdown in April 1930 and in June entered a Swiss clinic at Prangins. With a vague sense of guilt for not having prevented—or for having accelerated—their past dissipations, Fitzgerald stayed at her side and gave her unfailing support, neglecting his novel. His own private tragedy seemed a personal reflection of the economic crisis of 1929. Zelda was released from Prangins and allowed to return to Montgomery in September 1931; Fitzgerald went back to Hollywood for a few months, but in January 1932 his wife suffered her second breakdown. In an attempt to rebuild her personality, Fitzgerald even helped her to write and publish a novel (*Save Me the Waltz*), which Maxwell Perkins accepted on his recommendation. While Zelda was in a Baltimore hospital Fitzgerald had but little time to continue his own work. He rented a country house (La Paix) on the edge of the city, but in spite of short periods of reawakened creative ability, he found it very difficult to get on with his novel.[12]

He was at the very limits of emotional resistance (he was to call it "emotional bankruptcy"). On top of this, he realized with dismay that he had remained too far from the public for too long. When he made a solitary trip to New York in 1933, to be "physically" present in the city, he was aware that he appeared like a ghost from the past. He relieved his impotent bitterness in quarrels with Edmund Wilson and with Hemingway.

At the end of 1933 the novel was completed. Freed from the long nightmare of composition, Fitzgerald made a final attempt with Zelda and took her to Bermuda. On her return, however, she had a third collapse, and there was no longer any hope of recovery. *Tender Is the Night* had a limited success, and his private life had foundered on the shoals of misunderstanding and mental illness; the dream of the writer was wrecked, and so was his dream of eternal love. From then on, Fitzgerald's life was lonely and pathetic. He renounced the external signs of popularity, withdrew within himself, and fought his battle alone, against time and death. He would spend the next years in rebuilding his own personality, in refining new techniques, in trying desperately to reach a final artistic achievement. He had his own suffering to build on, and his solitude to shelter him. However cruel it might seem, Zelda's final hospitalization freed both writer and man from a yoke that might have proved fatal, and which certainly added nothing to his art nor to his psychological stability. Henceforth he was able to think of himself, which meant, above all, of his own artistic endeavors. Unlike Dick Diver in *Tender Is the Night*, he did not disappear into the warm darkness, but gave further proof of his artistic vitality with a final literary flowering.

3

The long silence between *Gatsby* and *Tender Is the Night* was not only the result of external factors, but was also due to uncertainty and to a crisis of literary inspiration. The difficulty with which he found his new "line" proves it. Freed from pressing family concerns, Fitzgerald started to write again, but he produced an abortive historical novel, of which he completed four chapters before realizing that the project was a blind alley. A keen artistic awareness would have saved him at once, but his inventive and evocative ability had become barren, and his psychological resistance was easily overcome. Zelda's crisis transferred itself to him (as was the case between Nicole and Dick in *Tender Is the Night*), and without any restraint, he drank immoderately and suffered his first collapse.

A short love affair brought only a momentary, passing relief, and his pressing debts did not make his life any easier. He published his last collection of short stories, *Taps at Reveille*, in 1935, but the true reawakening was still to come. When he moved to Asheville, and then for a short while to Hendersonville, North Carolina, he found himself in real poverty.[13] Back in Baltimore, he suffered an attack of tuberculosis, for which he had a certain predisposition, aggravated by overwork, and which had already shown itself in 1917. His stories began to be refused by the big magazines, and Fitzgerald realized that he had counted on resources, both physical and emotional, which he no longer possessed, "like a man overdrawing at his bank."

All that was left him was the courage of ruthless self-analysis. He had to look to the very bottom of the abyss to which he had slipped, to define exactly his own ills, to analyze his decay. He stripped himself naked in the three famous articles on his own crackup—"The Crack-up," "Handle with Care," and "Pasting It Together"—written at the end of 1935 and published the following year. It seemed an "exercise in self-pity," but Fitzgerald gathered enough self-knowledge from the experience to escape the evil. That was not all: such an experience furnished the basis for a maturer, more intense style and for a new awareness of life, which were brought to bear in the composition of *The Last Tycoon.*

The exorcism of ghosts is not the liberation of the spirit nor the resolution of problems; but it sets in motion the forces of renewal. Fitzgerald's troubles seemed to multiply. He had broken his arm and then slipped in the bath, lying four hours on the floor before being able to get help—this experience bringing on a form of arthritis. But a small inheritance left at his mother's death permitted him to settle some of his debts, and with great strength of will he went to work again at Asheville—writing short pieces, sketches, and stories. His final decision, however, was to return to Hollywood; this decision, no longer motivated by a wish to escape, restlessness, or dissatisfaction, represented a form of self-affirmation. He moved to Hollywood in July 1937. This time he was not compromising with the economic muse, but was responding to a need for experience, for direct contact with reality. It was an urge to live, a challenge to the dark night of his soul.[14]

The last three years of his life were marked by a reawakening of his creative forces and by his last desperate struggle with the specter of decadence. He worked with enthusiasm at various film scripts, minimized his social life, and succeeded in abstaining from alcohol. It was neither an easy nor a pleasant existence, nor a restful one. But his perceptive gift was sharpened again, and he succeeded as no one else had in giving us a picture of the histrionic world of Hollywood.

Of all the scripts that he worked at, none, for one reason or the other, was produced.[15] But his health was partly restored, with the aid of a quieting love affair, and he was able to write for himself. There is a tendency to depict this last phase of Fitzgerald's life as one of continual humiliation and constant dissatisfaction, as Budd Schulberg did in his brilliant novel, *The Disenchanted*. But Schulberg took into account only the very last phase of his stay in Hollywood. In point of fact Fitzgerald was able to resist the tensions of Hollywood and his own inner conflicts, to detach himself from the setting in which he lived, so that this last period of his life becomes interesting and important both from the human and the artistic point of view.

His relationship with columnist Sheilah Graham [16] had in many ways the effect of putting a little order into his life, and of permitting him to devote himself with greater tranquillity to the novel that he had begun. He organized the material for *The Last Tycoon* and wrote the first drafts of this uncompleted novel. He also wrote more than twenty brief sketches, which from their very brevity had intensity and a nervous conciseness of style.

After this interval, the rhythm of the oncoming ruin speeded up again. Fitzgerald quarreled with his agent, Harold Ober, and in February 1939 had a disastrous experience with the producer Walter Wanger. Accompanied by Budd Schulberg, he was sent with a film company to Hanover, New Hampshire, to film some scenes of the Dartmouth Winter Carnival. He had started drinking on the plane, and deeply wounded by the treatment he received there—he found that he had not even been assigned a room—he lost control of himself. In his drunken indignation he created a scandal first in Hanover and then in New York, where hotels refused him rooms and where he even had trouble entering a hospital. Whether or not there was a black list for alcoholics, it was a fact that from then on Fitzgerald had great difficulty in finding work with producers. He estranged himself even from Sheilah Graham. In the spring of 1939, after he had begun writing the final draft of his novel, a new bout of his illness confined him to bed.

Oblivious of his illness, of himself, and of his friends as well, and preoccupied only with his novel,[17] he wrote feverishly at an improvised desk in bed during the long hours of sleeplessness. He completed a script of his own story "Babylon Revisited," but when this was set aside by the producer, he returned more furiously than ever to his novel. "Do I look like death (in mirror at 6 P.M.)" he wrote in his notes; but in spite of a heart attack in November 1940, the composition of the book proceeded so untiringly that Fitzgerald could promise its completion for January 15. On December 20 he finished the first part of chapter VI: the next day he had his second and fatal heart attack.

The artist had overcome the weaknesses of the man; by cruel irony, premature death snatched away the full crowning of his achievement. "There are no second acts in American lives," he had written in the notes for his book. Brief as it was, Fitzgerald's life *had* a second act, and not one of mere repetition, as was to be the case with many others more famous than he, but one of genuine artistic renewal. One might say, it is true, that it was a second act that was interrupted before the last scene; but it differed from the first and it bore the mark of a new development. Ignored or obscured until recently, this second act now permits us to have a better idea, closer to the truth, of the writer's real stature and of his whole achievement.

Perhaps to no one but Fitzgerald, who called himself "a mediocre care-taker of most things left in *his* hands, even of *his* talent," could be better referred the disconsolate lament of William Empson in his poem "Missing Dates":

The waste remains, the waste remains, and kills;

but from that continued waste, which smothered and impoverished him before killing him, Fitzgerald the writer was still able to rescue a few shapes of beauty—faithful to his own deeper and better nature, despite external interferences or inner conflicts.

CHAPTER II

Early Success

> ... *and really if Scribner takes it*
> [TSP] *I know I'll wake some*
> *morning and find that the*
> *debutantes have made me famous*
> *overnight.*
>
> CU, p. 252.

1

An examination of Fitzgerald's literary career must begin with his prep school and university writings. However immature it may be, *This Side of Paradise* is not the sudden product of a literary infatuation; it came at the end of a long period of apprenticeship. The fact is important, because it serves to destroy the legend—which the author himself helped create—that he turned to writing as the only solution for his financial and emotional problems.[1] Undoubtedly, an incurable, almost morbid desire for success pushed him to the writing of the book, but Fitzgerald had already prepared himself in various early attempts.

His "Juvenilia" [2] consist of sixteen short stories, nine poems, five book reviews, a dozen satirical and humorous pieces, four little plays, and the ideas and lyrics for three musical shows. The germs of his later development are already here. Short-story writing increased his ability to plot. The songs and poems prepared him for the careful use of imagery. The theatrical experience gave him a feeling for the dramatic scene.

Fitzgerald's first story, "The Mystery of the Raymond Mortgage" (1909), was a detective story and has only curiosity value. His second, however, "Reade, Substitute Right Half," shows a certain liveliness of style, even if it is nothing more than a sketch. His contributions to *Newman News* have now been collected and published (together with his other juvenilia) by John Kuehl in *The Apprentice*

Fiction of F.S.[3] They deal mostly with school topics, as did those published during his college years.

Among the latter, "The Ordeal" (1915), the first draft of a story later developed with the title "Benediction," has but little value. More interesting was "Shadow Laurels," which was entirely in dialogue. Fitzgerald availed himself of a technique of presentation that was purely "dramatic," without using the established narrative convention. This explains why sections of pure dialogue were inserted in *This Side of Paradise* by way of dramatic interludes. "The Débutante," published in 1917 in *The Nassau Lit.*, was another short story written entirely in dialogue; it found its way almost unchanged into the novel. Such technical experiments are clearly based on the intense dramatic activity to which young Fitzgerald devoted himself in this period.

Fitzgerald had already composed an "original sketch" called *The Girl from the Lazy J,* a one-act skit of a half-hour's length for five actors. In 1912, while at Newman, he attempted a longer play in two acts, *The Captured Shadow.* There were twelve characters and the action developed through a whole series of complications after an initial bet of "the shadow"—the chief character, played by Fitzgerald himself—to keep the New York police in check for two weeks. It was a detective adventure play, in imitation of the famous pieces on Arsène Lupin. On the other hand, the successful attempt of the next year, *The Coward,* is a true western melodrama that takes place during the Civil War. Its principal character is a young southerner who refuses to wear a uniform and fight. The situation was difficult to develop: the conflict to be depicted was essentially an inner conflict, dependent on psychological evidence. Fitzgerald chose the easiest way out by introducing as many as seventeen characters, breaking the unity of time and stressing the spectacular aspect of the action. From melodrama the path led to comedy. In *Assorted Spirits* Fitzgerald returned to the unity of time (as well as of place) and the action was again based on conventional middle-class comedy situations, with a more limited number of characters (twelve). Better than the preceding plays, this attempt demonstrated how congenial to Fitzgerald's talent was the light and witty pace.

It was quite natural that this inclination brought him to contribute to three musicals staged at Princeton by The Triangle Club. It is rather difficult to establish the exact amount of his contribution to these. He appeared usually as the writer of the lyrics, but for the first of these musicals—*Fie! Fie! Fi-Fi!*—he was also responsible for the plot. It is not a mere coincidence, perhaps, that this musical is by far the best of the three. In a story-book version of Monte Carlo, Fi-Fi, who might be considered as a flapper before her time, succeeds in restoring to power the prime minister of the principality, who had been driven out by a usurper. In the maze of complications that follows, she gives the plot the minimum of unity required by the genre. Fitzgerald's imagination flares up in a brilliant series of lyrics, which already reveal that lightness of phrasing that would become one of his distinctive characteristics as a fiction writer. In *The Evil Eye*, which was produced the next year (1915–16), the plot was provided by Edmund Wilson, but Fitzgerald was able to adjust his lyrics to it and to achieve a personal success with them. The same can be said of *Safety First*, the third musical, to which he contributed a good twenty lyrics.

While writing so many lyrics for musicals, Fitzgerald was bound to take an interest in poetry itself. In this period of apprenticeship he wrote a group of verse compositions that at the time gave him a certain reputation. They range from the vague elegiac attempt of "Princeton—the Last Day," to the flippant reversal of a Keatsian theme ("To My Unused Greek Book"), from the little scene of Verlaine-like melancholy ("Rain Before Dawn") to the emulation of Gautier in "The Cameo Frame," from the twilight theme of "City Dusk" to the rough realism of "Marching Streets." The cadences and the tone are almost always of romantic origin, and they often bear a resemblance to Georgian poetry (especially in "My First Love")— just as the musical lyrics seem often derived from Wilde or Gilbert and Sullivan; but in certain cases, notably in "The Pope at Confession," the intensity of the foreshortening, the precision of the details, and the concisiveness of the presentation allow us to speak of an imagistic achievement:

> The gorgeous Vatican was steeped in night,
>   The organs trembled on my heart no more,
> But with a blend of colors on my sight
>   I loitered through a somber corridor;
> When suddenly I heard behind a screen
>   The faintest whisper as from one in prayer;
> I glanced about, then passed, for I had seen
>   A hushed, dim-lighted room—and two were there.

> A ragged friar, half in dream's embrace,
>   Leaned sideways, soul intent, as if to seize
>   The last grey ice of sin that ached to melt
>   And faltered from the lips of him who knelt,
>   A little bent old man upon his knees
>   With pain and sorrow in his holy face.[4]

It was not for nothing that the young student had marked in his anthology of English poetry the poems of T. S. Eliot and Pound, at that time hardly known. These early attempts show him already conscious of his craft.

If in the novel that he had under way at the time he had no scruples against using material which had already appeared in print ("Babes in the Woods," for instance, or "The Spire and the Gargoyle," two short stories of these same years),[5] he did so with full realization of what he was doing. His apprenticeship had already provided him with a few tricks of the trade: the secrets of dialogue, the need for plotting and for careful phrasing, the importance of imagery were now part of his artistic awareness. In his novel, youthful self-assurance coexisted with the clear signs of a long labor of apprenticeship.

2

With malice and exaggeration, *This Side of Paradise* was greeted at its publication as "The Collected Works of Scott Fitzgerald." [6] In reality, its organization was not dependent on his fragmentary early works; rather, he subordinated these to it. The book remains uneven and structurally uncertain, but it provided a frame in which pre-existing material found its natural place and blended harmoniously with the general theme. Its purpose was to give a comprehensive picture of college life, and the experiment can be said to have been successful, inasmuch as the best achievement of the novel is in its uniformity of tone and atmosphere. But it must be admitted at once that the success of the novel at the time of its appearance was due not so much to its artistic worth, as to a series of external circumstances that helped to make it celebrated for the wrong reasons.

By happy coincidence, Fitzgerald unconsciously suited the public taste. As he himself said later, the generation for which he wrote "bore him up, flattered him, and gave him more money than he had dreamed of, simply for telling people that he felt as they did . . ." [7] He found an immediate response in his readers because his own sincerity and openmindedness matched their desire for utter intellectual and emotional clarity. *This Side of Paradise* became at once, in the readers' minds, a book of protest and revolt in the name of liberty as a generic principle; it seemed to advocate freedom from money, from bourgeois morality, from Victorian hypocrisy, from religion, and above all from conformity. The book stripped the idols, prejudices, and lies of a society at the very moment that it felt an awakening need to examine all the conventions on which it was based. In a society in which antiprohibition feelings were increasing, in which the discussion of women's suffrage and emancipation began to spread, in which it became popular to talk of sex, Fitzgerald's novel, with its open references to petting and necking, to the unconventional behavior of the youngsters, with its amusing descriptions of "egotists" and debutantes, was bound to cause a sensation. His denunciation of the vulgarity of the new rich, his social criticism, and his frankness made Fitzgerald the mouthpiece and the leader of a revolution in customs and manners which was open to any suggestion and which was later to exceed the positions he had taken in the novel.[8] If it did not capture the elusive spirit of the times, the book reproduced instinctively the moment of transition from one generation to another and bore witness to a radical change of attitude among the young: and so it was that Fitzgerald came to be greeted as the herald of a new age.

There was some exaggeration in it. The merit of having expressed—but not of having transcended, as he was later to do—his own time does not hide the fact that the book's success was disproportionate to its real value. And we are more concerned with its value than with its success.

This Side of Paradise went through two incomplete drafts before acquiring its final form. The first draft was "completed" at the end of Fitzgerald's college years and given to Christian Gauss, who refused, as has been noted, to pass it on to a publisher. No trace remains of this version. According to Gauss's recollection, the first part was not very different from the first part of the published novel, while the second part was made up of a series of unconnected episodes, anecdotes, satirical pieces, and poems about Princeton, including the story—then incorporated into the book—"The Spire and the Gargoyle." [9] His recollection was not, perhaps, as exact as we would like, because the second draft, known as "The Romantic Egotist," differs in many places, especially at the beginning, from *This Side of Paradise*.

Of "The Romantic Egotist," "completed" at Fort Leavenworth, Kansas, in 1918, only five manuscript chapters (I, II, V, XII, XIV) and a description in a letter to Edmund Wilson remain. In his letter Fitzgerald spoke of twenty-three chapters in all, a mixture of poetry, vers libre, and prose, and added:

> It purports to be the picaresque ramble of one Stephen Palms [Dalius?] from the San Francisco fire thru school, Princeton, to the end where at twenty-one he writes his autobiography ... It shows traces of Tarkington, Chesterton, Chambers, Wells, Benson (Robert Hugh), Rupert Brooke and includes Compton-McKenzielike love-affairs and three psychic adventures including an encounter with the devil in a harlot's apartment ... I can most nearly describe it by calling it a prose, modernistic Childe Harolde ... (*CU*, p. 252.)

It seemed to him that "no one else could have written so searchingly the story of the youth of *his* generation"; but two points are here worth noting. The name of the hero seems clearly to be derived from that of Stephen Dedalus in James Joyce's *Portrait of the Artist as a Young Man;* on the other hand, the fictional conception of the book is completely disorganic. From the very beginning, that is, we must take into account the model provided by Joyce's book, and the opposite tendency to the "picaresque ramble," which can easily dispose of any plot restriction.

In spite of what is stated in the letter, however, "The Romantic Egotist" begins *in medias res*, and it is a first-person narrative. In Chapter I the protagonist is in an officers' training camp. He speaks with boring insistence of himself and of the book that he is writing (and which he should have already written), repeating slavishly, often with bad taste, the concepts expressed in the letter.[10] This "egotist, romanticist, and loiterer on the border-land of genius," marvels greatly at the very things he is relating; he has probably forgotten that they are supposed to be autobiographical, and thus he hands out counsels and admonishments, insists on statements of purpose, and end up by tiring everyone, himself included.[11] If the critic reads these pages now it is because they reveal the intentions and designs of the young author and the fictional ideal that he wanted to pursue: his aim was to strike an unconventional attitude, to excel with a brilliant and original tone, to be amusing and revolutionary. At this stage, however, his surprising self-assurance does not hide the fact that he has very little to say.

After the stage has been set, Stephen's "picaresque ramble" is related in a long flashback. The youth with his parents changes residence continually; he reads, goes to school, and performs one after the other all the exploits of young Fitzgerald himself, from the writing of stories and plays to the first tentative love affairs (Chapters I and II). As these events seem to precede the "San Francisco fire" of which he wrote in the letter, we may assume that this part comes without change from the first draft. If this is true, a faint but revealing echo of Joyce that can be discerned in these pages is of the greatest interest. Says Stephen in "The Romantic Egotist": "I'm trying to set down the story . . . of my generation in America [?] and put myself in the middle as a sort of observer and conscious factor" (p. 18 of the MS). This is not exactly the ambition of Stephen Dedalus, in Joyce's *Portrait*, ". . . to forge in the smithy of my soul the uncreated conscience of my race," but the undertone, at least, is analogous. And if we remember that Amory Blaine in *This Side of Paradise* thinks that he has been preserved "to help in building up the living consciousness of the race," we can assume with safety that the influence of Joyce played an important part in the preparation of the novel from the very beginning.[12] We shall see in a few pages the implications of this fact.

Chapters III and IV must have continued with the youthful adventures of the precocious "conscious factor," because with Chapter V we reach the university years ("Spire and Gargoyles"). Fitzgerald tried to give a faithful documentary picture of college life, going so far as giving a list of words typical of the place. The jump in the manuscript to Chapter XII brings us to the Eleanor episode (Part II, Chapter III, in *This Side of Paradise*), and we can again assume that the intermediate chapters went substantially as they were into the novel. But in "The Romantic Egotist" this episode seems to have a different thematic value than in the completed novel. It is the first conscious encounter of Stephen with evil, which presents itself under the guise of "the dark beauty" and is identified with the problem of sex. This same experience is repeated, but in a more vulgar key and without the pseudoliterary implication of the Eleanor episode, in Stephen's encounter with the devil in a New York apartment, where he had gone with two questionable girls and a college friend, as related in Chapter XIV.

In *This Side of Paradise* the original plan is broadened, although many episodes are included from "The Romantic Egotist," and the whole subject matter is divided into two parts, separated by an interlude. The first part retains the title of "The Romantic Egotist," while the second bears a title, "The Education of a Personage," which betrays the new informing idea of the novel. The story is told in the third person, thanks to a happy suggestion of the publisher, and it follows a certain line of development, even if the thematic difference between the two parts is a clear indication that the material was not completely unified in the author's mind. Fitzgerald seems to have faltered between two thematic possibilities which he was not able to reconcile in full. In the first part we are given a rather static portrait of the hero, Amory Blaine, who is a direct projection of the author himself and is contemplated in the ideal perfection of his egotism, more or less as Oscar Wilde had done in *The Picture of Dorian Gray*. In the second part the protagonist is carefully followed through an *education*, according to the imperfectly understood scheme of the *Bildungsroman*, of which Joyce's *Portrait* provided a late and artful example. Of course, this second part develops hints and germs already present in the first, but it centers on the *thematic* development of the episodes and on the inner development of the character itself. The general tone of the book, therefore, is much more unified than the episodes in the two parts; and if the theme is not properly focused, this is due partly to the author's inexperience and partly to an unresolved duality or plurality of models.

At the outset Amory Blaine is in the protective shadow of his mother, who instills in him a dangerous form of egotism, a tendency to dreamy sentimentalism, and a good deal of romantic restlessness. The idyllic and effeminate atmosphere in which he lives reminds us of the graceful and secluded world that Melville's Pierre inhabited before his tragic encounter with experience. But while Pierre seemed to be perfectly satisfied with his condition, Amory is already preparing himself for the "great adventure" which awaits him at college and in the world. In each case the protective and dominating presence of the mother is going to be replaced by other women or girls, whose influence will be of a different nature and will bring the hero to an awareness of evil and of human suffering.

In Chapter II we are already at the university. The egotist becomes, by a natural transition, an aesthete. The first literary discussions and the first cultural contacts alternate with the first petting parties and the first sentimental love of Amory for Isabelle. "The 'leading character' "—wrote Fitzgerald in a preface to the book [13]—

"loved many women, and gazed at himself in many mirrors"; one is tempted to say that even his loves are so many meetings before the familiar face of Narcissus in the mirror and aim only at a definition of his many-faceted portrait. An emotional and financial crisis (the death of his father) overtakes the aesthete, who reacts according to his nature, by settling down "to consider" (Chapter III); and his encounter with the devil (Chapter IV) has the same effect on him. After all his "considerations," he can do nothing but take a new course in love. Clara, the new girl, or the new mirror, represents for Amory an encounter with ethereal and supernatural beauty, with ideal and aesthetic perfection. With a kind of Pre-Raphaelite sensibility, one might call it, he sees himself in front of her as Joseph before the eternal significance of Mary. And such is the power of this deforming mirror that Amory remains for a while "Narcissus off Duty" (Chapter IV). This is almost the beginning of the end: and it is significant that this first part closes with an elegiac note on the fleeting moment and the approach of new dangers:

> No more to wait the twilight of the moon in this seques-
> tered vale of star and spire, for one eternal morning of desire
> passes to time and earthly afternoon. Here, Heraclitus, did you
> find in fire and shifting things the prophecy you hurled down
> the dead years; this midnight my desire will see, shadowed
> among the embers, furled in flame, the splendor and the sadness
> of the world. (*TSP*, p. 168.)

The interlude follows—a kind of shadowy period during which Narcissus is not only off duty but also out of sight (as was the case with typical Celtic heroes from Parsifal to Tristan), preparing himself for new trials to come. The new "adventures" force him to go through a painful "education." War has "spoilt the background" and "killed individualism": Amory has to come to grips with experience. The death of his mother has left him in a world turned upside down: it is now his task to keep or to deepen his character. It is no longer sufficient, as Monsignor D'Arcy had warned him, to be simply a "personality": the aesthete must recreate himself, must become a "personage," or be lost.

As in the first part, to a certain extent, the education of the character begins with an emotional crisis, which is represented by "The Débutante"—an episode completely set in dialogue. His love for Rosalind, no longer idyllic or idealized, but deeply suffered, provides no polite mirror to reflect the handsome image, but a polished stone that darkens the reflection. Rosalind abandons the aesthete (no longer an "egotist") for the same reasons that a whole series of Fitzgerald's heroines will later share, because she could not be "shut away from trees and flowers, cooped up in a little flat, waiting for him"; and Amory discovers that his own life is empty. His "experiments in convalescence" (Chapter II) mark the beginning of his inner growth. His uninterrupted drunken sprees do nothing but further break the cherished image of Narcissus, proud as he was of his isolation and aloofness. His flight from reality into literature—he gets involved in endless discussions of books and attempts to write— is only a means to confront in better awareness his own existence, to come to terms with his own experience: and, in fact, now he attempts to reconsider his whole life ("Looking Backward").

The next step of his education, or of his initiation to life, is bound to be his initiation into sex. This seems to be the purport—in this specific context, and in contrast with the probable meaning of its first draft—of the Eleanor episode (Chapter III). If Clara had been the daughter of light, Eleanor is at the same time the archetypal dark woman (born and educated in France: one is reminded of Isabella, again in Melville's *Pierre*), who is the symbol in so much of American literature of the complexity of experience and of the profane eros (from Hawthorne to James and to the modern novelists), as well as the *fille du feu* of Nerval. There is a spark of divine madness in her, and at the same time the sense of worldly materialism. Thus, Amory's worldly education is completed only after his encounter with Eleanor.

There is an initial danger in his relationship with Eleanor Savage (her last name is also significant), and that is a kind of aesthetic involution. Amory is attracted by some lines of Verlaine that she recites, enacts "the part of Rupert Brooke" with her, calls her Ulalume, reads Swinburne to her, allows her to play with the idea of being "Psyche, his soul," and so on. But Eleanor, even though a romanticist, is also "a small materialist" who does not believe in immortality; she gives herself to Amory on a summer's night. In this way she removes Amory from the bounds of adolescence, breaks the bonds of his aesthetic religiosity, and, above all, as Fitzgerald says, takes away his ability to regret. Their relationship ends as suddenly as it began, with a kind of "last ride together" in which the touch of divine folly deranges the mind of the heroine. Amory feels hatred for the girl and realizes that he has come to hate himself: the break with his exclusively narcissistic love is now complete. The original "portrait" is denied, and Amory's detachment from his former self is completed in Chapter IV, when he renounces his own social respectability with a gratuitous act and lets himself be discredited in public. The old ideal of the aesthete is shattered—the "collapse of several pillars" is an accomplished fact. As T. S. Eliot was later to say in *The Waste Land,* Amory has to shore up his fragments against the ruins.

In one of the last episodes he gives himself up to an endless "picaresque ramble," which has no possible outcome. Discovering now that he is a socialist, Amory starts an inconclusive denunciation of the capitalistic world, and the book closes with a whirlwind of revolutionary ideas. His long monologue is surprisingly ingenuous and is motivated more by a dissatisfaction with himself than with society. The socialism of Amory-Fitzgerald remains basically of an individualistic and sentimental kind,[14] and it is clearly the symptom of a psychological malaise which has more to do with *le mal du siècle* than with the exploitation of capitalism. It is the result of a typically decadent attitude toward the world and society; [15] nevertheless, Amory's education has reached its end. If nothing else, it has brought Narcissus to disillusionment and to self-knowledge. "I know myself, but that is all," says Amory in the end. And it is already a great deal to say—and to achieve—for someone who had begun with complacent aestheticism. Amory's education does not leave him much on which to build, but it at least had the effect of liberating him from a superstructure of egotistical complacency and of reawakening his sense of humanity:

> He found something that he wanted, had always wanted
> and always would want: not to be admired, as he had feared;
> not to be loved, as he had made himself believe; but to be
> necessary to people, to be indispensable. (*TSP,* pp. 286–87.)

There is still a trace of illusion and of egotistical complacency in the word "indispensable"—but in the wish to be "necessary" there is the whole sense of Amory's achieved education.

3

The parable of Amory is not very clearly developed in the book, although its general purport is clearly indicated in the text. The fact is that it must be carefully disentangled from the shapeless mass of episodes, repetitions, false starts and irrelevant speeches, literary reminiscences and influences that often encumber the page and obscure the meaning. But it is possible, I believe, to recognize a certain line of development in Amory's adventure, even if we have to disregard a whole set of secondary or collateral suggestions and many departures from the main theme. To account for the latter, we must briefly consider the contrasting literary influences under which the novel came to be written.

The presence of Oscar Wilde is clearly recognizable in the general tone of *This Side of Paradise,* although it would be difficult to find a specific coincidence of episodes in Fitzgerald's novel and *The Picture of Dorian Gray.* But Oscar Wilde's was a suggestive source for Amory's decadent attitude toward the world, and through his influence Fitzgerald found it easier to express in the novel a certain aspect of decadentism, which was both historically and psychologically true.[16] The atmosphere in which Amory's portrait becomes credible is the typical atmosphere of the English *fin-de-siècle,* with its enthusiasms for Verlaine and Rimbaud, for impressionistic writing and symbolistic poetry, for an ideal Renaissance and a decadent form of Hellenism. English decadence idealized the figure of man in tired attitudes and blasé forms, or reproduced it, almost emasculated, in the pages of *The Yellow Book;* the Pre-Raphaelites had identified it in their paintings with a pale medieval phantom; Oscar Wilde himself had seen in man nothing more than an exquisite poseur. Together with a predilection for Tennyson's drowsy poetry and for Swinburne's languid sensuality, these aspects of the decadent movement exercised a notable influence on practically all writers who flourished at the beginning of the new century—on Tarkington and Cabell—on young Faulkner and even on Dos Passos, and they are clearly discernible in T. S. Eliot's and Ezra Pound's early poetry as well. They permeated the whole cultural atmosphere which Fitzgerald *had* to absorb while at college, and it is small wonder if in his first book he repeated these forms, these attitudes, and these formulas to the point of satiety.[17]

Especially in the first part of *This Side of Paradise,* the portrait of Amory is clearly based on an awareness of the decadent tendency of a whole generation, and only the model provided by *The Picture of Dorian Gray* can explain how Fitzgerald was able to achieve such a unity of tone and such consistency of attitude in relating Amory's character to its milieu. But the static quality of the picture was gradually developed, in the second part, into a process of inner growth, whose literary model must be found elsewhere. The shift of interest is consistent both on the psychological level—Amory's education is completed only when he has renounced his decadent attitude—and on the sociological level, because the years that followed the "interlude" of the war saw a gradual disintegration of the *fin-de-siècle* tradition. But the transition from one theme to another is rather abrupt, and it can be explained only by keeping in mind that it was made possible by a massive intervention of a new model: James Joyce's *Portrait of the Artist as a Young Man*.

Joyce's influence cannot be properly reconciled with the initial influence of Oscar Wilde, and though it suggested the informing idea for the second part of *This Side of Paradise,* the thematic unity of the book was seriously compromised. Joyce's *Portrait,* furthermore, was an exacting model to follow, and it is probable that Fitzgerald did not understand in full its implications.

A Portrait of the Artist as a Young Man might be described as an avant-garde *Bildungsroman,* in which the education of the protagonist is represented as a process of liberation from the rule of religion, of middle-class conventions, and of established literary sources. Through his rebellion, Stephen Dedalus reacquires a natural spontaneity of attitude toward the world. His odyssey is an odyssey, as it were, *away from* the domestic background, not a return or a safe landing, but the breaking of all ties. His education ended by destroying all the idols of the past and by accepting the disquieting emptiness of the moment—as had been the case with Henry Adams, on a strictly intellectual level.

Amory comes to the same conclusion, but with the difference that he is much less complicated than Stephen Dedalus, both on the personal and on the intellectual level. Even though he too is of Irish descent, the weight of culture and tradition from which he has to free himself is much lighter than that on Dedalus. He has to free himself from Wilde alone, not from many centuries of middle-class Catholic stratification. His struggle is with Narcissus, not with Saint Thomas; the narrow streets of Princeton have none of the labyrinthine quality of the streets of Dublin. One might say that while Joyce's novel is "a portrait of the *artist* as a young man," Fitzgerald's work has no other pretension than that of being a "portrait of the artist as a *young man*." In the first the protagonist *is* an artist, caught in the crucial years of his intellectual growth; in the second, he is merely a young man whose youthful crisis is disguised under the pretence of his being an artist. Amory ends by feeling that "he was leaving behind him his chance of being a certain type of artist. It seemed so much more important to be a certain type of man." [18] At this same stage of his development, Dedalus had reacquired the freshness of mind necessary for the great artistic adventure that was in store for him.

The difference between the two figures—and therefore between the nature and quality of the two books—is constitutional, and this is also due to the unresolved duality of models that Fitzgerald had in mind. The part of the book which we have called à la Wilde determines the peculiar development of Amory's education. Having begun with a picture of an aesthete, Fitzgerald was bound from the very start to follow the theme of the gradual humanization of Amory, to whom he could not confer a shade of the complexities that make up the greatness of Dedalus. Hence the dualism of inspiration and structure which is the fundamental fault of the book. The attempts at reconciling the two different models were clearly unsuccessful, and the more so because the dualism of the material obviously brought with it an unresolved dualism of narrative techniques.

In spite of Fitzgerald's statement, Byron's *Childe Harold* has very little to do with *This Side of Paradise*. But in the same letter and elsewhere he had hinted at a number of literary influences, and among them those of Compton Mackenzie and H. G. Wells cannot be overlooked. To many readers and reviewers the novel seemed an imitation of Mackenzie's *Sinister Street*, and it has in fact much in common with that book. The similarities, however, are more of general atmosphere and of situation, than of informing idea. Fitzgerald himself, in a letter to Frances Newman, stressed the autobiographical nature of the story and of its character, rather than the literary origins; and he was right in referring to Oscar Wilde as his own and Mackenzie's *common* source.[19]

The influence of H. G. Wells is much more important, especially for the technical devices used in the book. Wells exercised an influence on fictional technique in clear opposition to that of Henry James, with whom he had had a long debate on the art of fiction between 1911 and 1915. In an essay on contemporary fiction, he had welcomed the advent of a new type of novel, the "novel of amplitude," freed from any restriction of form, which was to develop according to a "rambling discursiveness." H. G. Wells stressed four major points: a preponderance of character over action, the irrelevance of thematic unity, the personal intrusion of the author in his work, the need for "saturation" and for the open discussion of scientific, social, and philosophical problems in the novel. Some of his statements have now become commonplace: "The distinctive value of the novel among works of art is in characterization . . ."; "Nothing is irrelevant if the writer's mood is happy . . ."; "Nearly all the novels that have, by the lapse of time, reached an assured position of recognized greatness, are not only saturated in the personality of the author, but have in addition quite unaffected personal outbreaks . . ."; "[The novel] is the only medium through which we can discuss the great majority of the problems." [20]

James had answered with an essay on the "new novel," in which he refuted the points advocated by Wells and repeated his own conviction that the novel needed a "center of interest"—either a narrator inside the action, or the author himself, who was to tell the story from a chosen point of view—and that the principle of *selection*, not of saturation, was the only guarantee of thematic unity.[21] Piqued and resentful, Wells wanted to reaffirm his principles in a spectacular way, and brought forth a strange book called *Boon, The Mind of the Race, The Wild Asses of the Devil, and the Last Trump,* in which a whole chapter was devoted to a vicious attack against James's fictional ideal. James's selection was to him simply a case of omission; his preoccupation with the right word was a waste of time, and his rigorous application of the point of view resulted in a complete absence of "blood and dust and heat."

The argument went on in private, in an exchange of letters between the two writers. James reproached Wells for his want of taste (Wells had even appended to his chapter in *Boon* a parody of James's style), and Wells shed crocodile tears in an abject apology. He called his writing "a waste-paper basket"; James could then remind him that it is unusual and unadvisable to print and publish what had better *stay* in a wastepaper basket. Wells insisted that fiction was like a great window open to the world; it was easy for James to rejoin that windows need frames: "The fine thing about the fictional form to me is that it opens such widely different windows of attention, but that is just why I like the window so to frame the play and the process!" [22]

The controversy had taken place in England, but its echoes had reached America, and as James E. Miller, Jr., has shown,[23] the terms "saturation" and "selection" were known and discussed in all their implications among critics and reviewers. While there is no evidence that Fitzgerald had read James at that time, there is ample evidence that he was infatuated with H. G. Wells. He often referred to Wells in his letters and in the notes for *This Side of Paradise,* and in 1917 he had written that *The New Machiavelli* by Wells was "the greatest English novel of the century." What is more, Fitzgerald had read *Boon* and had thought it "marvellous." He was well aware, as is evident from his letters, that Hugh Walpole and Compton Mackenzie were faithful disciples of Wells,[24] and we must assume that Fitzgerald had drawn a lesson from him. The lesson was precisely that of "saturation" as a fictional method. We could not find a better definition for the type of novel represented by *This Side of Paradise.*

All four points that Wells had stressed as attributes of the new novel can be found in Fitzgerald's book. First, the *"rambling* discursiveness" of the narration is more than evident—in fact, it had been described as a "picaresque *ramble."* Second, as all the interest is centered on Amory, the action is subordinated to his characterization. Third, many episodes have no thematic relevance, the author's intrusions are continual, and it is the personality of the *author* that "saturates" Amory and the book itself. More than once Fitzgerald appears openly in the book to change the mood or the development of the story, and toward the end it is no longer Amory but rather Fitzgerald who exposes his own "philosophy of life." In this last case the novel has been turned into a vehicle for the discussion of social and philosophical problems—exactly as Wells had maintained that it should.

Furthermore, the novel has no unity of form. A purely "dramatic" interlude alternates with a descriptive sketch, and a descriptive sketch in turn develops into pure dialogue. Sensational openings ("She paused at the top of the staircase . . ."; "CLARA. She was immemorial . . .") are followed by documentary reports; letters and reading lists are inserted in the text without explanation or transition, poems and songs, summaries and interludes are set one against the other. There is a little of everything in the book, and much more than there should be. And just as psychological analysis ends in prescriptions, the introspective moments end in exchanges of questions and answers:

> *Question.*—Well—What's the situation?
> *Answer.*—That I have about twenty-four dollars to my name.
> *Q.*—You have the Lake Geneva estate.
> *A.*—But I intend to keep it.
> *Q.*—Can you live? etc. etc. (*TSP,* p. 276),

and the dialogue breaks into stream of consciousness:

> One Hundred and Twenty-seventh Street—or One Hun-
> dred and Thirty-seventh Street . . . Two and Three look alike—
> no, not much. Seat damp . . . are clothes absorbing wetness
> from seat, or seat absorbing dryness from clothes? . . . Sitting
> on wet substance gave appendicitis, so Froggy Parker's mother
> said. Well, he'd had it—I'll sue the steamboat company,
> Beatrice said, and my uncle has a quarter interest—did Beatrice
> go to heaven? . . . probably not. (*TSP*, p. 278.)

In the great "amplitude" (or confusion) recommended by
Wells, then, we perceive again the influence of Joyce. In point of fact,
if the general principles are derived from Wells, Joyce's impressionistic technique was also imitated by Fitzgerald, and even on the level
of technique we might say that *This Side of Paradise* bears the signs
of an unresolved dualism of inspiration. An anonymous reviewer had
remarked that Fitzgerald was "following in general technique what
we might call the Impressionistic Novel shadowed forth in James
Joyce's *Portrait* . . . ," [25] and Edmund Wilson had praised it to Fitzgerald "because of its rigorous form and its polished style and because
the protagonist is presented with complete detachment." Certainly,
Joyce's book offered an example of "rigorous form," and it is clear
that Fitzgerald must have felt it, in spite of his general allegiance to
the precepts of Wells.

We might say, therefore, that just as on the thematic level the
influence of Joyce is superimposed on the influence of Wilde, on the
technical level the "amplitude" and the discursiveness of Wells came
to be mitigated by the impressionistic model of Joyce's *Portrait*. The
lack of thematic unity was bound to be reflected in a lack of stylistic
uniformity, and it is only within the single episodes of the book that
the various tensions give way and Fitzgerald can speak for himself.

In spite of all dissections, however, *This Side of Paradise*, as
Edmund Wilson remarked, "does not fail to live": and it lives because
of its youthful freshness and self-assurance, and thanks to the redeeming quality of its prose. We would not say that in the novel Fitzgerald
was able to achieve "epigrammatic beauty," "emotional depth," and
"a breath-taking quality of language," as a fine novelist like John
Marquand believes.[26] But he had already mastered a mature and
fluent prose, sweet and modulated, light and harmonious. It can be
melancholy and dreamy in its sentimental moments:

> The last light fades and drifts across the land—the low,
> long land, the sunny land of spires; the ghosts of evening tune
> again their lyres and wander singing in a plaintive band down
> the long corridors of trees; pale fires echo the night from tower
> top to tower: Oh, sleep that dreams, and dream that never
> tires, press from the petals of the lotus flower something of this
> to keep, the essence of an hour (*TSP*, p. 168),

or full of the sense of sudden change and death, sustained by a
nervousness of expression and by an inner movement:

> So the grey car crept nightward in the dark and there
> was no life stirred as it went by . . . As the still ocean paths
> before the shark in starred and glittering waterways, beauty-
> high, the moon-swathed trees divided, pair on pair, while
> flapping nightbirds cried across the air . . .
> A moment by an inn of lamps and shades, a yellow inn
> under a yellow moon—then silence, where crescendo laughter
> fades . . . the car swung out again to the winds of June, mel-
> lowed the shadows where the distance grew, then crushed
> the yellow shadows into blue . . . (*TSP*, p. 94.)

It is a prose that excels in moments of the most intense sentimental participation—the Isabelle or the Eleanor episode—and
which can expand into the slower rhythm of recollection and self-
analysis:

> There were days when Amory resented that life had
> changed from an even progress along a road stretching ever in
> sight, with the scenery merging and blending, into a succession
> of quick, unrelated scenes—two years of sweat and blood, that
> sudden absurd instinct for paternity that Rosalind had stirred;
> the half-sensual, half-neurotic quality of this autumn with
> Eleanor. He felt that it would take all time, more than he could
> ever spare, to glue these strange cumbersome pictures into the
> scrapbook of his life. (*TSP*, p. 250.)

Gertrude Stein had no hesitation in proclaiming young Fitzgerald "the only one of the younger writers who wrote naturally in
sentences." [27] Even at the early stage of his development, this would
be difficult to deny, and in the confusion of purposes, literary influences, and models, this was his first true and original success.

CHAPTER III

The Romantic Ideal

*The compensation of a very early
success is a conviction that life
is a romantic matter. In the best
sense one stays young.*

CU, p. 89.

1

Soon after the publication of *This Side of Paradise* Fitzgerald felt that
he "was now a professional," and a true mania for writing developed
in him. His popularity grew, and the magazines that had refused his
short stories before were now eager to publish them. Most of the
time these stories were hurriedly written—on the spur of the moment,
often for purely financial reasons and without any pretense of artistic
elaboration. It would be difficult to trace in them a consistent line of
development. One might say that Fitzgerald was groping his way in
the dazzling light of his own blinding success, and in this arresting
euphoria he was not above repeating motives that had already been
amply exploited in the novel. He realized the poor quality of most of
his stories, but he was discouraged by the fact that the public seemed
to prefer the ones he thought the poorest, and he felt somehow compelled to please his readers.[1] With this ambiguous attitude, he let the
good be smothered by the mediocre.

In *This Side of Paradise* Amory improvised a "philosophy of
life," uncertain and inconclusive, but clearly indicating a revolution
in manners and morals. All his various girls had proved to be flappers.
This was one of the many signs of the coming age of jazz: and Fitzgerald's stories were organized against the background of this golden
age, between the two fictional possibilities provided by the flappers
and their immature philosophers.

"Benediction"[2] is centered on the little crisis of one of these
flappers who has run away from home to marry her "philosopher";
after meeting her brother, who studies in a seminary, she is brought

to reconsider her step and reacquires a sense of traditional values. The story is interesting because it shows clearly that the writer was aware of the moral problems arising from the code of behavior of his youngsters. "Bernice Bobs Her Hair," [3] on the other hand, gives us a picture of the thoughtless behavior of these flappers, and the story has a purely humorous development. The situation revolves around youthful malice. Bernice agrees to bob her hair on the advice of her cousin (who has her own reasons for suggesting it), and when this expedient for greater popularity fails, Bernice takes her revenge by cutting her cousin's hair. Here the drama seems to be about as important as the length of the girls' hair—as if the idea for the story might have been suggested by *The Rape of the Lock*—and the story ends with a youthful shrug of the shoulder. Fantasy and farce are predominant in "The Offshore Pirate," [4] together with a tendency to the spectacular *dénouement;* "The Camel's Back" [5]—written, Fitzgerald tells us, "during one day in the city of New Orleans, with the express purpose of buying a wrist watch which cost six hundred dollars"—represents a further step toward farce. The protagonist goes to a masked ball in a camel's costume in which another man is hidden. A whole series of misunderstandings results in a mock marriage which turns out to be real, and in the end the man has the great satisfaction of winning back his girl. The whole thing is clearly a *divertissement;* in "Porcelain and Pink" [6] we are on the lower level of popular farce, and the trimmings match the mood. The attention of the reader is directed to a bathtub, from which a pink flapper tells her story in a careless way; and the flapper is represented here in her most prosaic activity, with a minimum of artistic elaboration. She is there simply to be watched; the general tone is again that of the college musicals—the story is laid down as pure dialogue and with the necessary stage directions.

The theme of flappers and philosophers can also be dealt with in a more mature way, especially if it is based on motives already present in *This Side of Paradise.* In "The Jelly-Bean" [7] the "philosopher" of idleness, who is the protagonist, lives through a crisis of "education" when he comes in contact with the flapper. He saves her from a gambling debt, but she turns away from his love to marry another on the very same night; the "jelly-bean," after the transitory elation of success, is brought to reconsider his life by the bitter disillusionment that he has suffered. The motive of the protagonist's "education" is also openly present in "Four Fists," [8] in each of the

four separate episodes that make up the story. The four fists by which
the protagonist is hit on four crucial occasions in his life constitute as
many phases of a long process of education, culminating in the
awakening of his sense of moral and social responsibility. The development of the plot is in this case rather mechanical, however, and
there is a lack of organic unity in the story, since the four episodes
are not properly related to each other.

A deep moral sense and a budding social awareness, structurally
united in an organic whole, went into the writing of the surprisingly
successful "May Day." [9] Just as the novel proposed to be the history
of a generation, this long story is intended to be the history of a period,
"the general hysteria of that spring which inaugurated the Jazz Age
(1919)." A series of apparently unrelated incidents is woven into a
pattern and unified by the particular historical background in which
they are set. The story opens with a quick sketch of the background
and then introduces one after another the adventures of various characters. Gordon Sterrett, ruined by the war and by his weakness, is
desperately trying to borrow some money that will save him; Philip
Dean, enriched by the war, turns down his request for a loan; Edith,
who had once been Gordon's girl, recoils from him, horrified at his
degradation, when she meets him at a party. To the same party,
after dragging through the city on a drunken spree, come Rose and
Key, two poor soldiers, who end up in a closet from which, symbolically, they come out only to steal drinks, or to meet Peter Himmel,
Edith's neglected escort. Gradually, the mood of the party changes
from gaiety to hysteria. Edith goes to visit her brother who works for
a socialist paper and is caught in the office when a mob of demon-
strators give vent to their restlessness and rage. This new, frightening
experience brings about a profound change in Edith. Her brother is
wounded; one of the two soldiers is killed. Edith watches with horror
as Philip and Peter continue their spree, going from one bar to
another, while Gordon goes back to the vulgar Jewel and commits
suicide. Begun with a documentary purpose, "May Day" becomes an
artistic achievement because of its dramatic presentation of a series
of events and its careful plot—the soul, as Aristotle said, of the action.
It is, in fact, the masterful disposition of the various episodes and the
way in which they are related and woven together that make the
story interesting. There are no loose ends, no incongruous parts in
the story, and each thread is taken up and given its final twist at the
end with an economy of means that makes it possible for a vast frame

of events to find its focus. Fitzgerald faced the structural problem of a skillful plot-disposition with full aesthetic awareness.[10] For the first time he made use of the technique of foreshortening which Henry James had advocated and which he was later to develop with greater skill. There is a corresponding maturity in the perception of the theme. Fitzgerald often confused himself with his characters, but here he assumed an objective viewpoint that permitted him to combine a wide frame of reference with a particular relief given to each separate scene and to its thematic relevance. To give a picture of a particular historical moment, he did not avail himself of the reactions of a single character, but instead made up that picture by resorting to distinctly varied characters. This was a step forward from *This Side of Paradise.*

Amory's motivations were taken from Fitzgerald's own private stock of limited experience. Here the motivations of the characters have a common basis—the *malaise* caused by the war—and are defined according to the different psychological make-up of contrasting characters and to the varying environments from which they sprang. The historic background—the aftermath of the war, that would inspire the great American writers of the period from Faulkner in *Soldier's Pay* to Dos Passos in *Three Soldiers,* from E. E. Cummings in *The Enormous Room* to Hemingway—is a kind of determining factor in the behavior of the characters, but the subtle shades of social distinction among them are equally important. The difference between Philip and Gordon is the result of their contrasting psychological natures, but it also has something to do with the difference in the social milieu from which they spring. The two run-down soldiers contrast their abjectness with the thoughtless carelessness of the two rich "philosophers" of the jazz age. Edith, untouchable in her aristocratic aloofness and in her selfishness, is the counterpart of Jewel, who is vehemently attached to Gordon by her insecurity and need for support. The socialist ideas of Amory, it should be remembered, were of an emotional and sentimental origin. In "May Day," the social contrast is represented in an objective way and becomes the focal point of the central episode in the newspaper office. The experiences that are brought to bear on the story reveal a clear perception of social matters, as will be the case with *The Great Gatsby.*

"May Day" is an isolated achievement among the commercial stories. But some of these deal with motives and themes that Fitzgerald was to exploit in his next novel, *The Beautiful and Damned,* and are therefore interesting as early attempts to come to terms with new subject matter. One gets the impression that Fitzgerald's artistic sensibility was still uncertain and that he wavered between various thematic possibilities. He abandoned himself to the inspiration of the moment, and his spirit *en disponibilité* did not refuse a single suggestion.

"Head and Shoulders" [11] deals with the theme of the reversibility of roles and the transference of vitality—the motive that inspired so many works of Henry James and which was to be of paramount importance in *Tender Is the Night*. The theme is here treated as pure *divertissement,* but its early appearance in Fitzgerald's fiction is worth noting. One character, an "intellectual monster," becomes in the end a circus performer, while his wife, who was a thoughtless actress, has an enormous success as an author. What interests us now, even in this rather mediocre story, is how the theme of the "education" of a character is gradually replaced by the opposite theme of the "deterioration" of a character. This change in Fitzgerald's fiction is apparent, even from the title, in "Dalyrimple Goes Wrong," [12] where the protagonist, a war hero, accepts one moral compromise after another until he finally becomes a gangster and begins, ironically enough, a political career. This story is undoubtedly one of the worst, but the "philosophy of life" which is here expressed is closer to Anthony Patch's than to Amory's, if all that Dalyrimple wants is to find happiness in money:

> Happiness was what he wanted—a slowly rising scale of gratifications of the normal appetites,—and he had a strong conviction that the materials, if not the inspiration of happiness, would be bought with money.

In "The Ice Palace" [13] the central theme is given by the social contrast between the North and the South, which will reappear to a certain extent in the third part of *The Beautiful and Damned.* A Southern belle arrives in a Northern city to meet her fiancé, and her contact with the coldness and the mental rigidity of the North proves fatal to her. Sally loses her way in the cellar of an ice palace, and when she finally succeeds in finding her way out of the place she has suffered such a shock that she feels that she might no longer adjust to normal life. The contrast between the North and the South is dealt with in a very superficial way, and it revolves round the banal idea of the difference in climate. But despite this obvious weakness, we notice a new tendency to use symbolical images (the ice palace itself) and a predilection for the tale of horror that might be traced back to an influence of Edgar Allan Poe. A nightmare quality informs the story, and the same can be said of "The Cut-Glass Bowl." [14]

In this story the idea of the central symbol might have been suggested by James's *The Golden Bowl* or by Poe's "Lenore," although in both cases the idea was probably taken from the Bible. The development of the story, however, tends to recreate a typically Hawthornian atmosphere of fatal gloom. The family at the center of the story undergoes a series of frightful adventures, which are all in direct relationship with the fatal bowl. The bowl had been broken in the very first scene, when the protagonist was discovered by her husband with another man, and it becomes clear that the cut-glass bowl is a symbol of human destiny. As one can see from his *Notebooks,* Hawthorne was very fond of identifying ideas with concrete things, abstract concepts with everyday objects, and this same preoccupation is present in Fitzgerald's story. But in his case, the symbolism is open and obvious, the style jumbled and forced, and we conclude that once again he followed models that he had imperfectly understood.

And yet, we are on the way to *The Beautiful and Damned,* both for the apparent use of symbolism and for the appearance of the theme of deterioration and decay. Even closer to the novel are two other stories of questionable literary worth: "'O Russet Witch'" [15] and "The Lees of Happiness." [16] The former deals with the pursuit of an ideal love by a modest worker, who remains faithful to a youthful image through the years, until he realizes that all the fascination and splendor of the woman he pursues is only a product of his imagination. For him, as it would later be for Anthony in *The Beautiful and Damned,* idealized love proves a deception. "The Lees of Happiness" has its initial situation as well as the motive of the protagonist's deterioration in common with the novel. Just when a successful writer believes that he has achieved the fullest happiness by marrying a beautiful actress, a cerebral hemorrhage reduces him to a mere dummy of a man. His wife remains with him for eleven years, and finally, at his death, she has no further desire for a life of her own. Her defeat is the result of the long wait that destroys the significance and the importance of her final liberation; and this is the sense of Anthony's and Gloria's adventure in the novel. In the story the conclusion stresses the serenity of the heroine's renunciation ("To these two life had come quickly and gone, leaving not bitterness, but pity; not disillusion, but only pain. There was already enough moonlight when they shook hands for each to see the gathered kindness in the other's eye."), and the tragic plight of the characters is determined by unavoidable circumstances. But the general tone of sadness is already that of the novel, especially in the central part, where the heroine watches helplessly the dissolution of her husband's personality, as Gloria was later to do in *The Beautiful and Damned*.

In these stories Fitzgerald already shows a clear inclination to represent weak or flawed characters, undermined by illusion, unequal to the struggle for existence. His flappers and philosophers reveal the fragility of their capacity for living, the precariousness of their careless and challenging attitudes. The flaw of evil is also present in the golden world of youthful indifference. If we have spent some time on these stories, whose artistic value would not always justify specific critical interest, we have done so because *The Beautiful and Damned*, like the previous novel, came at the end of a long period of apprenticeship or preparation. Gloria is in a way Anthony's "russet witch," and the "lees of happiness" will ruin both of them.

2

The theme of *The Beautiful and Damned*—written at the time of the stories just mentioned and published serially in *The Metropolitan Magazine* (September 1921–March 1922) before being issued in book form—is the dissipation and deterioration of the inner self. Two people, husband and wife, are equally guilty of an excessive indulgence in illusions and dreams. This idea of a motivated failure of the protagonists was in the author's mind since the very first conception of the new novel, even if he was thinking at the time of giving a new portrait of the young aesthete:

> My new novel—[he had written in 1920]—called *The Flight of the Rocket*, concerns the life of one Anthony Patch between his 25th and 33d years (1913–1921). He is one of those many with the tastes and weaknesses of an artist but with no actual creative inspiration. How he and his beautiful young wife are wrecked on the shoals of dissipation is told in the story. (*Letters*, p. 145.)

If ties with the "young artist" that Amory had been are still visible, we cannot say that the new novel was to continue his story, because Anthony Patch is bound from the start to become a failure, and his story is to be seen in close interdependence with the story of his wife. The interdependence of the two characters was emphasized in the title of the manuscript, which was called "The Beautiful Lady Without Mercy" and had furthermore an epigraph taken from Keats's "La Belle Dame Sans Merci." [17] This epigraph disappeared in the published version of the novel—the new title clearly indicating that both Anthony and Gloria were victims of a romantic conception of the world. But the main theme of the dissipation of the two characters remained as it had been conceived originally, all the more painful because their ruin is the result of an apparent, but deceptive material victory. Anthony and Gloria struggle against philistinism and hypocritical morality so as to be able to prolong their dissipation, but their victory, reached when it is too late, only serves to make the feeling of incurable defeat the more terrible. "The victor belongs to the spoils," reads the new epigraph: and there was never a more bitter and hollow victory than this one, which leaves the two characters among the spoils and remnants of their struggle and of their existence. It is a pathetic struggle, too weakly and too selfishly fought to become tragic, which reveals the flaws of decay and deterioration under the golden appearance of success. As with Amory in the earlier novel, the story of the two characters, so "beautiful and damned," is developed as a moral parable, linearly unfolded, though with a better feeling for the general structure. And the parable is precisely that of the youthful dreams and illusions that gradually become a lethargy and then a nightmare and are involved in an inevitable ruin.

The novel is divided into three books, [18] each in turn divided into three chapters. Each book represents a distinct moment in the development of the story, while the chapters themselves mark the progressive unfolding of the parable. From a complete abandonment to dreams at the beginning, the two protagonists fall to tasting the lees of an illusory happiness and find that the dreams have become nightmares. Just as in *This Side of Paradise*, a "portrait" of Anthony is given at the very beginning: he is a sophisticated and blasé aesthete, who lives in a comfortable ivory tower in a New York apartment. More mature than Amory and lacking his sentimental obsession with socialism, Anthony has the advantage of a certain culture (he reads Flaubert's *Education Sentimentale* ...), is independent and rich, and has his future assured by the prospect of a big inheritance. He is more refined than his predecessor and enjoys the close friendship of a small set of people, through whom he makes hesitant and timid approaches to the world. His real desire is to perpetuate his pleasant life; he is content to contemplate his own image (there is a touch of Narcissus in him, too) in the golden mirrors and polished surfaces of his house. His favorite retreat is the bathtub, and there he weaves immaterial dreams, castles in the air, reveries of himself contemplating sensual beauties, or playing imaginary violins:

> He felt that if he had a love he would have hung her picture just facing the tub so that, lost in the soothing steamings of the hot water, he might lie and look up at her and muse warmly and sensuously on her beauty... (*BD*, pp. 11–12.)

> He raised his voice to compete with the flood of water pouring into the tub, and as he looked at the picture of Hazel Dawn upon the wall he put an imaginary violin to his shoulder and softly caressed it with a phantom bow. (*BD*, p. 17.)

All his social and cultural attempts dissolve in that dreamy atmosphere. He feels compelled to do something, and he can think of nothing better than writing a history of the Middle Ages. He feels that he should allow himself some diversions, and he finds a girl, Geraldine, who offers him a new mirror in which to gaze at himself. She is held at a distance and kept for certain hours, because "she was company, familiar, and faintly intimate and restful. Further than that he did not care to experiment—not from any moral compunction, but from a dread of allowing any entanglement to disturb what he felt was the growing serenity of his life."

A "Flash-Back in Paradise," however, marking the birth of the "beautiful" Gloria, is sufficient to put the serenity of his life in jeopardy. Gloria is a new, more dangerous incarnation of the "debutante" or flapper, both careless and fascinating. She, too, is possessed by an illusory dream, the dream of a beauty to whom all is due, who accepts no responsibility and subordinates every other aspect of life to an aesthetic principle. To Gloria, "who took all things of life for hers to choose from and apportion, as though she were continually picking out presents for herself from an inexhaustible counter," it is enough for people to "fit into the picture." She does not mind "if they don't do anything." "I don't see why they should—in fact it almost astonishes me when anybody does anything."

Her meeting with Anthony is therefore perfectly logical and unavoidable. And yet, if the aesthete gives up his dream of detachment from the world, of aloofness and isolation, it is only to replace it with a new dream—the dream of eternal love. He knows very well that he is not "a realist," that Gloria requites his love because he is "clean," but greatly interested as he is by every girl "who made a living directly on her prettiness," there is no possible escape for him. It can be either "white" or "black magic," but Gloria fills him with dissatisfaction, then panic, and finally brings him to the altar.

Anthony and Gloria throw their illusions together, but the dream of one cannot but suffer in contact with that of the other. The illusion of love as an absorbing way of life collides with the ideal that sees marriage as a means of satisfying one's vanity:

> Marriage was created not to be a background but to need one—says Gloria—. Mine is going to be outstanding. It can't, shan't be the setting—it's going to be the performance, the live, lovely, glamorous performance, and the world shall be the scenery. (*BD*, p. 147.)

After the precarious "radiant hour" (that opens the second book), Anthony finds his serenity compromised, while Gloria finds herself without the much-coveted security. Her "tremendous nervous tension" contrasts with his utter cowardice. A new dream, that of an expected inheritance, keeps them together. But Adam Patch is not so eager to die, and he disapproves of their fast spending and reckless living. He keeps a close watch on them, while they are unconsciously preparing their ruin. Anthony tries in vain to go on with his book and has a short and fruitless working experience; Gloria plays with the idea of becoming a film actress, but her husband objects to it. His further attempt to write commercial short stories is also a failure.

Their dream becomes gradually an inexcusable form of lethargy, and after their refusal to have a child, this lethargy kills even the illusion of eternal love. "Gloria had lulled Anthony's mind to sleep ... [she] realized that Anthony had become capable of utter indifference toward her, a temporary indifference, more than half lethargic. ..." Only a childish vision of future happiness and security stirs them at times from their lethargy:

> That spring, that summer, they had speculated upon future happiness—how they were to travel from summer land to summer land, returning eventually to a gorgeous estate and possible idyllic children, then entering diplomacy or politics, to accomplish, for a while, beautiful and important things, until finally as a white-haired (beautifully, silkily, white-haired)

couple they were to loll about in serene glory, worshipped by the bourgeoisie of the land.... These times were to begin "when we get our money"; it was on such dreams rather than on any satisfaction with their increasingly irregular, increasingly dissipated life that their hope rested. (*BD*, p. 277.)

Their expectation could not rest on weaker foundations. In a highly dramatic scene, Adam Patch, the old millionaire, who is a prohibitionist and a supporter of a Victorian moral code, visits them at the climax of a drunken party. The blow proves fatal for him and for the hopes of Anthony and Gloria as well, because they are disinherited.

Then lethargy turns into a nightmare. Even Anthony realizes that he "had been futile in longing to drift and dream; no one drifted except to maelstroms, no one dreamed without his dreams becoming fantastic nightmares of indecision and regret." This realization, however, is only temporary, and the two react by attaching themselves desperately to the hope of winning back the inheritance. They have now to contest the will, but their struggle (related in the third book) is really on two fronts, because their inner tensions break the remaining ties of love and destroy all their serenity. Anthony welcomes the diversion offered by the war and enlists to escape, as it were, his own self and his contradictions, but even this illusion is wrecked by the ruthless impact of reality.

Stationed in a Southern military camp, Anthony ends by getting himself entangled in a sordid love affair, which is represented as "an inevitable result of his increasing carelessness about himself.... He merely slid into the matter through his inability to make definite judgments." This same inability is responsible for his breaking bounds to go and see his new girl, with the inevitable result of being stripped of his rank. Thus, even his respectability and self-respect are ruined, and he plunges again into a nightmare of helpless impotence and dissatisfaction. Meanwhile, Gloria, who has recognized the failure of their love ("That she had not been happy with Anthony for over a year mattered little"), falls back on the obstinate dream of her beauty. She flirts with old friends and new acquaintances, makes a new attempt to go into the movies, which results in bitter failure, and is unable to come to terms with reality. Not understanding that circumstances and people change, she reverts to childhood, dreaming of being a child again, of being protected, expecting "to wake in some high, fresh-scented room, alone, and statuesque within and without, as in her virginal and colorful past."

But the present intrudes; it offers only the pale image of an Anthony who, back from the military camp, spends his time in the house turning his back on every human or worldly contact. The aesthetic recluse has become the melancholy hermit of indigence and helplessness. Anthony spends his time wearily reading newspapers in the midst of disorder and filth, and now more than ever he has recourse to the deceptive relief of drinking. He too reverts to the dream of his past youth, and he too discovers that he is unfit for the present. Even his drinking aims at recreating an equivocal atmosphere of dreamy sentimentalism and decadent aestheticism:

> There was a kindliness about intoxication—there was that indescribable gloss and glamor it gave, like the memories of ephemeral and faded evenings. After a few high-balls there was magic in the tall glowing Arabian night of the Bush Terminal Building. . . .
> . . . The fruit of youth or of the grape, the transitory magic of the brief passage from darkness to darkness—the old illusion that truth and beauty were in some way entwined. (*BD*, p. 417.)

Anthony comes to realize that it *is* an illusion, but it is a devastating realization. His psychological balance is broken, and he resorts to pointless violence. He provokes Bloeckman, his former rival, to a fight, and when Dorothy, the Southern girl, comes to see him in New York, he suffers a nervous collapse. It is at this point that the news reaches him that he has finally won his suit against the will and that he owns thirty million dollars.

Their dream is realized, but only when it is too late. The slow and inexorable passing of time has made this victory *in extremis* a hollow one. With a touch of dramatic irony, the reversal of fortune overtakes the two characters only when their initial situation has been reversed. Anthony, sophisticated and blasé at the beginning, is now an empty shell who goes to Europe with a doctor at his side. Sparkling Gloria, who used to divide people into clean and unclean, now herself appears "sort of dyed and *unclean*."

3

If we read the story in this way—disentangling its meaning from the mass of obtrusive material and subsidiary aspects—it becomes clear enough that it is a parable on the deceptiveness of dreams, on the impossibility of evading reality through illusions, and on the painful destructiveness of time. The very evil that wears away the life of the flapper who refuses to grow up and the life of the "philosopher" who cannot come to grips with reality and experience is hidden in their youthful dreams, in their careless attitude of defiance toward the world, in their refusal to evaluate and accept the effects of time. Far from being the mouthpiece or the singer of the jazz age, Fitzgerald was its lucid accuser. He was well aware of its equivocal dangers, of its irresponsible attitudes, and he pitilessly exposed its disastrous consequences—even admitting that his denunciation was achieved almost in spite of his own intentions and was brought to light in the novel almost unconsciously.

If the meaning of the story told in *The Beautiful and Damned* must be identified with the gradual denunciation of Anthony's and Gloria's irresponsible progress of deterioration, and with an exposition of their guilty behavior toward themselves and the world, one cannot deny that in many passages Fitzgerald reveals a tendency to bestow on Anthony, if not on Gloria, a kind of moral greatness that contradicts the *objective* development of his adventure. At times Fitzgerald seemed to falter between a desire to show the "heroic" side of Anthony and a willingness to criticize his pointless endeavors. The story itself admits of no other possibility than a bitter denunciation of Anthony and Gloria, because their actions speak for themselves, and there is little doubt as to their purport. But at the very end of the book Anthony is represented in an ambiguous light and almost praised for his refusal "to give in, to submit to mediocrity, to go to work":

> Anthony Patch, sitting near the rail and looking out at the sea, was not thinking of his money [!], for he had seldom in his life been really preoccupied with material vainglory. . . . No—he was concerned with a series of reminiscences, much as a general might look back upon a successful campaign and analyze his victories. He was thinking of the hardships, the insufferable tribulations he had gone through. They had tried to penalize him for the mistakes of his youth. . . .
>
> Only a few months before people had been urging him to give in, to submit to mediocrity, to go to work. But he had known that he was justified in his way of life—and he had stuck it out staunchly. . . .
>
> "I showed them," he was saying. "It was a hard fight, but I didn't give up and I came through!" (*BD*, pp. 448–49.)

His last words are words of self-satisfaction and defiance, and his long struggle is here represented in a sympathetic light. This final reversal of the moral judgment is even more apparent in the magazine version of the novel, in which Fitzgerald not only defended the grandeur of Anthony's and Gloria's desperate attempt, but went so far as to exalt the validity of its motivation—"the freshness and fulness of their desire." "Their fault was not that they had doubted but that they had believed," Fitzgerald had written. Their only "disastrous extremes" were identified with "the exquisite perfection of their boredom, the delicacy of their inattention, the inexhaustibility of their discontent," and their figures acquired a halo of romantic suffering and purity. It is worthwhile quoting the whole final passage of the magazine version, which justifies, among other things, the title of the last chapter ("Together with the Sparrows") which was retained in the book:

> That exquisite heavenly irony which had tabulated the demise of many generations of sparrows seems to us to be content with the moral judgments of man upon fellow man. If there is a subtle and yet more nebulous ethic somewhere in the mind, one might believe that beneath the sordid dress and near the bruised heart of this transaction there was a motive which was not weak but only futile and sad. In the search for happiness, which search is the greatest and possibly the only crime of which we in our petty misery are capable, these two people were marked as guilty chiefly by the freshness and fulness of their desire. Their illusion was always a comparative thing—they had sought glamor and color through their respective worlds with steadfast loyalty—sought it and it alone in kisses and in wine, sought it with the same ingenuousness in the wanton moonlight as under the cold sun of inviolate chastity. Their fault was not that they had doubted but that they had believed.
>
> The exquisite perfection of their boredom, the delicacy of their inattention, the inexhaustibility of their discontent— were disastrous extremes—that was all. And if, before Gloria yielded up her gift of beauty, she shed one bright feather of light so that someone, gazing up from the grey earth, might say, "Look! There is an angel's wing!" perhaps she had given more than enough for her tinsel joys.[19]

The logical development of the story is here given a deliberate twist; and it is perhaps significant that this idea of a moral comment on his characters that would justify their struggle and explain its motivations came to Fitzgerald, it seems, at the last moment and in a sudden flash, since in the manuscript version of the novel the story closed simply with the return of Gloria to her Paradise:

> The stars greeted her intimately as they went by and the winds made a soft welcoming flurry in the air. Sighing, she began a conversation with a voice that was in the white wind.
> "Back again," the voice whispered.
> "Yes."
> "After fifteen years."
> "Yes."
> The voice hesitated.
> "How remote you are," it said, "Unstirred. . . . You seem to have no heart. How about the little girl? The glory of her eyes is gone—"
> But Beauty had forgotten long ago.

Such a conclusion probably belonged to an early conception of the novel, when Gloria (la belle dame sans merci) was to be represented as the main cause of Anthony's deterioration and ruin. But it makes it clear that Fitzgerald had not completely mastered his material when he published the novel and that his final rehabilitation of Anthony was due to a sudden impulse which reflected, somehow, a basic uncertainty as to his real stature and accomplishments. Traces of this wavering attitude toward Anthony can in fact be found in other passages of the book as well, and they must be acknowledged, even if it means recognizing that The Beautiful and Damned does not present a story as straightforward as one would like to have it.

Consider, for instance, the nature of Anthony's relationship with his few friends, especially at the beginning. It is clear that he enjoys an unquestionable superiority over Maury Noble and Richard Caramel, but even after his "downfall" Fitzgerald represents him as superior to both Noble and Caramel. It is true that Noble, in spite of his nihilistic tirade in the middle of the book (at the end of the chapter entitled "Symposium"), succumbs to a respectable, middle-class marriage, and that Caramel undertakes a brilliant career as a commercial novelist—a career which gives him fame and fortune, but does not redeem him from the limitations of his talent and the meanness of his compromises. Still, Anthony does not do any better than they: but by using these two figures, Fitzgerald apparently wished to set off in relief the purity, "the exquisite perfection" and the inaccessibility of Anthony, who remains true to his initial ideals without ever descending to a vulgar compromise. This is made quite clear in an episode toward the end, when poor Caramel is violently abused by Anthony, and Fitzgerald seems to watch the performance with great gusto.

The same might be said, with different qualifications, of Gloria, whose fascinating personality predominates in many episodes of the book and whose charm is felt both by Fitzgerald and the reader. But even if Fitzgerald's intent—conscious or unconscious—was to extol the "beauty" of his two characters by contrasting them with the mediocrity of middle-class life and ideals, we must still say that the remedy proposed is worse than the evil indicated and that this alternative to reality denies its own reasons, because the two protagonists are "damned" without hope by their actions and attitudes, as they are developed and made apparent in the story. And they are damned not only in the eyes of the world, or for moralistic considerations on the part of the readers, but because their story *is* a story of self-destruction, which naturally results in inner and outer ruin.

All this must be taken into consideration to understand the exact nature and quality of the book and its deeper meaning, in spite of the many misleading suggestions that we have to confront. *The Beautiful and Damned* is not "a distressing tragedy which should be, also, 100 per cent meaningless," as Edmund Wilson claimed, if we see beyond the surface into its *objective* line of development. And it is not a mere "muddle" in the presentation of the two characters, as Arthur Mizener maintained,[20] if we see their true natures behind the screen of their self-complacency. The book has a meaning and a significance, even if its theme is not rigorously focused and consistently developed to its logical conclusion.

The reason for this incongruity lies perhaps in the fact that Fitzgerald's attempt was too ambitious. Soon after his autobiographical *This Side of Paradise,* he was facing a new and complex theme which required a considerable amount of objective treatment. Amory had been a direct projection of the writer himself. To Anthony and Gloria he gave many characteristics, traits, and apprehensions of his own and of his wife, but he imagined his characters' experience as a possibility, rather than representing his own private experience. It was not simply a question of evoking or recreating a personal reality—it was rather a question of bringing to life an imaginary situation, which he had contemplated as a possibility, with no immediate connection with his own life, and which was to be represented in its objective development.[21] In this ambitious attempt Fitzgerald proved himself unequal to the exacting task of controlling the objective development of his characters according to a rigorous thematic principle. He tried to detach himself from his characters, to stand aside and unfold their story in all its implications, going so far as to pass a moral judgment on them. On the other hand, he sympathized with his characters and shared some of their illusions and not a few of their attitudes, with the result that he felt like justifying, incongruously, the greatness of their attempt. He had, in other words, to expose and denounce two characters who appealed to him, or to justify their beauty in spite of their damnation. He wanted to do both things, and the thematic unity of the book was seriously compromised. The double choice offered in the title is reflected in the lack of a consistent resolution of its conflicting motives. The objective and inescapable result of the action is that Anthony and Gloria are "damned": and they cannot be, therefore, as "beautiful" as the author tries to make them.

This is why we have to conclude that *The Beautiful and Damned* is a transitional novel. It lies half-way between a youthful success and the achievement of maturity. But if it is a novel of transition, it is so because some of the limitations of *This Side of Paradise* were transcended. Flappers and philosophers celebrate no triumphs in this novel. If they do seem to gain a victory, it is soon shown to be illusory and deceptive, a subtle form of irredeemable defeat, the snare of moral misery. Although sympathizing with the defiant attitude of his heroes, Fitzgerald feels the need to pass a moral judgment on them, and even in their glamorous and careless way of life he reveals the hidden flaw of failure and defeat. In spite of his enthusiasms, in *The Beautiful and Damned* Fitzgerald is concerned with exposing the inner meaning of life, not with reproducing its brilliant surface alone; he is concerned with suffering and the bitter aspects of experience, not with its playful manifestations. "I guess I am too much of a moralist at heart"—he was to write in his notes—"and really want to preach at people in some acceptable form, rather than to entertain them." [22] This inclination—if not yet this intention—is already present in his second novel.

4

This "moralistic" attitude and the theme of individual failure were so little of a personal and autobiographical nature that they can be traced back to a distinct literary influence. Edmund Wilson, in his essay already quoted, claimed that *The Beautiful and Damned* was an attempt in which Fitzgerald had tried to use the principles of a new school of writing that he called "ironical-pessimistic," and in this way it was to be connected with a literary movement whose spokesman was H. L. Mencken. In the light of more recent studies, James E. Miller, Jr., has again demonstrated that the origin of the book, as well as its "message," are to be traced directly to Mencken's influence.

Fitzgerald had "discovered" Mencken at the time of his first contributions to *The Smart Set*, and there are many indications of his growing admiration for this slashing critic of American philistinism.[23] Soon after its publication, Fitzgerald reviewed Mencken's *Prejudices: Second Series* (1921),[24] and a few months later he praised Mencken as the writer who had had the most beneficial effects on American literature. In an interview which he gave the next year Fitzgerald recognized his debt to Mencken, if not for *This Side of Paradise*, at least for his following works.[25]

This might have been a momentary infatuation: but it is significant that in the first essay of the volume which Fitzgerald had reviewed—an essay entitled "The National Letters"—Mencken had expressed some literary principles that the younger writer was clearly to follow in *The Beautiful and Damned*. These principles were expressed in the context of a severe criticism of the contemporary cultural scene, and Mencken's position was not so much an aesthetic as a moralistic one. He did not dwell on stylistic or technical problems (he actually denied their importance) and was more concerned with the choice of an acceptable subject matter for the novelist. He maintained that the interest of "superior fiction" lay in the representation of the conflict "between a salient individual and the harsh and meaningless fiats of destiny," in the struggle of a hero who is not "one who yields and wins, but one who resists and fails." Starting from the assumption that "the theme of the great bulk of superior fiction . . . [is] character in decay," he came to the conclusion that "in nearly all first-rate novels the hero is defeated. In perhaps a majority he is completely destroyed." [26] It was not so in America, but that was the way to be taken.

To this plea one might say that Fitzgerald answered in his own way. His interest in a "character in decay"—in a hero who "resists and fails," rather than yields and wins, who is defeated if not completely destroyed—might easily have been suggested by Mencken's statements, or at least confirmed by Mencken's analysis. In this instance, the influence would be all the more important, because it would explain better than anything else Fitzgerald's ambiguous attitude toward his characters in *The Beautiful and Damned,* which we have analyzed. Mencken's moralistic assumption was difficult to reconcile with his almost morbid preoccupation with decadence and decay, with the defeat of salient individuals. But he had stressed the value and importance of the struggle; and in *The Beautiful and Damned,* while showing Anthony's and Gloria's decay and defeat, Fitzgerald had defended to the very end the value and the greatness of their struggle, even when the struggle itself became a sign of their decadence.

Mencken was, therefore, probably responsible for the particular type of story that the young novelist wanted to attempt, and at the same time he created some difficulties for the young moralist. Fitzgerald himself complicated those difficulties when he chose a specific literary model from among those suggested by Mencken—Theodore Dreiser's *Sister Carrie.* Mencken's influence was purely thematic: it suggested a certain type of story. Dreiser's influence, on the other hand, was both thematic (the progress of deterioration and failure of two characters) and stylistic: and for this second aspect, the choice was unhappy. The atmosphere of decadence evoked in the last section of *The Beautiful and Damned* recalls in many ways the atmosphere toward the conclusion of *Sister Carrie,* while the heaviness and monotony of style is in both cases a typical example of "pathetic fallacy." [27]

Fitzgerald's model, as in *This Side of Paradise,* was imperfectly understood and only partly followed, but its influence is clearly discernible. The deterioration of Hurstwood, in Dreiser's novel, has many points in common with Anthony's deterioration and decay: the lack of a regular job, the sordid rooms in which both men waste away their lives, the friends who are shabbier and shabbier, the inner dejection and helplessness, the want of cash, and then the mean arguments, the hopeless drinking, the newspapers read in a gloomy half-light, the drifting along the empty streets, and so on. Hurstwood himself is represented as a "pilgrim adream"—his dream, too, becomes a lethargy and then a nightmare. But in Hurstwood's case, many important economic and social factors were responsible for his ruin. If his destiny is determined by his own weakness—his hamartia, his tragic flaw—it is also the result of the concurrence of external circumstances, such as the ruthless laws of the business world and the deep-rooted social prejudices of middle-class philistinism, to which Carrie's desertion must be added. His destiny is therefore tragic, not merely pathetic as is the destiny of Anthony and Gloria, whose weaknesses are not matched by a corresponding conflict of outer forces. Gloria identifies herself with Anthony's fatal lethargy, but Carrie does not do so with Hurstwood's. And whereas Carrie's vitality permits her to make a new life for herself in the theater world, Gloria's similar attempt to go into the movies is bound to failure, just because she cannot accept the basic rules of the game. Anthony hasn't the justifications of Hurstwood, nor Gloria the virtues of Carrie—who is guilty as well, but for other reasons irrelevant here. Anthony is not rebuffed by the world but by his own and Gloria's refusal to accept reality.[28]

Through Dreiser—and Mencken, almost *malgré lui*—Fitzgerald was linking himself with the finest vein of American naturalism, but he did it with rather poor material and with imperfect knowledge of it. From naturalism, moreover, he derived a questionable stylistic lesson. Compared with the previous novel, *The Beautiful and Damned* shows that Fitzgerald was availing himself of the same narrative technique, although with the advantage of a more harmonious structure. The quality of his language, however, is greatly compromised.

As in *This Side of Paradise,* the action is based on the development of the characters, even if we note that the development is here a negative one, a process of deterioration. The action, in other words, is subordinate to characterization; there are frequent intrusions of the author himself, and although there is no open discussion of philosophical or social problems (with the notable exception of Maury Noble's speech in the chapter called "Symposium"),[29] yet the novel serves as a vehicle for the exposition of a social problem. The principle of inclusion or discursiveness is finally responsible for the excessive length of the book. There is little selectivity in these pages, and secondary episodes or characters are not always relevant to the main theme. The satirical section about Gloria's parents in the first part, a great many scenes in the second, and most of the events in the third could easily be foreshortened to the great advantage of thematic unity. Maury Noble and Caramel, for example, are given excessive importance in the general economy of the novel. The links between one episode and another are often casual, and even their disposition in short sections within the chapters is not due to a desire for clarity, but to an attempt at a kind of kaleidoscopic pattern of isolated facets, which in the end compose an enormous, confused fresco. It is a serious criticism for a novel of which the writer himself was to say: "I devoted so much more care myself to the *detail* of the book than I did to thinking out the *general* theme." [30] Moreover, the old device of alternating parts of pure dialogue ("The Men," "A Flash-Back in Paradise," "The Ushers," "The Broken Lute") with proper narration is used with little functional precision. The same device had been used by Melville in *Moby Dick* (Chapter 36, "The Quarter Deck") and by Joyce in *Ulysses* for crucial scenes. Fitzgerald uses it in "The Broken Lute"—the turning point of the book, but here the pure dialogue does nothing but slow the rhythm and loosen any form of dramatic tension. It is not the crowning of a mounting tension that breaks down into dramatic dialogue because of its intensity; it is only a dull and clumsy beginning (see the long stage direction that sets the scene), followed by an anticlimax—the "retrospect" section— in which the emotional reaction of the characters to the preceding scene is wearily analyzed. It is the same as dividing the comment from the action, depriving the one and the other of their proper force and significance.

This awkward procedure, to which must be added a documentary tendency that is typically naturalistic in kind,[31] deadens the lightness of touch and the "impressionism" that are distinctive features of *This Side of Paradise,* while the general heaviness of tone is increased by the poor quality of the language. Fitzgerald seems to have lost his gift for "writing naturally in sentences." Here his sentences are long and twisted, elaborate and overloaded with images, full of round-about expressions and far from fluent. They follow one another with the same heaviness that we find in the worst passages of Dreiser, and they are charged with the same overabundance and pomposity found in Thomas Wolfe's style. They appear like the clumsy sentences of someone who, faced with a theme superior to his resources, neither perfectly understood nor controlled, tries to hide his difficulties under complicated grammar and wordiness.

To justify our criticism, it would be enough to quote a single passage at random. Whoever turns back in this study to the many passages that have been quoted to illustrate the possible meaning of the book can hardly fail to realize how heavy, pretentious, and stilted the language of Fitzgerald has become, sometimes reaching the extremes of the ridiculous and absurd. It might have been, originally, a way of depicting the absurdities of his characters or the falsity of their attitudes, but then we must say that Fitzgerald was carried away by his own intent and fell into his own trap. What little poetry there was in *This Side of Paradise* has vanished here; only its underlying irony remains, relegated to secondary purposes (the characterization of Adam Patch, for instance) and sounding mannered, if not false.

The refusal of any preoccupation with form, in keeping with Mencken's precepts, and the complete allegiance to the principle of an omniscient and omnipotent author, advocated by H. G. Wells, are at least partly responsible for it. When every form of foreshortening and selection is renounced the writer is exposed to such dangers. There is only a single moment, toward the end of *The Beautiful and Damned,* when Fitzgerald very timidly attempts foreshortening: all of a sudden, he lets us see Anthony and Gloria through the eyes of two other passengers on the ship which is taking them to Europe. This single scene, from a limited point of view, is filtered through the impressions of the bystanders, and it is the only one which can be said to possess dramatic intensity. It can be taken as a sign, whether consciously or unconsciously, of the method that would make possible the dramatic achievement of *The Great Gatsby.* It is too little, however, to enliven this novel, so interesting in many ways, but hopelessly deadened by its own heaviness. The interest of *The Beautiful and Damned* lies in the germs of thematic renewal that it contains and in the new moral awareness that it betrays. Much of this interest is given by its half-way position between *This Side of Paradise* and *The Great Gatsby;* on the aesthetic level, our judgment clearly must be severe.

CHAPTER IV

The "Tragic Pastoral"

This isn't just an epigram—life is much more successfully looked at from a single window, after all.

GG, p. 169.

1

There is a remarkable difference in quality between *The Beautiful and Damned* and *The Great Gatsby*. But the road from the ambitious early attempt to the later achievement is short, going by way of an unhappy experience in the theater and the writing of a comparatively limited number of stories.

The project for a real play, something quite different from the college musicals or the adolescent melodramas, engaged the writer for more than a year. The results, however, were unequal to the effort expended, and *The Vegetable, or from President to Postman* (published by Scribner's in 1923) was a complete failure.[1] Popular success escaped Fitzgerald in the theater, as it had escaped, in spite of his greater efforts, Henry James. But even in this unlucky attempt, a critic can detect at least one positive element of renewal, a stage of a process through which Fitzgerald moved to a maturer position as a writer.

The Vegetable is only a light comedy, pleasingly written with the vague intention of staging a political satire. Nevertheless, if we examine its motives more closely, we can see that the subject of the play is again an indictment of the fallacy of dreaming, a denunciation of our irrational illusions. The play lacks a unified development and a truly dramatic pace. It often descends to pure farce; but its informing idea and its final "message" is a definitive affirmation of realism and inner sincerity such as cannot be encountered previously in Fitzgerald's works.

The single ambition of the protagonist, Jerry Frost, who works for a railroad company, is to become a postman. This ambition seems ridiculous to his wife, father, and sister-in-law, all of whom contribute to making his life miserable with their continual upbraiding. Harassed and distressed by their reproaches, he nevertheless remains faithful to his ambition. After being visited by a bootlegger he dreams of becoming President of the United States. Most likely, he has drunk too much; all of the second act of the play takes place presumably in his dream, as in Shaw's *Man and Superman*. To Jerry Frost this long dream sequence soon becomes a frightful nightmare. He has been pushed to make war by ambitious generals and has been barred from the treasury by his miserly father; he has given up the whole state of Idaho, which has risen in rebellion against him, in exchange for some unknown islands and can only laugh when a Supreme Court justice, followed by all the Senators, stands up at hearing a jazz song which he takes for the national anthem. He has made fun of the army, political oratory, the inner divisions of Europe, and the American federal system. But this is not the life that Jerry Frost had wanted; it is a life that has been imposed on him. Thus, when he is accused of high treason, his sudden awakening to everyday reality is a form of liberation to him. Having learnt his lesson, in the third act he flees from home and does not reappear until he has become what *he* had wanted to become—a happy, self-satisfied postman, who can assert his own independence and personality over his relatives. His wife has been taught a lesson, too, and she welcomes her husband home.

It is clear that the plot is forced and mechanical, and it is equally evident that the three acts do not add up to a structural unity. Neither the central situation nor the method of presentation is original. The satire is often crude and the frequent *boutades*, puns, or wisecracks are clearly derived from the more brilliant ones of Oscar Wilde and Shaw. The discredit into which the play has fallen is, therefore, understandable: but in our context, it is worthwhile emphasizing the real novelty of intent with which Jerry Frost is portrayed.

Jerry Frost is the down-to-earth man, having no excessive illusions or ambitions in life, who asserts himself through the "realistic" side of his nature. In his acceptance of his own limitations, he achieves happiness and self-respect, after both of them have been put in jeopardy by absurd dreams or impossible pretentions. On the title page of the published version of the play Fitzgerald had placed an epigraph taken from "a current magazine": "Any man who doesn't want to get on in the world, to make a million dollars, and maybe even park his toothbrush in the White House, hasn't got as much to him as

a good dog has—he's nothing more or less than a vegetable." Jerry
Frost, then, remains a "vegetable," and Fitzgerald intended perhaps
to make fun of him as well. But this "vegetable" shows us the absurdity
of the American myth of success. Frost's self-realization is in his doing
what his innermost spirit tells him he wants to do. He does not get
very far in the world, and he does not make a million dollars. But his
character betrays a positive, realistic side—the side that was so lacking in Anthony and his predecessors.

The serious aspect of his character, set against the background
of a flippant farce with satirical intents, is perhaps one of the reasons
for the play's failure. The "moralistic" assumption—either latent or
consciously present—is difficult to reconcile with all the superficial
elements that were included in the play to suit the popular tastes or
the requirements of Broadway. But even this ambiguity and uncertainty represented a step forward. Jerry Frost has the virtue of
accepting reality as it comes and is content with what he can get,
without indulging in impossible dreams, pointless struggles, or Pyrrhic
victories. He lives in the realm of everyday life, not in the eternal
"carnival by the sea." He pays the penalty for his weakness in the
second act, but then his wisdom triumphs over the world's folly, and
he can become what he wanted to be—a simple, happy, efficient postman. He has realized his fate by accepting the simple virtues of his
nature, and this "realistic" solution seems quite new in Fitzgerald's
works.

It was still a way of burning incense before Mencken's disdainful
frown, and in fact, Fitzgerald joined Mencken again in the denunciation of the vulgarity and ridicule of the contemporary popular myths.
He offered Mencken a tribute of great esteem, and possibly a personal
form of alliance. This coincidence with Mencken's crusade, however,
is a passing one, and fortunately too, because the young writer had to
follow his own intimate creative development by beating new paths
and different roads. Yet even this temporary coincidence was a further
step toward maturity. Even in *The Vegetable,* perhaps, Fitzgerald
was experimenting with a form of dramatic foreshortening, of quick
and concise action, of immediacy of response, such as he was later to
achieve in *The Great Gatsby.* In this rather marginal experiment, in
the waste of energy itself, not everything was lost,—just as not everything was lost in the stories which were written during, or soon after,
the composition of the play. In most of them Fitzgerald was dealing
with themes and motives and availing himself of techniques that he

had already thoroughly exploited in the previous works. But a slow development toward the new novel is at times discernible, and this makes the stories interesting and significant, even when their purely aesthetic value seems rather poor.[2]

For the most part they are commercial stories, written for money, "fantasies" thrown together in a few hours, dealing with situations and characters which are wearily brilliant, repetitious, or pointless. It is clear that the writer had neither the time nor the willingness to try new things. Like a trump card, he held the novel up his sleeve, while satisfying for a while the public taste. And if the public had a taste for frivolity, Fitzgerald knew that he had better condescend to frivolity and repetition.

"The Popular Girl,"[3] for instance, deals again with the theme of the flapper, while "Rags Martin Jones and the Pr-nce of W-les"[4] reworks the formula of the rich boy who has to stage an elaborate fantasy to win the love of his flapper—as was the case in "The Offshore Pirate." "Gretchen's Forty Winks"[5] avails itself of autobiographical elements, while "Not in the Guide Book"[6] is a kind of advertising copy. "Dice, Brass Knuckles and Guitar"[7] is nothing more than a series of vapid humorous notes, and "Our Own Movie Queen,"[8] suggested and at least partly written by his wife Zelda, is nothing more than social chatter.

They are *divertissements* which are not even amusing, and they often melt into "fantasies," if we want to adopt Fitzgerald's definition for many of them. In "John Jackson's Arcady"[9] we are confronted with the theme of the prodigal son, whose homecoming brings peace and new faith to the long suffering father, who had been on the verge of despair. "The Curious Case of Benjamin Button" is merely an exercise in ingenuity. The germ for this story (which Fitzgerald found in a remark of Mark Twain and then in a note of Samuel Butler) is provided by the idea of a man born old, who grows younger as the time goes on, until he becomes a child. Once the situation is set in motion, each comic or farcical episode is possible and justifiable—if we accept the premises.[10]

Even a "fantasy," however, can serve a better purpose or can be put to a larger task, as is the case with the well-known story "The Diamond as Big as the Ritz,"[11] where the theme of overpowering wealth is dealt with on the level of romantic fable. The story, foreshortened in eleven brief sections, follows the fantastic adventure of a boy who is a guest and at the same time a victim of an extremely wealthy family living in a secluded valley, and it is anything but negligible, either from the point of view of its theme or of its artistic realization. It is in fact a variation on the motive of excessive wealth seen as the corrupting element which destroys both the dream of love and the need for purity. We are closer here to *The Great Gatsby* than to *The Beautiful and Damned,* because this same motive will be given fuller development in Fitzgerald's next novel. But here the theme is unfolded and, as it were, analyzed in its bare form, in its essence, without the concurrence of other elements. The corrupting power of money is gradually revealed to the boy, but his discovery becomes the focal point of the tale, toward which every other interest is centered. As in the two novels the end of the fable is complete ruin, so great that it turns upside down the fabulous valley and destroys almost all its inhabitants. Only the boy, John, who remains uncorrupted despite his acceptance of the impossible dream of a boundless luxury, and his innocent girl-friend, purified by love, save themselves. The "moral," of course, is that only purity of mind and sincerity of emotion resist the subtle corruption of money, and this is the lesson that Nick Carraway will learn, but with greater scepticism, in *The Great Gatsby.*

In bringing out the moral sense of such a parable, unfolded in its barest essence, there was the danger of making an abstract study of it, or of preaching a lay sermon about it. Fitzgerald avoided this danger, however, exactly because he gave the story the air of a fable or of a fantastic dream. Seen as such, the dream becomes credible because it is complete and isolated in its own frame, with no direct relationship with reality. The dreamy atmosphere sets off, as though in a show case, the events of the story, which acquire a kind of abstract and unreal distance. They are seen as detached from everyday life, perfectly consistent within their own frame of reference, and they are contemplated through the dazzled eyes of the boy. This focal length permits the action to unfold in obedience only to its own rationale, quite apart from any transposition on the level of actuality, which would have flawed the absolute purity of the fable:

> Afterward John remembered that first night as a daze of many colors, of quick sensory impressions, of music soft as a voice in love, and of the beauty of things, lights and shadows, and motions and faces. There was a white-haired man who stood drinking a manyhued cordial from a crystal thimble set on a golden stem. There was a girl with a flowery face, dressed like Titania with braided sapphires in her hair. There was a

room where the solid, soft gold of the walls yielded to the pressure of his hand, and a room that was like a platonic conception
of the ultimate prison—ceiling, floor, and all, it was lined with
an unbroken mass of diamonds, diamonds of every size and
shape, until, lit with tall violet lamps in the corners, it dazzled
the eyes with a whiteness that could be compared only with
itself, beyond human wish or dream. (*Stories*, pp. 11–12.)

Such a perspective required from the author a certain capacity
for objective detachment and an awareness of the possibilities provided by the use of symbolic devices. Fitzgerald proved equal to the
occasion, so that the central idea of the story—the isolation and
distortion of values which are typical of the very rich—is made
evident by the symbol of the huge diamond and of the secluded
valley, which is first the retreat and then the instrument of ruin for
those who had found every reason and justification for living in it.[12]
The symbolism, it should be noted, is still mechanical and rather
simple here. And yet Fitzgerald's intuition—that the very rich are
different and isolated from the rest of the human race and that they
have to pay a penalty for it—is developed with rigorous consistency.
For the first time, Fitzgerald was able to use a "controlling center"
with thematic precision, by having the story recorded by the protagonist and filtered through his impressions. He set the center of
interest in the sensitivity of the boy, and in this way he could confer
a dreamy atmosphere on the story, and develop its theme as it
gradually opened itself to John. If Fitzgerald, because of his total
disinterest, could not tell the *how* and the *why* of so much wealth, he
was able to make it visible and present through the dazzled and
bewildered reactions of the boy; and this is quite sufficient for us to
feel the inescapable burden under which the characters in "The
Diamond as Big as the Ritz" must be buried.

The same theme, as we have hinted, was to reappear in *The
Great Gatsby;* but it had to be dealt with, if not yet completely
resolved, in realistic and not merely "fantastic" terms, before being
ready for a maturer treatment. A breakaway from fable devices is
already recognizable in "The Adjuster" and in "The Baby Party," [13]
which takes up a theme of domestic comedy, developed along the
slender thread of an argument between two old friends after a quarrel
among their children. But it is also significantly present in three more
stories—"Winter Dreams," " 'The Sensible Thing,' " and "Absolution"—which bring us up to *Gatsby*.

The first two of these stories can be properly seen as attempts to come to terms with the new material that Fitzgerald was to utilize in the novel. They are, in a way, preliminary studies or tentative sketches, leading to a fuller awareness of the possibilities of a given subject matter. They might even serve by way of introduction to the novel, with all the merits and defects that introductions usually have. While clarifying many points that would reappear in *Gatsby*, they might predispose or condition our interpretation of the novel from an all-too-narrow point of view. In both of them we find the motive of a youthful dream of love which can be realized only when enough wealth has been somehow accumulated, and in both of them the financial success of the poor hero brings only the failure of the ideal of love. In "Winter Dreams" [14] there is no doubt about the eventual failure. Young Dexter, although he has risen from caddy on the golf course to successful industrialist, is still unable to win the lasting love of irresponsible Judy, and his illusion of eternal beauty collapses when he discovers that the girl herself has lost all her charm. Money alone has not permitted him to fulfill his childhood dream. Like Anthony, he has tried to find an escape into the army, and like Anthony and Gatsby, he has failed to realize the "destructiveness of time." He has not been able to stop the fleeting moment of beauty and love, and nothing is left him but a deep regret for a youthful illusion which the present has shattered:

> "Long ago," he said, "long ago, there was something in me, but now that thing is gone. Now that thing is gone, that thing is gone. I cannot cry. I cannot care. That thing will come back no more." (*Stories*, p. 145.)

The ending of the story is more melancholy, perhaps, than hopelessly romantic, even if we are reminded of Poe at his least successful, and the style does not always reach the heights of the emotion that it would convey. In " 'The Sensible Thing,' " [15] on the other hand, George O'Kelly, suddenly enriched, obtains an apparent victory in winning back the love of Jonquil, who had left him because he was poor. But even for him this apparent victory is but a sign of a subtler defeat, since it is won at the cost of an incurable loss: the loss of sentimental freshness and youthful emotion. For George O'Kelly as well, the passing of time had deprived his love of any charm and significance, and the longed-for wealth cannot bring back the lost moment:

But for an instant as he kissed her he knew that though he search through eternity he could never recapture those lost April hours. He might press her close now till the muscles knotted on his arms—she was something desirable and rare that he had fought for and made his own—but never again an intangible whisper in the dusk, or on the breeze of night. . . .

Well, let it pass, he thought; April is over, April is over. There are all kinds of love in the world, but never the same love twice. (*Stories*, p. 158.)

In this second story, moreover, the theme is developed with greater skill and with a better awareness of its implications. In "Winter Dreams" the protest was hopelessly sentimental, and stylistically, it was resolved in awkward repetitions and digressions, with a deadly monotony of diction. " 'The Sensible Thing,' " instead, seems to be more evenly balanced and better organized from a structural point of view. It portrays people that are at least more credible than those in the preceding story. George and Jonquil are more cautious and less given to talk than Dexter and Judy, and they are seen against a more realistic background. They refrain from the excited tone and the exasperated individualism of the earlier characters, and in the end they are willing to accept a form of compromise. Their refusal to make great scenes results in a melancholy humanity, such as we will meet again in the character of Gatsby. In the novel, however, the story developed from these slender suggestions into tragedy and even myth: here the writer was preparing and adjusting only the materials, the canvas, and the thread for the story that he was to weave. But we are slowly approaching that condition of happy perception that is responsible for the greatness of *Gatsby;* and with "Absolution," according to Fitzgerald's own admission, we have a discarded prologue of the novel itself.[16]

The interest of this story might be limited to its role as a possible explanation for the character of Gatsby; but one cannot neglect the fact that some technical devices of the novel are first encountered here. A young boy is driven by his father's harshness to tell two lies in confession, while the priest who hears them is involved in a deep moral and religious crisis. But what might interest us here is the fact that the story is practically represented by a long flashback sequence (the same technique used for relating Gatsby's and Daisy's past in the novel); the crisis of the priest, moreover, is not properly analyzed, but rather suggested by a careful correspondence of symbols (the

Swedish girls, for instance, that appear at the beginning and at the end). Gatsby's "mystery" is not explained by this story, but here we can find all the premises for the technical and stylistic maturity of the novel, just as in the previous two stories we could easily recognize the first signs of its theme. But early thematic attempts and stylistic warnings cannot explain the balanced perfection of *The Great Gatsby*. We can only say that the ferment of ideas and the wealth of motives that can be found in these stories serve to set off in relief its unique quality.

2

In *The Great Gatsby* the motive of an impossible dream of love, which riches cannot fulfill after the right moment has passed forever, finds its definitive consecration. Fitzgerald reveals the tragic implications of that dream by organizing the plot around an agonizing conflict of the moral and social order and by enlarging its meaning on the symbolic level of legend and myth. The story of Gatsby and Daisy, Nick and Jordan, Tom and Myrtle has a common origin with the similar adventures of so many of Fitzgerald's heroes and heroines. But it is no longer dependent on contingent reasons, nor is it the result of psychological distortions which are typical of individuals who turn their backs on reality. The story is rooted in an objective frame of references and thus acquires an individual, realistic meaning which is immediately apparent on the literal level. But it attains an even larger significance on the symbolic level by carrying to its tragic solution a conflict of characters which has a "universal" implication and a representative value. Hence its legendary and, at least partly, mythic quality, although we have always to remember that both legend and myth are resolved in, or spring from, the actual development of the story.

To impose on the book widening circles of symbolic meaning, it was necessary to represent its motives in a clear perspective and through a careful plot contrivance. And as, perhaps, in no other case, it might be said that the very structure of the book—rhythmic and dramatic, perfectly balanced and rounded-off—is responsible for its thematic richness, its amplitude of meaning, and its aesthetic achievement.

Only a careful examination of this structure—a thematic analysis, that is, developing step by step with an analysis of the manner of presentation—can render justice to the original and revolutionary quality of the novel. It is the method of presentation as well as its substance which is new, and this fact must be duly stressed; it is only in this way that T. S. Eliot's well-known statement about the novel—that *Gatsby* was "the first step that American fiction has taken since Henry James . . ." [17]—can be meaningful.

At the time of composing his third novel, Fitzgerald felt that he had "grown at last." To both Edmund Wilson and John Peale Bishop he wrote of his new work with enthusiasm. He was convinced that he was writing something "wonderful," "something *new*—something extraordinary and beautiful and simple and intricately patterned." [18] His inspiration came so quickly as he worked that he finished the book in only ten months. In November 1924 the manuscript was already in the hands of the publisher, and yet he continued smoothing and polishing it so that in February of the following year he modified the structure of Chapters VI and VII by cutting and adding material and by rewriting an entire episode. It was only when the book was published on April 10, 1925, that Fitzgerald's labor to give it an organic form was completed. [19]

According to the outline that he had made, [20] Fitzgerald divided the material into nine brief chapters, in such a way that the climax comes in the fifth chapter (the "dead middle of book," as he called it). The first four chapters act as a slow introduction and preparation, while the last four mark the development of the story to its tragic conclusion at a quickened pace. In this brief span, by a masterful use of foreshortening, are encompassed the events of a single summer and the facts that precede them. These are evoked and reconstructed by the narrator, Nick Carraway, who learns about them and tells them in bits and pieces. Many flashbacks alternate in this way with the straight narration, and they give the motivations for the events represented, as well as provide a fuller basis for their understanding. From the dramatic immediacy of the present we are brought back to the past and referred to what might explain or motivate the action, reminded of its premises, recalled to its psychological reasons. In this superimposition and reciprocal influence of the two temporal levels, we are already confronted with an amplitude of perspective which makes the novel breathe.

In the first three chapters—to follow the action more closely in its development—the main characters are defined in their respective milieux and according to the moral or social positions that they represent. They are not described or "portrayed," however, as in the previous novels, but are represented *in* action and *through* their actions. Fitzgerald presents them at three different parties, given in different places at distinct times, in order to show immediately their various psychological natures, their diverse aspirations and ambitions, and the different social environments from which they spring and which they somehow embody. The method of presentation is, in other words, typically dramatic; the various characters are defined in action during three big scenes, as Nathaniel Hawthorne had done in *The Scarlet Letter*. Hawthorne's novel had been actually built on and around three "theatrical" scenes, which were staged on a "scaffold" (a kind of stage), and it could be easily staged in the theater. Melville had used the dramatic method of presentation in *Moby Dick*, and his novel has been often staged in the theater. The tendency to organize a novel in dramatic form, or to stress its dramatic possibilities with the use of theatrical devices, is actually present in most American fiction. It was to reappear in all its force in the last great novels of Henry James, who actually passed through a theatrical experience before writing them, and who built a theory of the "dramatic scene." This amounts to saying that at the very beginning of his new novel Fitzgerald had placed himself squarely within a fictional tradition, or at least trend, whose premises and assumptions were already firmly established.

Early in the novel Nick Carraway is defined as the *perfect* narrator. He has learned from his father to suspend judgment (which is an essential element for "objectivity"), he has been accustomed to listening to people who take him into their confidence, he maintains a "sense of the fundamental decencies," and possesses a good share of human sympathy and understanding. He can be "within and without, simultaneously enchanted and repelled by the inexhaustible variety of life." A son of the Middle West, he is now working in the East, having come back from the war disenchanted, but not feeling at ease in a surrounding which is foreign to him. Hence the precious detachment of his vision. But it is he who hints at Gatsby and suggests him, he who puts us in contact with Tom and Daisy Buchanan, who live on the other side (the fashionable side) of a bay on Long Island Sound. He thus becomes a participant in the story, a kind of fictional "go-between," who can be at the same time "within and without."

At the first party, Tom and Daisy betray to Nick their innermost natures. Strong and immeasurably rich, self-reliant, careless and ruthless, reactionary and arrogant, Tom has a "touch of paternal contempt in his voice." Daisy is also careless and self-reliant, but she is sophisticated and mildly genteel. She dawdles with Nick and her friend Jordan Baker, she teases Nick and is witty at times. And yet, under the cover of their genteel manners and the courtesy of their social talk, Nick, who feels himself "uncivilized" and would prefer "to talk about crops or something," does not fail to perceive a very different reality. Tom keeps a mistress, who telephones him at dinner, Jordan eavesdrops shamelessly, Daisy has sudden fits of impatience. Nick's first impulse is to "to telephone immediately for the police." His detachment from the Buchanans is not only social or geographic, it is moral. He draws back "confused and a little disgusted" before what seems to him "a rather distinguished secret society," and it is through his eyes that we have the first glimpse of Gatsby, alone and thoughtful in his garden, on the other side of the bay.

We have then, in the second chapter, a description of the "valley of ashes," halfway between the bay and New York. It is a desolate spot, a kind of waste land, overlooked by a gigantic pair of eyes on an advertising sign—a chance symbol,[21] but none the less effective, of the spiritual bareness and blindness of the world. This forms a prelude to the sordid atmosphere of moral disorder which broods over this chapter, and at the same time it offers a kind of thematic anticipation, for the final tragedy will take place in that valley. Myrtle, Tom's mistress, lives there, and he takes her to their apartment in New York, dragging Nick along. The second party, in New York, takes place among vulgar and squalid people, in an atmosphere of moral disorder: Nick gets drunk, and in this way he records the events in a distracted and confused narration which reflects the intrinsic and moral disorder of the scene. This second party contrasts greatly with the "genteel" party in the first chapter and reveals the complete baseness of Tom, who, while amusing himself all the time with Myrtle, has no intention of divorcing Daisy. Like an autocratic and violent master, he wants to keep both women.

Gatsby now appears on the scene, after many hints and indirect suggestions. He is also shown (in Chapter III) against the background of a party on the grounds of his fantastic house ("a factual imitation of some Hôtel de Ville in Normandy"), to which a "menagerie" of people comes uninvited. There is an aspect of vulgarity in Gatsby's party, too, for his unknown guests behave "according to the rules of behavior associated with an amusement park." In the eyes of Nick, who has been regularly invited, the pretentious pomposity of this wealth is not lost. But Gatsby, far from participating in the drunken sprees of his guests and from identifying himself with the crowd of people, is melancholy and aloof. His isolation has something suspect and at the same time attractive about it. We sympathize with his evident timidity, his subdued tone, with the self-conscious courtesy with which he asks for an interview with Jordan Baker, who is present at the party. A comic automobile accident ends the elaborate "pageant" of his party, and this is a forewarning of the tragedy that will take place further along in the story.

Nick and Jordan wearily begin an affair and as "mediators" between the main characters, they make a meeting—or rather a collision—possible between East and West Egg, between Tom's and Daisy's "hard malice" and the dreamy vulnerability of Gatsby. In the fourth chapter, we have the preparations for the meeting. Gatsby reveals more and more of his contrasting aspects of modesty, ambiguous power, and questionable respectability, until Jordan discovers his secret—his lifelong love for Daisy. He has made his fortune for her, and for her he has bought his house in West Egg and given his parties (in the hope of meeting her by chance). This dubious gangster, who is supposed to be a murderer or a spy, reveals thus the dreamy aspect of his nature, his sentimental dedication, which in part redeem his coarse manners and his shady background, while Daisy's aloofness and carelessness are already marked by the fact that she has never yet appeared at one of his parties.

It is significant that their first meeting has to take place in the neutral ground of Nick's house (Chapter V); when the three of them move to Gatsby's enormous mansion, Gatsby after a passing moment of enthusiasm, of overwhelming self-satisfaction, begins to entertain a doubt "as to the quality of his present happiness." "Fulfilment destroys the dream"—as Fitzgerald himself was to write. A long-cherished, sentimental illusion can be shattered by a mere brush with reality, or at least reduced to smaller dimensions. Gatsby's enormous dream is bound to suffer from any contact with reality.

This conflict between the expectations of Gatsby and the objective situation, however, is not simply an inner conflict. In the four chapters that follow it becomes also a conflict between external forces and social interests. Gatsby is ruined not only because of his inability to accept reality as equal to or sufficient for his dream; he is also defeated by Tom's "hard malice" and Daisy's irresolute carelessness.

The sixth chapter marks a pause in the narration. In the galley proofs, Fitzgerald described at some length the relation between Gatsby and Daisy, who told Nick of her willingness to "run off" with Gatsby. But in the final revision Fitzgerald chose to let the reader guess at the nature of the relationship, and to fill the void he skillfully added the "truthful," although incomplete, story of Gatsby's past.[22] We learn thus that Gatsby is a self-made man, an unscrupulous parvenu with no distinction or social background. He had met and lost Daisy in his youth, and his lifelong aim has been to recapture her, to become again acceptable to her. But he has no social or cultural tradition, and he remains a "newly rich" outsider. The point is important: it is from this angle that Tom chooses to attack Gatsby when he begins to suspect the truth.

At another party in Gatsby's mansion (Chapter VI), Tom, who has already snubbed him cruelly in the course of a casual encounter, manages to show him his utter hostility and contempt. This party should have marked Gatsby's triumph, but it proves a failure. Humiliated by Tom, Gatsby discovers with dismay that Daisy is unhappy and uncomfortable among his guests;[23] yet even in his disillusionment, he clings desperately to his impossible dream of "repeating" the past. The present does not come up to his expectation, and Gatsby abandons himself to an idyllic evocation of his first meeting with Daisy—his only way of actually "repeating" the past.

His faith, however, has been shaken, and he can no longer rely on his dream for support: he becomes an easy prey. He closes his house to please Daisy,[24] but he wants to come to a showdown with Tom—he wants Daisy herself to deny her past, to repudiate her love for Tom. On a sultry August afternoon, in the presence of Nick and Jordan, Gatsby confronts Tom in open battle (Chapter VII). But the struggle is not only for Daisy: each of the two wants to preserve and reaffirm his own attitude to life, the inner motivations of his own behavior, and Daisy's irresolution can only favor the man who is not utterly dependent on her. Enraged by the double prospect of losing wife and mistress at the same time (he has had a quarrel with Myrtle), Tom is ruthless in his attack. With the physical strength of an athlete and hardened by his lifelong habit of command, Tom succeeds in striking Gatsby's weakest points until he makes him incapable of further resistance. In his purity Gatsby wants to be sincere and honest, and he reveals to everyone the secrets of his past, regardless of the consequences. He wins Nick's approval, but not

Daisy's. Faced with these unpleasant revelations, and with Gatsby's avowal of a complete, unchanging love, she keeps her ground and does not move to meet him.

Abused by Tom and wounded by Daisy, Gatsby has already lost his battle. The automobile accident that happens under the spectral eyes of Dr. Eckleburg in the valley of ashes—on the ground that brings together both victors and vanquished—merely seals Gatsby's defeat. Daisy, who is at the wheel of Gatsby's car, runs over Myrtle who has rushed toward the car believing it to be Tom's, and Gatsby takes upon himself the whole responsibility for it. Shaken by these events Daisy hides behind the protection of her husband, without telling him the truth, and she remains with him, while Gatsby "is left standing there in the moonlight—watching over nothing":

> Daisy and Tom were sitting opposite each other at the kitchen table, with a plate of cold fried chicken between them, and two bottles of ale. He was talking intently across the table at her, and in his earnestness his hand had fallen upon and covered her own. Once in a while she looked up at him and nodded in agreement.
>
> They weren't happy, and neither of them had touched the chicken or the ale—and yet they weren't unhappy either. There was an unmistakable air of natural intimacy about the picture, and anybody would have said that they were conspiring together. (*GG*, pp. 274–75.)

Disturbed by this sight, Nick tells Gatsby of his admiration for him, but Tom puts Myrtle's husband on the track of Gatsby, who is murdered in the swimming pool (Chapter VIII). The murder might even seem superfluous, since Gatsby has already completed the cycle of his destiny. But fate is so bitterly cruel to him that it has in store the final humiliation—only Nick and a chance visitor attend his funeral (Chapter IX), and the latter recites a disconsolate epitaph on Gatsby: "The poor son-of-a-bitch." Nick has broken his affair with Jordan, and in a final scene, a sort of elegiac fading-away, he is left to reconsider the story. He has learned a personal lesson, and he is now qualified to see the tragic and symbolic dimensions of the story, to bring forth its moral and universal significance—as a latter-day Horatio over Hamlet's body.

Thus, the tragic dimension of the story becomes evident through a careful plot disposition, while Nick's reconsideration (or the author's reconsideration filtered through Nick) allows us to see its inherent richness of symbolic connotations. Superficially, the novel deals once more with the failure of a dream of love, which cannot be fulfilled or made to last by the acquisition of money. But Gatsby's failure has a deeper and more complex motivation in a subtle interplay of human and social conflicts, and his constitutional weakness finds a tragic counterpart in them. Gatsby, too, is a hopeless dreamer, like Anthony before him, and he clings stubbornly to his impossible illusion. But he has been strong enough to shape his own life and to acquire sufficient wealth, and his struggle for success is a real one, ruthless and even dishonest. He *might*, after all, win his battle, because he has prepared himself for it. But in his very strength, his sentimental purity is impaired. Gatsby builds his own fortune and puts himself, as it were, in a bargaining position with Tom and Daisy, because he has somehow fulfilled her expectations of luxury and wealth. He is in any sense a self-made man, but he wants still to spring from "a Platonic conception of himself" and remain pure in his motives, at least.

His motives, however, may be pure, and yet he has to resort to dubious means to make his fortune; he is thus brought to foul the purity of his actions, and the "foul dust that floated in the wake of his dreams" envelops him in the end. If he is still a dreamer, in other words, he can accept the ethics of the "pioneers" and conform to it. If he is not linked with his parents, he is linked with Dan Cody ("the pioneer debauchee, who during one phase of American life brought back to the Eastern seaboard the savage violence of the frontier brothel and saloon"), and he shares the basic assumptions of Dan Cody's ethics. He can be faithful to his dream, but to fulfill it he has to revert to questionable means, renounce his scruples, compromise with the world and its evil ways.

He is no longer a "youngster" or a "philosopher," and he cannot be a "young girl," as has recently been suggested by a modern critic.[25] He is definitely superior to Anthony, and he lives in a world of mature achievement, where one's wealth is no longer "easy money." On the practical side, he is a grown man who knows how to attain his practical aim. But for this very reason, the purity of his motivation is compromised by an acceptance of the ways of capitalist society. In this cleavage, therefore, between the innocence of his dream and the corruption of his practical ways, is to be found Gatsby's hamartia, his tragic flaw.

If this were all, however, Gatsby would be bound to become a pathetic failure, like Anthony. His failure *is* tragic, instead, because his attempt is thwarted by Tom's and Daisy's organized forces. His inner and psychological conflict coincides with an overt struggle where he is again bound to fail because his psychological and practical resistance has been weakened and because his dream interposes too much on his straightforward path. Daisy, of course, is no longer a flapper—or she is a flapper still, but with a far greater power of offense than her predecessors. If, like Gloria, she has made her choice, and has chosen security and wealth, four years with Tom have hardened her character and made her careless and ruthless in her malice. Gatsby's dreamy attachment has no chance with her.

He asks too much of her, far more than she could actually give him, and this sentimental claim makes him partly responsible for her reaction. But she has taken on Tom's "hard malice" and his sense of spiteful superiority, and she comes to identify herself with him when he attacks Gatsby. In this sense Gatsby counts on her as an ally when he is actually confronted with another enemy. On the other hand, Tom is the dramatic antithesis of Gatsby. Born rich, he cares only for himself and his possessions (including Daisy, not so much as a wife but as someone or something that belongs to him), and he makes almost a natural right of his constitutional corruption. He has so successfully shaped Daisy's mind that she accepts his values and can even tolerate his frequent and open infidelities. At the crucial moment, only in Tom can she find a support for her weakness and her cowardice. Quite rightly, Nick puts them together in his moral judgment:

> They were careless people, Tom and Daisy—they smashed up things and creatures and then retreated back into their money or their vast carelessness, or whatever it was that kept them together, and let other people clean up the mess they had made. . . . (GG, p. 300.)

After the car accident, as we have seen, they appear to Nick to be "conspiring together." And it has been a conspiracy, even if unconscious, in which Gatsby has been trapped. He has "paid a high price for living too long with a single dream," but he has also been defeated by the organized opposition of his antagonists. He has been brought against a wall of incomprehension, and he could not strike through their masks. He wanted to repeat the past, and the present itself fails him. He wanted to make up for his loss, and a greater loss awaits him. He wanted to be true to his own inner self, without realizing that the conflict was so much more of contrasting social and moral positions than of mere persons.

In Gatsby's moral ambiguity there is a also a touch of greatness. If this greatness lies in the unspoiled purity of his feeling, despite his soiled hands and his service of "a vast, vulgar and meretricious beauty," it is of no avail if confronted with the corruption of those traditionally "very rich," with the shamelessness of those who still know how to use force and exercise a *droit de seigneur*. "They are a rotten crowd—Nick shouts to Gatsby—. You're worth the whole damn bunch put together." He is confronted with a rotten crowd, and they are instrumental in bringing about his defeat: his failure is no longer the result of his own weakness alone. Nick makes this clear with his passionate outburst and with his moral opposition to Tom and Daisy. Gatsby is crushed in a moral conflict between two contrasting conceptions of the world, which is reflected in his geographical division from Tom and Daisy. Gatsby's mansion and Nick's cottage are on this side of the bay (both geographically and symbolically), while Tom and Daisy weave the threads of their net across the water, in East Egg or in New York.

This geographic opposition makes the moral division of the four characters symbolically concrete, but even their social contrasts are brought to bear in the development of the story. Gatsby, who is compared and equated with Trimalchio, remains a parvenu to the end. And this social detail speeds, if it does not actually determine, his ruin. Tom is opposed to Gatsby as a rich man by birth and tradition who hates and holds in contempt the lack of taste and manners of the newly rich. Tom himself is coarse and vulgar, of course, besides being corrupt (his relation with Myrtle admits of no doubt about it), but with Daisy he knows how to strike a detached attitude, how to impress her with his superior manners and superficial aloofness. He can be effectively ironical about Gatsby's display of wealth, his yellow car, the "menagerie" of people who frequent his house, the gaudiness of his dress, the vulgarity of his parties. Gatsby's "elaborate formality of speech just missed being absurd," we are told, and his pseudo-British expression "old sport" annoys Tom greatly. Daisy absorbs from her husband some of his annoyance and fastidiousness, and she feels uncomfortable at the party to which Gatsby invites her. She feels uneasy, too, about his display of wealth, and it is significant that Gatsby's first move after they have met is to rid himself of the "menagerie." [26]

During that hot summer, we have to remember, Daisy lives in dark and cool rooms, "shadowed well with awnings." Gatsby does not feel at ease in her house (Chapter VII), and there is a social disparity between them that Daisy could overcome in her youth, but which she finds difficult to accept now. The social tone of Tom, Daisy, and Jordan is sophisticated and blasé, and they have no sympathy for Gatsby, with his childish and impulsive sentimentality. Gatsby is outside their world from the very beginning, and his attempt to separate Daisy from her "aristocratic" background and surroundings is doomed to fail. The disparity of social levels from which they spring makes it impossible for him to satisfy her deeply rooted need for gentility and social distinction.

This social contrast between the opposing characters plays a remarkable part in *Gatsby*, and it is therefore clear why Gatsby's defeat, determined as it is by a complex interplay of inner and outer factors, becomes tragic and not merely pathetic. Too many forces, besides his sentimental weakness, are at work against him for him to escape his doom. He is doomed for having lived too long with a single, impossible dream, defeated by social opposition, trampled down by a world of moral corruption and carelessness. But if he does not escape his fate, a "possible" redemption is clearly indicated, and a gleam of hope is left at the end.

The many conflicts that cause the ruin of Gatsby leave Jordan as well as Tom and Daisy unchanged. But to Nick they open the way for a beneficial return home. Both Nick and Jordan (narrator and *ficelle* on the technical level) do not in fact remain on the edges of the plot, but participate in it, contributing to its clarification and at the same time involved in its development. Their own affair, wearily begun and dragged on, sets off in relief Gatsby's absorption in his love for Daisy; it is highly significant that Nick is moved to break off his affair with Jordan when Gatsby's love is painfully wrecked. Detaching himself from Jordan, who belongs completely to Tom's and Daisy's world and, like them, is "careless" and "incurably dishonest," Nick perhaps avoids a similar destiny. At the same time, Gatsby's ruin, while saving Nick from a protracted compromise on the moral level, drives him home to the Middle West, where his innate "honesty," still uncorrupted, can find a better ground in which to flourish. Before it is too late, Nick leaves the East, which has the likeness of a nightmare for him now—and his choice is a moral one, a way to salvation. In the East, owing to his intermediate position between the various characters, he has been offered many allurements that might have meant ruin for him as well. Jordan was after all a trap, which might have brought him on Tom's and Daisy's side. Tom and

Myrtle had tried to involve him in their corruption (Chapter II).
Daisy had fascinated him, too, with her beauty and her verve. Gatsby,
on the other side, had offered him a job ("a rather confidential sort
of thing") that would have drawn him into his world of questionable
business transactions. And yet Nick resists all the various suggestions
and maintains his intermediate position without compromising his
own integrity. His only concession to *their* code of behavior is his
short-lived affair with Jordan. Thus, Nick is free to condemn the
conduct of Tom and Daisy, even if at the end he can be persuaded to
shake their hands. He feels strongly attracted by Gatsby and defends
the purity of his hopeless attempt and his generous behavior, without
sharing his assumptions. He is willing to let him meet Daisy in his
own cottage, he is sensible of his "greatness," but he refuses his moral
compromise between pure motives and shady means. He stays with
him to the bitter end, but then goes home, and his return to the
Middle West is a clear proof of his independence of judgment and
moral integrity.

He saves himself through Gatsby's ruin; in his incorrupted
honesty Nick is given the task of commenting on the story and of
throwing into relief its legendary or mythical aspects. If he goes back
to the Middle West, it is because it represents for him the positive
side of a moral dilemma. In the geographic contrast between East and
West, Nick perceives symbolically a wider significance: this contrast
foreshadows a moral one between corruption and innocence, between
economic power and homely virtues, urban sophistication and close-
ness to nature, "culture" and simplicity. As custodian of tradition and
moral values, the West finds in its contact with the East the negation
and perversion of these values. It is in this sense that Nick's choice
becomes meaningful:

> After Gatsby's death the East was haunted for me . . . ,
> distorted beyond my eyes' power of correction. So when the
> blue smoke of brittle leaves was in the air and the wind blew
> the wet laundry stiff on the line I decided to come back home.
> (*GG*, p. 298.)

If he returns home, it is because the story which he has witnessed
implies a typical parable in which East and West are set up as two
contrasting moral polarities:

> I see now [says Nick] that this has been a story of the
> West, after all—Tom and Gatsby, Daisy and Jordan and I,

were all Westerners, and perhaps we possessed some deficiency in common which made us subtly unadaptable to Eastern life. (*GG*, p. 298.)

All of them are excited by the East, but the East has "a quality of distortion." West Egg appears to Nick "as a night scene by El Greco," and so it must have appeared to Gatsby as well. Some of the characters have succumbed to the East, some have adapted themselves to it, some flee from it to save themselves and find shelter in the West. The West itself, of course, is tainted by the far-reaching tentacles of the East,[27] and Nick is right in observing that *his* Middle West was "not the wheat or the prairies or the lost Swede towns, but the thrilling returning trains of *his* youth." The returning trains come from the East with a burden of insinuating and subtle corruption— and it might be worth remembering that in college Nick belonged, after all, to the same society that Tom did; he might have been as predisposed to corruption as Tom was. But if Nick was not (at the very beginning, Gatsby represented for him "everything for which *he had* an unaffected scorn"), it is also because, in spite of his words, he was faithful to "the wheat" and "the prairies."

The point is that this complex adventure transcends, in its deeper nature, the literal limitations, the mere formulation of the facts as they are on the page. Going on with his disconsolate comment at the end, Nick realizes that Gatsby's illusion can be identified with the illusion or the dream of the early Dutch settlers, entranced by their vision of the New World:

> As the moon rose higher the inessential houses began to melt away until gradually I became aware of the old island here that flowered once for Dutch sailors' eyes—a fresh, green breast of the new world. Its vanished trees, the trees that had made way for Gatsby's house, had once pandered in whispers to the last and greatest of human dreams; for a transitory enchanted moment man must have held his breath in the presence of this continent. . . .
>
> And as I sat there brooding on the old, unknown world, I thought of Gatsby's wonder when he first picked out the green light at the end of Daisy's dock. He had come a long way to this blue lawn, and his dream must have seemed so close that he could hardly fail to grasp it. He did not know that it was already behind him, somewhere back in the vast obscurity beyond the city, where the dark fields of the republic rolled on under the night.

Gatsby believed in the green light, the orgiastic future
that year by year recedes before us. . . . (*GG*, p. 301.)

The houses, as we see, become "inessential"; what matters is
that Gatsby's story is identified with that of the pioneers. The trees
have vanished, but his dream or his illusion repeats, in a modern
context, their dream, which might have been after all an illusion, of
building a new life for themselves, a new place in history where they
could renew the past. The "green light" cherished by Gatsby is not
only on Daisy's dock—it is also the green light of the "orgiastic
future." And that future recedes before us, year by year, if it is not
already behind us, in the past, "in the vast obscurity beyond the city,"
in the dark fields.

In this way, Gatsby's adventure is based on a traditional motive
of the American experience, divided between the yearning for innocence and the compromises of reality, between the idyllic vision of
the West and the corruption of the urban civilization of the East. All
experience in America—whether historical, legendary, or literary—
seems to be characterized by a pendular movement between these
two poles: Fenimore Cooper and Thoreau, Mark Twain and Hemingway, Robert Frost and so many modern writers have all relied on that
contrast for their works. *The Great Gatsby* clearly belongs to this
tradition, both for its literal theme and for its larger symbolic significance. In his well-known preface to the novel,[28] Lionel Trilling
speaks quite rightly of the legendary and mythical aspect of Gatsby's
story. The legend is that of the "young man from the provinces,"
thwarted by his contact with the city (the East). The "myth" is the
typical American myth of the geographic and moral juxtaposition
between the two poles of the nation to which a symbolic meaning is
attached: the innocence of the flowering fields of wheat, the corruption and sterility of the city.

According to a well-known definition of Jacques Barzun,[29] all
the characters, whether real or imaginary, who express and embody
destinies, aspirations, or attitudes typical of man, or of a particular
section of mankind, are to be considered "mythical." In this limited
sense of the word, *The Great Gatsby*, both in its action and in its
characters, can be said to be mythical. They do express and embody
"attitudes, aspirations, and destinies" in many ways typical of the
American experience; and thus they allow us to detect in the "literal"
sense of the story a larger significance of symbolic connotations.

3

The Great Gatsby says or suggests all this. And it does it with a maturity and an economy of expressive means which must be duly emphasized, because they represent an important step forward and a real turning point in Fitzgerald's fiction.

The maturity lies in Fitzgerald's detachment of vision, in his objective rendering and in his skillful construction of the plot. The economy of means is achieved through a perfected use of foreshortening and of the "dramatic scene." The superior quality of the language gives the final touch to the book.

Gatsby vibrates with the intensely personal participation of the author, who infuses into his characters the warmth and depth of his own feeling. But this does not imply an immediate identification of the writer with his characters, as could be said of Amory or, to a lesser degree, of Anthony. Although making use of his own experiences, as every writer does, Fitzgerald *lent* them to his characters in *Gatsby* without linking himself to them. He projected them in imaginary figures who move by their own force and live their own "life" independently of him. Gatsby's dream might have been, partly, Fitzgerald's own dream, too. But it becomes step by step the dream of a whole nation, as we have seen, and it acquires a meaning which exceeds any autobiographical interpretation. Gatsby was originally drawn from a man Fitzgerald knew; [30] Daisy seems to have very little in common with Zelda, while Nick, Tom, Wilson, Myrtle, Wolfsheim, and the other characters are all objective creations. The fact that they are "filtered" through the eyes of a narrator undoubtedly added sharpness to Fitzgerald's objective rendering; and this is the first and all-important technical device which accounts for his detachment of vision.

The narrator gives a personal flavor to the story, and at the same time he allows the writer to attain a balance between the representation of character and incident. Henry James had already warned that in a successful work of art there is no possible distinction to be made between characters and incidents: "What is character but the determination of incident?—he had written—What is incident but the illustration of character?" [31] Too often, in the preceding novels, the fusion between these two elements had failed because the character was defined a priori by a "portrait," and the story unfolded according to the initial *donnée*. In *Gatsby* the two components are harmoniously developed in close relationship. The action is represented through "dramatic scenes" in which the characters are "illustrated" by their actions, and the incidents are in turn "determined" by their inner psychologies. Both incidents and characters are shown as they appear to Nick, and he can define them only by seeing them in a single moment of vision, where no distinction is possible between what the characters *do* and what they *are*. What they do tells us what they are; and what they are shows us what they can do. Nick is the only one to be defined at the beginning, on account of the obvious function that he has to perform: then the dramatic scene is responsible for the parallel development of the story and of the characters.

In this view, the supposed deficiencies of the book are easily accounted for. Edith Wharton, relying on her own method of composition, held that we should know more of Gatsby's past and his early career. And Fitzgerald himself agreed with John Peale Bishop that there was "a BIG FAULT" in the novel: he had given "no account (and had no feeling about or knowledge of) the emotional relation between Gatsby and Daisy from the time of their reunion to the catastrophe." He felt that he had concealed the fault with "blankets of excellent prose." [32] But in the light of what has been said it is evident that the ambiguity of the relation between Gatsby and Daisy is revealed indirectly by the events that follow, when his dissatisfaction with the bourgeois compromise of secret adultery is contrasted with her careless indecision. There is no account of their relation, but its deeper sense is dramatically made evident; and in the same way, Gatsby's clumsy attempts to regain and then defend the possession of Daisy are a clear indication of the instability and suffering of his youth. What is not "reported" is clearly suggested, and sometimes the suggestion carries more weight and significance—as in these cases—than would a diffuse treatment. As we know, moreover, these "omissions" were deliberate: Fitzgerald did not use "Absolution" as a prologue to the novel, and he cut out of the proofs his references to the relation between Gatsby and Daisy. In both cases, again, nothing was lost if we keep in mind the particular type of foreshortening that Fitzgerald used in the story.

The technical devices he used in *Gatsby*—foreshortening, the dramatic scene, the narrator, the mutual interdependence of character and incident—account for the formal perfection and the novelty of the book, and they must be properly understood if one wants to avoid the pitfalls of rash criticism. It is at this point that the influence

of Henry James and Joseph Conrad becomes of paramount importance. If it was not a completely conscious influence, it was an indirect
lesson that Fitzgerald drew from both writers, and in particular from
Conrad, and neither of them can be ignored if we want to see the
reasons that account for the success of *Gatsby* and for its novelty in
the corpus of Fitzgerald's works.

His infatuation with Wells and Mackenzie had lessened, his
interest in Dreiser had dwindled away, and he had discovered the
ethical purpose of Mencken's "literary revolution." [33] In the short
period between *The Beautiful and Damned* and *Gatsby* Fitzgerald
had become interested in other writers—in Anatole France, Stephen
Crane, Willa Cather, Edith Wharton, and, above all, Joseph Conrad.[34]
They were all writers who were particularly interested in, and even
obsessed by the problems of literary form, who strongly believed in
the craft of fiction and in the art of the novel. Writing about *The
Beautiful and Damned,* Edmund Wilson had maintained that Fitzgerald "had been given imagination without intellectual control of
it" and that he had labored under "a desire for beauty without an
aesthetic ideal." Responding to the advice of his "intellectual conscience," in his third novel Fitzgerald had set himself the task of "an
attempt at form," refraining carefully "from trying to 'hit anything
off.'" [35] He had developed a form of intellectual control over his
material and proposed to himself an aesthetic ideal which can be
traced back to the informing principles not only of Conrad or Edith
Wharton but of their "master," Henry James.

Henry James had strongly advocated, both in theory and in
practice, the principle of the *"craft* of fiction" and of the *"art* of the
novel" by stressing the need for a formal awareness on the part of the
writer. He had emphasized in his essays on the novel and in his
prefaces the necessity of an indirect approach through the use of a
narrator involved in the story, or of a disinterested observer, who
would filter the story itself through his impressions and feelings. He
had then inferred from it the principle of the "dramatic scene," with
the corollary of foreshortening and of the limited point of view.
Eliminating the principle of an omniscient author, and consequently
his personal intrusions in the novel, he had reduced the value of the
great fictional "frescoes" in favor of a dramatic type of novel, in which
a series of quick and meaningful scenes—"pageants" or *tableaux
vivants*—would resolve and exhaust the complex shades of the action
and define the psychologies of the characters. He detached himself

in this way from a typically nineteenth-century tradition and opened the way to the modern novel. His ideal, as has been noted, was to endow the novel with dramatic immediacy, to represent the action in its unfolding, "here and now." The practical result was an awareness of the need for selection and the fictional importance of a dramatic structure. As Joseph Warren Beach has remarked:

> The dramatic method is the method of direct presentation, and aims to give the readers the sense of being present, here and now, in the scene of action. . . . Description is dispensed with by the physical stage setting. Exposition and characterization are both conveyed through the dialogue and action of the characters.
>
> .   .   .
>
> The restricted point of view is listed among the elements that make for the realization of the dramatic ideal. . . . The fundamental impulsion to dramatic concentration in general is the desire to secure in the novel something equivalent to the dramatic present in the play. The limitation of time tends to produce the effect of the dramatic Now; the limitation of place, the dramatic Here; the "center of interest" concentrates the attention, as in the drama, upon these particular people or this particular person now present here. And finally, the restriction of the point of view carries to its full logical outcome the esthetic idea of the limited center of interest.[36]

Willa Cather, Edith Wharton, and Joseph Conrad not only knew, but conformed to these principles in their works. Conrad himself had enlarged the task and the role of the narrator involved in the story, by bestowing on him the ability of "imagining" scenes at which he had not been present, and by admitting the principle of a concurrence of several narrators of the story. Furthermore, driven by a desire for verisimilitude, Conrad had advocated the principle of the "chronological muddlement," arranging his stories not as a chronological sequence of events, but as a series of gradual discoveries made by the narrator. Ford Madox Ford, who worked with Conrad and collaborated with him on some early novels, has left us an enlightening explanation of this theory:

> It became very early evident to us that what was the matter with the novel, and the British novel in particular, was that it went straight forward, whereas in your gradual making acquaintanceship with your fellows you never do go straight

forward. You meet an English gentleman at your golf club.
He is beefy, full of health, the moral of the boy from an
English Public School of the finest type. You discover gradually
that he is hopelessly neurasthenic, dishonest in matters of small
change, but unexpectedly self-sacrificing, a dreadful liar. . . .
To get such a man in fiction you could not begin at his beginning and work his life chronologically to the end. You must
first get him in with a strong impression, and then work backwards and forwards over his past. . . . That theory at least we
gradually evolved.[37]

There is no evidence that Fitzgerald had read much of James
when he wrote *Gatsby*, although he knew *The Portrait of a Lady* and
What Maisie Knew (and possibly James's own prefaces to them). But
he had read *A Lost Lady* (1923) and *My Ántonia* (1918) by Willa
Cather—two novels in the Jamesian manner that have points in
common with *Gatsby*—and had become an even greater admirer of
Edith Wharton.[38] Moreover, we have every reason to believe that he
was perfectly acquainted with Conrad's methods, and while writing
Gatsby he had "just re-read," by his own admission,[39] Conrad's
preface to *The Nigger of the 'Narcissus.'* In this well-known and
important preface, Conrad had expounded his "impressionistic"
principles ("Fiction . . . appeals to temperament. . . . Such an appeal
to be effective must be an impression conveyed through the senses.")
and had maintained that the art of fiction "must strenuously aspire to
the plasticity of sculpture, to the colour of painting, and to the magic
suggestiveness of music." The task which the writer had to achieve
was "by the power of the written word to make you hear, to make you
feel— . . . before all, to make you *see*." In a "single-minded attempt"
of this kind the writer would "hold up unquestioningly, without
choice and without fear, the rescued fragment before all eyes in the
light of a sincere mood . . . and disclose its inspiring secret: the stress
and passion within the core of each convincing moment." All the truth
of life was then to be found in "a moment of vision, a sigh, a smile." [40]
Conrad's principles were clearly based on certain assumptions of
James's theory of the novel, and through his words, therefore, Fitzgerald could have at least a glimpse of James's lesson.

In this way the process of evolution that brought the author to
an awareness of the *craft* of fiction and of the novel as an art form
becomes clear, and in the technical and formal excellence of *Gatsby*
we are able to single out some precise derivations. For his narrator,

Fitzgerald used the "modified point of view" developed and advocated by Conrad. Nick is not present in all the scenes, and he reconstructs what he has not witnessed through other sources: Jordan Baker, the *ficelle* (who tells him about Daisy before her marriage), Gatsby (who reveals to him some of his own past), Gatsby's father and servants, Michaelis (who reports to him Wilson's desperate behavior). In addition, Nick draws upon his imagination when he describes Gatsby's death and his youthful idyll with Daisy. From Conrad, again, Fitzgerald got the technique of the "chronological distortion" of the events, beginning with a "strong impression" of the protagonist and of the situation, and then moving "backwards and forwards" to unravel the past from the present, the truth from the appearance, the motivation from the act. The chronological order of *Gatsby* is not so complicated as that of *Lord Jim*, for example, but it does give the reader the sense of a "reconstruction," as close as possible to the truth, of the events.[41] Typical of Conrad, too, is the predilection for the indirect allusion, the ability to suggest character and situation by simple hints, the "magic suggestiveness" of the "written word" which allows Fitzgerald to hold up "unquestioningly" his rescued fragments and to disclose "the stress and passion" within the core of his convincing moments. As a matter of fact Fitzgerald went even further, by availing himself of open symbolism (the monstrous eyes of Dr. T. J. Eckleburg—the image of an impotent god, or rather of a satisfied devil—the "green light" on Daisy's dock, the valley of ashes, etc.); and at this point an influence of James, however indirect or unconscious, must be taken into consideration.[42]

The technical device of a *ficelle* (Jordan Baker), who somehow supports the narrator in his task, seems to be clearly derived from James, even if Fitzgerald gave Jordan not only a *technical* function in the novel, but a thematic significance as well, in contrast with the requirement of the "master" himself. And the use of foreshortening and compression, of the dramatic scene filtered through an observer, is perfectly in keeping with James's principles and with James's advice to suppress all the substance and all the surface in favor of an allusive treatment:

> To give the image and the sense of certain things while still keeping them subordinate to his plan, keeping them in relation to matters more immediate and apparent, to give all the sense, in a word, without all the substance or all the surface, and so to summarise and foreshorten, so to make values both

rich and sharp, that the mere procession of items and profiles is not only, for the occasion, superseded, but is, for essential quality, almost "compromised"—such a case of delicacy proposes itself at every turn to the painter of life who wishes both to treat his chosen subject and to confine his necessary picture.[43]

The Great Gatsby is governed by this principle and informed by this "delicacy." The picture is "confined" and the chosen subject is "treated" so that its art becomes "exquisite." "The mere procession of items and profiles" is almost compromised, but the values have been made both rich and sharp. The foreshortening is so conscious, and the compression so much sought after, that the effect comes close to James's aesthetic ideal—"to the only compactness that has a charm, to the only spareness that has a force, to the only simplicity that has a grace—those, in each other, that produce the *rich* effect."

In this complex interplay of literary influences or suggestions Fitzgerald was nonetheless able to speak with his own voice, and he explored the ways of the dramatic scene or of the "magic suggestiveness" with his own vehicle—a highly refined and mature prose, musically alive, sober and controlled in its diction but rich in effectiveness. In *This Side of Paradise* the stylistic pattern was given by the sentence. In *The Great Gatsby* it is represented by the period, almost a rhythmic clause rounded-off and self-contained, subtly scanned in the transitions from one sentence to another, opening at times in effective flow. Of the many possible illustrations (and quite a few are already there in the previous pages), two will suffice at this point. One is the central scene of the accident, when Myrtle Wilson is run over by Daisy at the wheel of Gatsby's car, a scene compressed and foreshortened, seen from a close angle of vision:

> The "death car" as the newspaper called it, didn't stop; it came out of the gathering darkness, wavered tragically for a moment, and then disappeared around the next bend. Mavromichaelis wasn't even sure of its color—he told the first policeman that it was light green. The other car, the one going toward New York, came to rest a hundred yards beyond, and its driver hurried back to where Myrtle Wilson, her life violently extinguished, knelt in the road and mingled her thick dark blood with the dust. (GG, pp. 268–69.)

The crucial incident of the novel is given in three quick sentences. It opens with the sight of the speeding car, which has already a connotation of death, and whose swerving is actually reproduced in the movement of the first sentence. The car disappears immediately, and in the second sentence we have a pause, marked by the appearance of that clumsy name—Mavromichaelis—which seems almost a personification of the absurdity of things. There is a vague hint at the color of the car, the sudden mention of the policeman, and then "the other car" rushes on the scene in the third sentence—another image of speed which comes slowly to a standstill. Following the steps of its driver, we are brought to the cruel discovery of Myrtle's body, weirdly kneeling on the road, and the scene closes on that gruesome image of her *thick, dark blood* mingling with the *dust.* The three sentences seem to mark the three steps of a musical progression, scanned in the last line by the sharp beat of the monosyllables.

This passage might be linked with the scene when Gatsby's body is found in the swimming pool:

> There was a faint, barely perceptible movement of the water as the fresh flow from one end urged its way toward the drain at the other. With little ripples that were hardly the shadows of waves, the laden mattress moved irregularly down the pool. A small gust of wind that scarcely corrugated the surface was enough to disturb its accidental course with its accidental burden. The touch of a cluster of leaves revolved it slowly, tracing, like the leg of transit, a thin red circle in the water.
>
> It was after we started with Gatsby toward the house that the gardener saw Wilson's body a little way off in the grass, and the holocaust was complete. (*GG*, p. 287.)

In this case, we are given at first an almost elegiac image, modulated in four short sentences on the suggestion of a faint and peaceful movement ("faint, barely perceptible movement of the water," "fresh flow," "little ripples," "hardly the shadows of waves," "a small gust of wind that scarcely corrugated the surface," "the touch of a cluster of leaves"). Then our attention is drawn on "a thin red circle in the water," and here the undulating and dancing movement is interrupted by the clean, cruel break of a matter-of-fact enunciation: "It was after we started with Gatsby. . . ."

With equal skill a single sentence is sufficient to suggest Wolfsheim's moral character, when he is made to say: "I understand you're looking for a business gonnection [*sic*]." " 'Her voice is full of money,' " Gatsby says of Daisy, and in that single phrase we perceive

the depth of his love and his disconsolate disenchantment, his awareness of her basic weakness. Many other of these brilliant touches
could be quoted to illustrate the concision and the "magic suggestiveness" of Fitzgerald's language in *The Great Gatsby*. After the effective
and witty list of Gatsby's guests—a *tour de force* which tells us more
about them and about Gatsby himself than an elaborate description—
Fitzgerald can bring Nick back to his role of sober narrator with a
sharp statement: "All these people came to Gatsby's house in the
summer." In the summer: this single statement, far from being a
casual remark, conveys all the melancholy sadness of Gatsby's "tragic
pastoral"—of a memorable novel, to which Arthur Mizener's definition seems perfectly appropriate.

CHAPTER V

Transition Stories

> *I was thirty. Before me stretched*
> *the portentous, menacing road of*
> *a new decade.*
>
> GG, p. 267.

1

From the long time lapse between the publication of *The Great Gatsby* (1925) and the publication of *Tender Is the Night* (1934), one might infer that Fitzgerald's creative vein had exhausted itself. In fact, this was a period of silence and artistic impotence only superficially. The author's creative powers did show signs of weariness and fatigue, and there were plenty of objective reasons to account for it: his wife's illness and her eventual hospitalization with its disastrous consequences for his tranquillity of mind and his literary activities, his own sense of instability and bewilderment after the ruinous collapse of the "Golden Twenties," his psychological strain and poor health, his increasing financial obligations. His favorite subject matter, now that the boom was over, lost all its interest, and, for that matter, he had exhausted it artistically. The writer had to find new sources of inspiration in the painful experiences of those sad years, and consequently to renew and vary the formal and technical patterns through which he was to express himself. In this difficult and exacting task Fitzgerald wavered for a while and lost his momentum, frequently taking refuge among the specters of the past for sentimental and, more often, purely economic reasons. But he did continue to search for new subjects and to experiment with new techniques, working with stubborn dedication and unflagging commitment to his craft. At the end of nine, long years he was to show that he had found a new, elusive artistic reality.

Fitzgerald began working on a new novel as soon as he had finished *Gatsby*, and he also wrote a great number of stories during the next few years. At least some of them, dealing with motives later

developed in the novel, redeem his frequent concessions to the economic muse and his unfortunate harking back to the past. The signs
of renewal become apparent after 1930, when the ghost of the past
has been exorcised in "Echoes of the Jazz Age"; but even earlier, in
the stories where the suggestions of the past are still predominant, one
can perceive at times the partial apprehension of maturer themes.

In "The Rich Boy" and "The Last of the Belles" Fitzgerald's
creative power seems clearly on the wane, and yet he has taken a
different attitude toward themes that were already familiar to him.
"The Rich Boy" [1] codifies, as it were, the poetic and moral feeling
with which the author up to that time had considered the very rich.
It is, in fact, a kind of parable on the isolation and impotence of the
very rich, which is embodied in the pathetic story of Anson Hunter.
His unlimited wealth has given Hunter a sense of superiority and
aloofness (that "came to him when he realized the half-grudging
American deference that was paid to him in the Connecticut village"),
a desire for predominance and a vague contempt for everyday life
("he disdained to struggle with other boys for precedence—he
expected it to be given him freely"), and an excessive indulgence for
his own faults. When he grows up this attitude results in complete
isolation from his fellow creatures and ends by compromising his
sentimental love for Paula, who might have given him a happy
domestic life. Wealth separates him from happiness; instead of fulfilling his dreams, it becomes an obstacle for his self-realization. For
him, as for Gatsby and for his predecessors, the awakening comes too
late. The link of this story with previous handlings of the same motive
is evident, and yet it lacks the quality of dramatic development and
inevitability of situation. In spite of Fitzgerald's statement ("there
are no types, no plurals"), he wanted, here, to represent the plight of
a whole social class, and it is sufficient to quote its beginning to see
his attempt to trace a nice distinction between the very rich and
common people:

> Let me tell you about the very rich. They are different
> from you and me. They possess and enjoy early, and it does
> something to them, makes them soft where we are hard, and
> cynical where we are trustful, in a way that, unless you were
> born rich, it is very difficult to understand. They think, deep in
> their hearts, that they are better than we are because we had to
> discover the compensations and refuges of life for ourselves.

Even when they enter deep into our world or sink below us,
they still think that they are better than we are. They are different. (*Stories*, p. 177.)

Hemingway's flippant rejoinder—"Yes, they have more money"—
is quite irrelevant here, and it shows only that he had not understood
Fitzgerald's deep awareness of the social and psychological differences brought about by wealth. But owing to this general formulation,
"The Rich Boy" becomes a kind of essayistic comment rather than a
story; it suffers from a lack of dramatic intensity, and it has none of
those poetic moments that enlivened an earlier story on the same
topic, "The Diamond as Big as the Ritz." The method of presentation,
moreover, is rather clumsy in "The Rich Boy": the writer begins with
an initial "portrait" of Hunter, which determines and conditions the
subsequent development of the story, as in Fitzgerald's early fiction,
while the use of a "narrator" involved in the story is not completely
controlled. The narrator deals openly here with the events of the
story and intrudes with superfluous observations and explicit comments, so that finally he destroys the structural unity that he should
actually give the story.[2]

"The Last of the Belles"[3] takes up again the motive of the
flapper, and here too the principle of the "narrator" is technically
imperfect. The interest of the writer is almost exclusively directed
upon him in the first and third sections of the story, resulting in a lack
of structural harmony. Furthermore, the narrator participates too
openly in the action, and he colors it with a kind of elegiac sentimentalism which contrasts with the unusual course taken by the
events. The "last of the belles," Ailie, who at the beginning of the story
has so much in common with Gloria and Daisy, differs radically from
them in that she accepts reality in the end. She is brought to give in
before the requirements of life and her emotional feelings by marrying
her modest suitor. This means renouncing, after a whirling, brilliant
life, the frivolous ideals of a flapper, and it is already a clear indication
of the break-up of a sentimental world of selfish pleasure. And the
crisis which has brought her to refuse the false values of the flappers
shows that the writer was becoming aware of a new reality, more
common and domestic, less brilliant and glamorous, that was confronting him. There is no point in the disconsolate comment of the
narrator:

All I could be sure of was this place that had once been
so full of life and effort was gone, as if it had never existed,

and that in another month Ailie would be gone, and the South would be empty for me forever. (*Stories,* p. 253.)

The last of the belles *is* gone—and this is the important aspect of the story, almost a new departure in Fitzgerald's fiction. The flappers give way under the pressure of everyday life; and "aesthetes" and college "philosophers" discover in their adventures the signs of an unfamiliar, unexpected experience of gloomy suffering. In "A Short Trip Home," [4] a student from Yale wins the love of his girl, Ellen, only after having gone through a nightmarish experience and after having rescued her from the evil influence of an actual ghost ("He was dead. He was dead as hell—he had been dead all along") who had been pursuing her. The heedless, superficial world of the college youngsters betrays the hidden presence of evil; more than the apparition that had frightened Amory, the ghost that throws its dark shadow over the whole story recalls the devilish figure that haunted Miriam in *The Marble Faun* of Hawthorne. And this fact is significant. If the obsession with evil of the great nineteenth-century novelist is echoed in the supposed singer of the Jazz Age, it is only because Fitzgerald has turned to his own bitter experience for inspiration, because he has started to reconsider his fictional material. And he deals with this new experience with technical skill, making a child the narrator and allowing him, as a "controlling center," to discover the evil influence that has haunted Ellen. The story is seen through the eyes of Ellen's little brother, who gradually discovers corruption, as had been the case with Maisie in James's novel.

The actual presence of evil in our lives also plays a preponderant part in "One Interne," [5] which deals with the same theme on a more realistic level. There is only a reference to a possible happy ending here, and the young protagonist can hope for the love of his girl only when she has freed herself from an obscure relationship with a thirty-five year old doctor (the ghost in the preceding story was the same age). In this case, however, Doctor Durfee does not hide under his mask an incorporeal being or a mysterious incarnation, nor is he a new Rappaccini. But his disquieting figure hides a dubious soul and suggests that mysterious and wicked element which seems to be inherent in life. It is the girl, Thea, rather than the youth, Bill, who has to disengage herself from his influence; but for both of them life is a source of apprehension and pain.

That love triumphs is no longer important, and if it can bear such a burden of anxiety, it is so because the writer has surrendered himself to the evidence of facts and recognized the obsessive presence of evil. One must add that the story remains a literary exercise, lacking a precise informing idea, and that Fitzgerald was trying to organize more material than was possible without including a "center of interest." But in these stories there is already a clear reflection of Fitzgerald's own experience of suffering as he followed his wife from one clinic to another, and of his foreboding fear of disaster. We can therefore acknowledge the fact that his fiction was developing in the direction of *Tender Is the Night*.

"The Bridal Party," [6] once more, is a variation on the theme of *Gatsby*. Like many of his predecessors, the protagonist, Michael, who is hopelessly poor, is deserted by his flapper Caroline. But the novelty of this story, as in "The Last of the Belles," lies in the conclusion. Even though Michael becomes suddenly rich (this time more easily than ever, through an inheritance), Caroline ends by marrying her fiancé Hamilton, who finds himself without a cent on the eve of the wedding. She reaffirms her faith in the man who is strong and sure of himself, despising Michael's weakness, which cannot be changed by money. Her responsible choice shows that new values must now be taken into account and, in some ways, foreshadows Nicole's choice in *Tender Is the Night*. Her "realistic" decision, moreover, leads Michael to reconsider his position and free himself from illusions and regrets—a first step, as we know from *This Side of Paradise,* toward maturity: "The ceremonial function [Caroline's marriage], with its pomp and its revelry, had stood for a sort of initiation into a life where even his regret could not follow them."

We are undoubtedly confronted with new "germs" and suggestions; but sometimes, as Fitzgerald himself warns us, "a ghostly rumble among the drums, an asthmatic whisper in the trombones" swing him back into the past.[7] Out of this return is born a compact series of stories, woven around two fixed characters, Basil and Josephine, who are the posthumous incarnations of "philosopher" and "flapper." The nine stories about Basil Lee and the five about Josephine represent almost a short novel, although Fitzgerald refused to have them published in collected form.[8] They hark back to distant events of his own childhood, with the same intention of tracing the crucial phases of the "education" of the two characters that inspired *This Side of Paradise*. Young Basil must pass through the "conquest of the successive worlds of school, college and New York"; Josephine has her first experiences as flapper even before the word itself was coined.

These stories have been taken as a clear indication of Fitzgerald's waning power and of his decline as a writer, and it must be admitted that his "reversion" is rather childish and naive, after the long stretch of road he had covered. And yet even these stories have their significance and place in Fitzgerald's fiction if they are interpreted as the author's turning toward what must have appeared to him as an oasis of freshness in the midst of his utter dejection. They have been described as "escapist" stories, and Fitzgerald was undoubtedly driven by a desire to escape his plight and to take shelter in the uncorrupted world of childhood. But he brought with him into that shelter the awareness of the bitter lesson he had learned. The childhood and adolescence to which Fitzgerald turned his attention are no longer seen as a longed-for Eden which had been lost; they are seen "through a glass darkly"—filtered, as it were, through his present suffering. They are no longer a world of simple innocence or repose, but rather they offer as a whole a panorama where his conscience brings to the surface the hidden presence of evil and disillusionment.

As Arthur Mizener has rightly remarked,[9] in these stories Fitzgerald "combined the innocence of complete involvement with an almost scientific coolness of observation." He was involved emotionally in the world of his youth, and he conveyed the sense of his intense participation; at the same time he was able to evoke the past from the point of view of the present and judge it in the light of his new awareness. This double perspective results in an odd kind of irony and detachment, and it has something typically Jamesian about it. The second level—the ironic judgment—is suggested rather than fully realized, but Fitzgerald was able all the same to reconcile it with a kind of intimacy; and in this aspect is laid the significance and the aesthetic value of these stories. His intimacy does not prevent him from a recognition that the principle of evil is already active in the idyll of youth; boys and girls act out of malice or spite, and the suffering that they cause may in itself become a maturing experience. Moreover, these stories are deeply rooted in a definite social context. With both Basil and Josephine the scene of the various episodes is usually a small provincial town, an unfashionable prep school, outside the fringes of the great universities or of the big cities in the East. And it is a setting bristling with motives and fictional possibilities, sketched with precision, which by its nature makes the adventures of the two youngsters, otherwise unbelievable, rather plausible. They become representative, in other words, of an experience that is typically American, or better still typically Middle Western.

With this premise, a few remarks on the single stories will be sufficient to illustrate the mechanics of the various situations and to make them familiar to the reader. "The Scandal Detectives," [10] the first in the series about Basil, tells of a boy's prank: envious of the charm and self-assurance of Hubert Blair, the "beau" of these stories, Basil and a friend take their revenge on him by sending him anonymous threats and frightening him in the dark. Hubert is made fun of because he takes the threats seriously and then enlarges fantastically upon his supposed danger, while in fact the ambuscade has miscarried in a comic way. An element of real interest is provided by the antagonism between Basil and Hubert: a small town dandy on one side and on the other the sensitive, intelligent youth, who usually gains his victory over Basil, in spite of Basil's imaginary triumphs. This motive will reappear in the following stories; here it is interwoven with a subtle notation of the suspicious atmosphere of the small town, embodied in the ridiculous figure of Hubert's father, whose satiric portrait gives some substance to the thinness of the plot. At such an early stage of his "education" Basil is somehow brought to recognize that he is conceited and to renounce his ambition of becoming a "gentleman burglar" like Arsène Lupin. In the next episode, "A Night at the Fair," [11] by succeeding in wearing long pants for the first time and by refusing to have anything to do with the girls picked up at the fair, Basil stands out from the rest of his friends. He remains "faithful" to Gladys—the good girl, both rich and proper—even if Gladys too lets him down at the end. His disappointments follow one upon the other in "The Freshest Boy" and "He Thinks He's Wonderful"; [12] either at prep school or back home, Basil is unpopular, and he ruins his chances of social success through his arrogance, his presumption, and his false self-assurance. In the second of these stories the prospect of a pleasant vacation is ruined by his endless and absurd talks ("he had undone the behavior of three days in half an hour"), and he has learned a painful lesson. In the first, which might be considered the central story in the Basil group, he gives a demonstration of courage and seriousness by remaining in his school when he could have escaped his unpopularity by going to Europe. He has learned that he has to find out and avoid the reasons for his unpopularity and "that life for everybody was a struggle, sometimes magnificent from a distance, but always difficult." Through his stubborn resistance he wins back the respect of his fellow students, and his final achievement is to be called by his own name, and no longer by nicknames.

Two more partial victories are won by Basil in "The Captured Shadow" and in "The Perfect Life." [13] In the first Basil succeeds in producing his play, though he has to lower himself to a compromise with Hubert and then fight his opposition. The play is a success all the same, and Basil is even brought to recognize the absurdity and uselessness of all his schemes: he begins to see things in their true perspective and in their actual value. In the second story he is initiated into a life of "perfect morality," and he runs the risk of becoming an insufferable "prig," but he succeeds at the very end in making himself socially useful to others by preventing an ill-advised elopement. Once the many obstacles of prep school and small town are overcome, Basil is confronted with the greater obstacles of college and big city. In "Forging Ahead" Basil is forced to find sufficient means to go to Yale ("the faraway East, that he had loved with a vast nostalgia since he had first read books about great cities"). He has to submit himself to humiliations and compromises, work hard with his own hands until a mechanical solution releases him from his burden when the financial fortunes of his family are suddenly restored. His efforts have shown that he has reached a certain maturity, and he can again be "faithful" to his girl. And in the last episode, "Basil and Cleopatra," [14] he takes a further step in his education by renouncing the obsessive ideal of a sentimental love. Here the war of the sexes becomes the chief element of the story, but at the edge of manhood and on his way to college, Basil turns his back on the world of youthful emotion and enters a new, virile world, free from his many prejudices and weaknesses. Acquiring popularity among his companions, he can now rely on his psychological balance and pass judgment on the weakness of his rival, resist the lure of a new sentimental involvement, and turn to the future:

> There was a flurry of premature snow in the air and the stars looked cold. Staring up at them he saw that they were his stars as always—symbols of ambition, struggle and glory. (*AA*, pp. 68–69.)

His "education" is still incomplete, of course, but he has achieved a better awareness of life than Amory did, and he has gone through a series of painful trials that will prevent him, as it were, from

following the steps of his predecessor at college. His emotional freshness, his very simplemindedness carry in them a touch of a greater
engagement: it is hardly believable that he will repeat the mistakes
of Amory, assume the mask of the "aesthete," strike an "egotistical"
attitude. In the supposed limbo of infancy and adolescence, Basil has
already discovered the secret flaw of falsehood and conflict and has
become aware that life, at any stage, is a painful struggle.

It is not so for Josephine. In her group of stories, starting from
a beginning in many ways similar to that of Basil, she is born and
remains a "flapper" to the very end. She does not go through a real
progress of "education"; although she may come in the end to her own
form of self-recognition, it is a less keenly felt and suffered one, and
less conclusive than Basil's. She does not build her own future, and
she plays a disturbing part only in the game of existence or in the war
of the sexes. This lack of development in her character is partly due
to the writer's intent, but it is for the most part imposed upon him by
the very situation in which he had to place Josephine. To trace the
line of Basil's development it was sufficient for him to rely on his own
childhood memories and to represent his own process of growth. To
give shape and substance to Josephine, he had to exert all his imaginative power to project an objectively realized character. Fitzgerald
succeeded in making Josephine representative, by conferring on her
some of the typical characteristics of the American girl—such as her
need to dominate men, to feel herself all-important and to show off her
emotional and social power—and by projecting her figure on a small-
town background that would permit her to play that role and exercise
her influence. But just because Josephine is representative, there is
no warmth of feeling in her character and no sympathetic participation in her adventures on the part of the author. Moreover, her
portrait is drawn with a mildly satirical intention, and these satirical
features prevent the proper development of an "education." Fitzgerald's objective perception of her shortcomings and of her basic
wickedness allows him a greater detachment of vision, but insisting
on the fatuous and egotistical sides of her character, he was driven to
give us a rather static portrait.

It is not without significance that he abandoned Josephine much
earlier than Basil and that he brought her to a "conversion" that is
both dubious and doubtful. In "First Blood," sixteen-year-old Josephine succeeds in drawing the attention of her sister's fiancé,
Anthony, on herself, and when Anthony pledges his undying love she

immediately loses all her interest in him. Almost the same trick is played in "A Nice Quiet Place" on Sonny Dorrance, a rich boy who is for a while ensnared by Josephine's "speedy" attitude, and only when Josephine has become "A Woman with a Past," [15] in the third episode, after having been expelled from school, is she brought to the sudden realization that personal conquests cannot be based on the sacrifices of others. For the first time she has tried to attract a man and failed, and her attempt to break an engagement this time comes to nothing. She is left therefore with the simple truth of her own statement that "one couldn't go on forever kissing comparative strangers behind closed doors." The flapper seems to have learned her lesson, but one can easily imagine that after a while she will continue in her disturbing career. This is in fact what happens in the fourth, uncollected story—"A Snobbish Story." To emphasize her change in the direction of seriousness Josephine becomes involved again with an older man, this time married. Her defiance of Chicago society, however, remains the typical gesture of protest of a flapper who has *not* grown up; and even if she is brought to "Emotional Bankruptcy" in the fifth story (also uncollected), we are still left with the suspicion that she will not mature further than that. Her "youthful cockiness" is lost when she realizes that her love affairs are like "a game played with technical mastery, but with the fire and enthusiasm gone"; but she is still looking for a man who is a leader and "with lots of experience," and *her* final "education" resembles Amory's. She seems to accept the wisdom of experience, but she is in fact left with a *tabula rasa:*

> She was very tired and lay face downward on the couch with that awful, awful realization that all the old things are true; one cannot both spend and have. The love of her life had come by, and looking in her empty basket, she had found not a flower left for him—not one. After a while, she wept.
>
> "Oh, what have I done to myself?" she wailed. "What have I done?" [16]

She has done nothing that we did not expect of a flapper, and, if she knows herself, that is not all: this premature vamp will continue in the illusion of both spending and having. Slave as she is of herself, Josephine will substantially remain what she has always been, whereas Basil did suffer a kind of "education."

There is more bitterness here, perhaps, than regret. If the past has been recaptured, it shows that the principle of evil and conflict is present everywhere, even in the golden years of youth and adolescence. Confronted with this discovery, the writer seems to withdraw in dismay, and it is again significant that his best care is devoted to Basil, who can still be saved. In this sense, the variety of motives and the consistent development of the education theme contribute to a better artistic achievement in the Basil stories than in the Josephine group. There is more love for and concern with Basil, while Fitzgerald seems to bear Josephine a grudge. And there is a greater chance for fictional development in dealing with a character who is painfully attaining his own integrity and finding his right way in the world. The sequence stops, however, before any real conclusion is reached, and the value of this experiment should not therefore be overestimated. At the same time it must not be overlooked or brushed aside in haste, as has been quite often the tendency. Fitzgerald's *recherche du temps perdu* does not land him in *le temps retrouvé*, and there is no reason why we should expect it. The various adventures of his youths do not attain the same profound significance of moral initiation as do the adventures of Nick in Hemingway's *In Our Time*. Nevertheless, Fitzgerald's return to the past has proved, if nothing else, the impossibility of any evasion from the present and has shown that suffering is already present in the supposed lost Eden of childhood. It is just the same, then, or probably better, to confront the present without looking back, to find in the foreboding experience of those years the reasons for survival or possibly the way to salvation.[17]

2

The present was poor in consolations but rich in warnings: Fitzgerald was well aware of it, and this was already a new beginning for his maturer fiction. Glamorous New York, upset by the crisis of 1929, was now "a lost city"; Ring Lardner had died without fulfilling his expectations.[18] And as adolescence was already far in the past, only "echoes" were left of the Golden Twenties. In his essay "Echoes of the Jazz Age," [19] Fitzgerald evoked that world with nostalgia and a sense of participation; but he described its collapse, too, in a kind of pitiless post mortem, and his analysis became lucid in the extreme, cold and unimpassioned, almost scientific, when he had to record the disastrous consequences of the past euphoria. The present was different, tragic and tormented:

> By 1927 a wide-spread neurosis began to be evident, faintly signalled, like a nervous beating of the feet, by the

popularity of cross-word puzzles. I remember a fellow expatriate opening a letter from a mutual friend of ours, urging him to come home and be revitalized by the hardy, bracing qualities of the native soil. It was a strong letter and it affected us both deeply, until we noticed that it was headed from a nerve sanitarium in Pennsylvania.

By this time contemporaries of mine had begun to disappear into the dark maw of violence. A classmate killed his wife and himself on Long Island, another tumbled "accidently" from a skyscraper in Philadelphia, another purposely from a skyscraper in New York. One was killed in a speak-easy in Chicago; another was beaten to death in a speak-easy in New York and crawled home to the Princeton Club to die; still another had his skull crushed by a maniac's axe in an insane asylum where he was confined. These are not catastrophes that I went out of my way to look for—these were my friends . . . (*CU*, pp. 19–20.)

There is no palliative for this reality, no possibility of escape, except perhaps the staunch resistance of personal integrity: and this seems to be the conclusion reached by Fitzgerald when he has succeeded in exorcising the past. The new reality that confronts him now is no longer marked by the motives of love and money, of dream and youthful illusion; even its legendary possibilities have vanished. And if the heart rebels for its own reasons, the mind must listen to and obey its reasons as well. Faced with the collapse of his former world, the author can be less involved or assume an attitude of detachment, but his lucid analysis allows him a fresh start. Turning to the present and to everyday life, availing himself of his own private experiences of suffering—his two stays in Hollywood, his life as an expatriate and his self-deception, his efforts to preserve his integrity as a man and as an artist in spite of his wife's illness, and so on—he was to find new and richer material for his fiction, both for the stories and for the novel which was under way at the time.

"Every attempt—as T. S. Eliot was to claim in *Four Quartets*— is a wholly new start," and Fitzgerald's new start was toward a material marked by human suffering, immediate in its appeal, which found it vehicle of expression in a bare style, burning with inner fire and intensity.

Personal charm is no longer sought after by his characters, and it can even become an impediment. In the story called "Magnetism," [20] George Hannaford has to rely on, but at the same time to defend himself from, his "magnetism." His personal charm and his perfect manners are of the greatest help in his career as a movie actor, but for that very reason he has to defend himself from the obvious consequences of them: he is pursued by an actress and blackmailed by his secretary, and his domestic peace is almost ruined. In the end he manages to escape safely, thanks again to his magnetism, but the warning as to its intrinsic danger is none the less explicit. The same danger was to waylay Dick Diver in *Tender Is the Night,* and to its bitter end. Hannaford is still able to save himself and to preserve his personal integrity with an act of self-assurance.

In "Outside the Cabinet-Maker's," [21] the protagonist reaffirms his personal integrity in a quiet and domestic way. In this beautiful little sketch, which shows what delicacy of feeling and bareness of style Fitzgerald could attain, there is practically no action: the sketch catches a glimpse of a father with his daughter, attached to each other by boundless love and affection, in a moment of intimacy and expectation. He buys her a doll's house and almost identifies himself for a while with her fanciful expectation. We are reminded for a single moment of Dick Diver with his children—for a single moment because any external intrusion would shatter the perfect balance of this sketch. There is a hint of impending tragedy in the story, and no more; perhaps Fitzgerald wanted to imagine an oasis of rest in the whirlwind of life, to project an illusion of safety, which would redeem the utter dejection of his mood. Everything here, however, is suggested, rather than made explicit, with an unmatched delicacy of touch. And as Arthur Mizener has remarked:

> "Outside the Cabinet-Maker's" is, both in substance and technique, a wholly mature story. Only a writer who had seen that the significant values of experience exist in all experience could have said so much with material so magnificently homely and familiar; only a writer who had known and could remember what it felt like to see and had completely accepted the blindness of middle age could have presented that little girl's murderous innocence without romantic irony; only a writer with the most delicate sense of how meaning inheres in events could have kept his story so unpretentious; only a writer whose dramatic sense was a function of his understanding could have managed the ending of this story without leaving an impression of technical trickiness.[22]

When panic has spread, however, and violence has been loosed, one's integrity becomes a laborious conquest—when it is not actually lost. In "Two Wrongs" and in "Babylon Revisited" [23] we have two examples of this further development of the theme. The principle of the "transference of vitality" (which will become the central motive of *Tender Is the Night*) permits in "Two Wrongs" the affirmation of a personal integrity, but only at the expense of the parallel sacrifice of another. Bill McChesney, a successful producer at the beginning, comes to Europe where his integrity is shattered by the contact with an elusive reality that he is unable to control. His wife builds up her character on his gradual degradation. Bill lets himself be swallowed by a questionable environment—as Dick will do in the novel—with its pseudo-aristocratic Europeans and expatriate Americans, utterly neglecting his wife Emmy, ruining his health and his reputation, while Emmy, in New York, becomes a successful ballet dancer. In her husband's dissipation Emmy finds the spur to a life of liberty and self-affirmation. When she is told that Bill cannot recover his health, she chooses to follow her own destiny as a dancer: if she has suffered a "wrong" from Bill, Bill will now suffer one from her. But this is not owing to the law of compensation on which Emerson had theorized so enthusiastically; here we are faced with the mysterious motive of the dissipation of energy which is accompanied by the parallel birth of new forms of vitality. The motive of the "transference of vitality" is clearly foreshadowed here: reality has reasons that are sometimes cruel, and the writer's task is to record them in their objective display. No enthusiasms or severe judgments are introduced into the story—only a kind of mature understanding pervades every detail. That is the burden and the lesson of experience, and the lesson is none the less bitter if, as in "Babylon Revisited," the conclusion is less pessimistic. Here the protagonist, Charlie, succeeds in reacquiring his lost integrity, but he has a penalty to pay and sacrifices to make before his ordeal is over.

In "Babylon Revisited" the tragedy of the Golden Twenties reaches its highest artistic realization. Convinced that the "snow of twenty-nine wasn't real snow," Charlie is forced to realize how real it was and how much of his life and of his world has been swept away by the whirlwind. A playboy during the Twenties, to the extent of becoming at least partly responsible for his wife's death, Charlie has returned to a ghostly Paris (the Babylon of the past) after the tragedy has canceled every trace of the boom, to try to get his daughter Honoria from his sister-in-law, Marion, who has been her custodian. Having tirelessly rebuilt a position for himself, Charlie would now like to have his own home, but he is looked upon with suspicion and mistrust and thwarted in his attempt to get Honoria back. In an ash-gray Paris, no longer full of light and excitement, he is faced with Marion's belief that he has not mended his ways and that he might begin drinking again, and when an unfortunate misunderstanding seems to confirm her suspicions she refuses to give up the girl.

Marion is also driven by a kind of personal resentment for his past happiness and wealth, when she could hardly provide for her own family, and from this point of view her refusal is both selfish and cruel. Cruel in particular, because Charlie's redemption has been fully paid for, as we can see by watching him with his daughter in Paris—no longer in bars and bistros but in the boulevards and respectable cafes. But against Marion's ruthless opposition, Charlie emerges a new, vigorous man. The past is not completely dead, and in the crucial point of the story it rises through the ghostlike figures of Charlie's former acquaintances to demand new victims. After this bitter trick of fate, he is about to begin drinking again, to lose hope and abandon himself to a darker, deeper dissipation. And yet, he finds strength enough in himself to resist the temptation and cling more than ever to his hope of regaining Honoria. He is resolved to have her back, and when he leaves the bar without accepting another drink, we know that he can go back to his task and sooner or later succeed in his attempt. "He would come back some day; they couldn't make him pay forever . . . he wanted the child, and nothing was much good now, beside that fact." His long sacrifice will continue until his penalty has been fully paid, but he has acquired a new form of integrity and the sense of human values. His catharsis has been made possible, and the collapse of the Golden Twenties has not destroyed everything. On the ashes of that world at least one is left who in his struggle for a noble aim finds it possible to reassert his own personality and to discover the sense of his human condition.

The story is developed with complete economy of means, without any concession to easy writing or to elaborate devices, and it achieves a perfect structural balance and tightness. A few brief hints are sufficient to evoke the past, which hangs heavily and menacingly over the whole of the story. A few scenes illustrate Charlie's situation, and the crucial point is reached almost immediately, without undue haste or omissions. The climax of the story has all the force and the absurdity of an inescapable tragic knot, and when the tragedy leans toward a possible happy solution the figure of Honoria acquires a symbolic light of redemption and eventual salvation. Like Pearl in

The Scarlet Letter, or, better still, like Maisie in *What Maisie Knew,* Honoria stands between the contrasting parties, between wickedness and purity of intentions, malice and self-denial, and she is entrusted with all hopes of salvation for her elders.

Dick Diver, again, wanted to save himself through his son. Still another child, in "Family in the Wind," [24] becomes the only means of salvation for the protagonist. In a setting that, like old Europe, bears all the marks of its inner dissolution—the South—another lonely survivor, Dr. Janney, who has long ceased to practice medicine because he has grown cynical and has suffered a psychological trauma, finds himself confronted with the ghost of the past. Against the background of a tornado—which has the same symbolic purpose and significance as the "snow of twenty-nine"—Dr. Janney is called to operate on the man who has caused the death of the girl he had loved. After having once refused, he succeeds in overcoming his rancor and performs the task; if he has thus reacquired his professional and human integrity, it is chiefly because during the tornado his feelings have been stirred by the sight of human sufferings and by an encounter with an orphan girl. Taking up his profession again, Dr. Janney fulfills his responsibility to himself and society and decides to devote himself to that lonely girl. Among the "winds of the world" his task will be now to protect others; when he leaves the Southern town his departure is neither an evasion nor a flight but an affirmation of will and an acceptance of life:

> He settled down in his seat, looking out the window. In his memory of the terrible week the winds still sailed about him, came in as draughts through the corridor of the car—winds of the world—cyclones, hurricanes, tornadoes—gray and black, expected or unforeseen, some from the sky, some from the caves of hell.
>
> But he would not let them touch Helen again—if he could help it. (*Stories,* p. 435.)

"Family in the Wind" is perhaps less balanced than "Babylon Revisited," from the structural point of view, but it is written in the same bare and effective language. And it is worthwhile noting that Fitzgerald's preference for motives where the force of will and the humanity of his characters triumph over an adverse or desolate reality is a clear indication of his human and artistic vitality in a period when his personal sufferings were particularly heavy. In the midst of despondency he wanted, perhaps, to renew a message of hope or to project his own possibility of salvation before the gloomy sadness of his own crack-up enveloped even those figures that he cherished most.

In "Crazy Sunday," [25] set in Hollywood, the protagonist succeeds once more in preserving his integrity, although on a human level that is less suffered and painful. But he seems to be the last one to win his battle; after him the forces of dissolution will get the upper hand. Invited among important people and in the midst of a complex game of interests, a young scriptwriter, Coles, attracts the sympathy of an actress married to a producer. Although unfaithful himself, the producer is extremely jealous of his wife Stella, and Coles must keep a fine balance between the demands of both to avoid ruining his career. There could be a mechanical solution, when the actress throws herself into the arms of Coles at the news of her husband's death in an airplane accident. It could be the final big scene of a popular film, and it did happen in life, but Coles resists his first impulse to stay, and even though he is in love with Stella he goes away. There is a clear hint that he might return, but in the crucial moment he has had enough strength to refuse an equivocal involvement and to assert his honesty of feeling. By refusing an easy solution he seems to escape evil and possible ruin, but he is the last character in our sequence who succeeds in doing so. The others who remain to be examined—before coming to *Tender Is the Night*—prefigure Dick Diver's final surrender.

"Crazy Sunday" is not as good as the previous stories because Fitzgerald has not clarified his attitude toward his characters. The exact relationships between them are not properly explained, their motivations are obscure, and their merits and defects are not clearly indicated. There is also a structural disharmony between the first part of the story, which is rather humorous, and the second part; moreover the device of the airplane accident to remove the producer from the scene is an easy and mechanical solution, a kind of *deus ex machina* to get things in motion again. And yet several motives and several situations that will reappear in the novel that follows are already brought together in this story. Just as Dick loves his wife but is attracted to Rosemary, so Stella loves her husband but would like to find a solution for her troubles with Coles. Coles has the same feeling as Rosemary of being a "pawn" in a cruel game (and we should note here that in the first draft of the novel Rosemary was to be a young Hollywood technician). If Nicole, suffering from a father complex, is inferior to and dependent on Dick, here it is the producer who suffers from a mother complex, which makes him dependent on Stella. And so on. We are confronted with significant analogies, both for the inherent similarity of some motives, and for the similar way in which they are brought together and handled. The same can be said of two other stories which are clearly to be considered as "preliminary studies" for certain situations and themes in *Tender Is the Night*.

Neither "The Rough Crossing" nor "One Trip Abroad" [26] is worth much as a story from a strictly aesthetic point of view; their value lies in their open links with the subject matter of the novel, whose long process of elaboration receives new light from them. "The Rough Crossing" is set on a liner en route for Europe, and it deals with two characters, Adrian and Eva, who are retracing the steps of their honeymoon during a particularly critical period in their marriage. As will be the case with Nicole in *Tender Is the Night*, Eva is dependent on the love of her husband, while Adrian, in search of new experiences, is attracted by young Miss D'Amido. She offers him her young love in the same words that Rosemary will use in the novel ("I fell in love with you the moment I saw you"); during a storm, Eva is so upset by the prospect of Adrian's infidelity that she walks on deck and is in danger of being swept overboard. Adrian is thus brought to reconsider his conduct, and when he has saved his wife from the impending danger he goes back to her. Their domestic peace is restored, and Adrian's final comment ("It was two other people") stresses that their quarrel has been only an episode of their married life, "minimized" by the outer "array of calamities." But the sudden explosion of their inner conflicts is already a prelude to the deeper contrast that will alienate Nicole from Dick in the novel.

In "One Trip Abroad," the heroine bears Nicole's name, and the informing idea of the story is already that of an emotional *épuisement* and of a broken marriage. After a few episodes set in Africa the scene shifts to Europe, where the neurotic dissipation of Nelson and Nicole finds new incentive among a set of expatriates. A first argument between them, which has taken place in a small African town, might have been the sign of youthful restlessness, but in Europe a whole series of misunderstandings follows, culminating in a violent scene when Nicole finds her husband kissing a young girl, Noel (this same name will reappear in the third draft of *Tender Is the Night*). As in the novel, the only solution looked for is escape. But Nelson's and Nicole's flight from Monte Carlo to Paris does nothing but precipitate further discord and division, bringing the dissipation and deterioration of the couple to its extreme consequences. Nelson takes to drinking, and they are eventually swindled by a fake European aristocrat and end up in Switzerland (where the novel begins) in a desperate attempt to prop up their lives from complete ruin. During a storm (the same device used in "The Rough Crossing") they see for the last time a ghostly couple which has haunted them with recurring appearances throughout the whole story and which is a spectral counterpart of themselves:

> "Did you see?" she cried in a whisper. "Did you see them?"
> "Yes!"
> "They're us! They're us! Don't you see?" (*AA*, p. 165.)

They are brought, perhaps too late, to a final realization of their complete dissolution. Bound to their destinies, Nelson and Nicole do not even find enough strength to separate; in *Tender Is the Night* Nicole will find enough force in herself to assert her physical vitality with Tommy Barban.

The motivations in these two stories are often insufficient, the psychological explanations are inadequate, and the influence of the European scene is imperfectly brought to bear on the action, in spite of Fitzgerald's own warning that "the geographical element must not be slighted." [27] We are still at the level of a preliminary study, which nevertheless reveals the new preoccupations and fictional concerns of the writer, even better, perhaps, than the finished novel. The Jazz Age has given way to an age of crisis and uncertainty. Human integrity is the victim of deep lacerations, eaten by the worm of inner evil, of personal weaknesses, of restlessness. The theme of "education" must be turned over—in the new reality, only motives of deterioration and personal ruin are fit material for artistic elaboration. The naturalistic writers had already been aware of this at the end of the nineteenth century; in the Thirties, a whole group of "engaged" writers was becoming aware of it, from Farrell to Caldwell, from Dos Passos to Steinbeck.

Fitzgerald, too, had come to realize it from personal experience and from his acute sense of the times. In those long years between *The Great Gatsby* and *Tender Is the Night* he had discovered or created a new, exacting subject matter. The germs and the first shapeless trials are clearly to be found in the stories; in the novel that followed they found their elaborate and laborious consecration.

CHAPTER VI

The "Intricate Destiny"

> *The dramatic novel has canons*
> *quite different from the philo-*
> *sophical, now called psychological,*
> *novel. One is a kind of tour de*
> *force and the other a confession*
> *of faith. It would be like*
> *comparing a sonnet sequence*
> *with an epic.*
>
> Letters, p. 363.

1

If *The Great Gatsby* is a dramatic *tour de force*, *Tender Is the Night* might be described, in a Jamesian sense, as a "loose and baggy monster." It presents so many characters and such a complex of motives and themes that there is difficulty in establishing its exact. value and its artistic significance. But the difference between the two novels is less substantial than we are made to believe. Fitzgerald himself thought that he had used different canons and had written a different type of novel. But he managed, through whole series of endless modifications, to bring *Tender Is the Night* within the more congenial "line"of development which runs from *Gatsby* to *The Last Tycoon*. As we read it today, *Tender Is the Night* does not represent a deviation from the main line of his fiction, but constitutes a bridge passage, showing an unquestionable continuity of themes and inspirations. Even in the complexity of its motives and the variety of its thematic variations, the informing idea seems to be the same as in the preceding novel. In the same way, it is the precise structural disposition of the plot that accounts for its artistic achievement. At least superficially, the theme is once more provided by the concept of the young, sentimental idealist corrupted and ruined by contact with the carelessness and selfishness of the leisure class, by involvement in the world of the very rich. And once more, a careful plot contrivance is responsible for bringing to light the latent and symbolic possibilities of that theme, even if in this case it was laboriously achieved.

The novel bristles with episodes and characters, in an ambitious attempt to give the "picture" of a whole world and to follow closely, in their gradual developments, the life stories of a group of characters without relying too much on principles of economy and structural tightness. A depth of realization is combined with an extensive treatment of the subject matter, explored and illustrated in its details and organized according to its inner growth. Only at the very last, and not conclusively, did Fitzgerald manage to tighten the structure and to get a firm grasp of the theme.

As Fitzgerald published it in 1934 after seven or eight years of painstaking composition, *Tender Is the Night* gives the impression of a vast and chaotic fresco, written in compliance with the "pictorial" method advocated by James in his early writings. The main concern seems to be for the "creation of imaginary psychologies" according to the formula advocated by Ortega y Gasset,[1] and the manner of presentation apparently goes back to the well-established tradition of the nineteenth-century novel. A group of characters is set in a well-defined and recognizable historical and social situation, and their psychological reactions are followed until these give substance to, and provide a development for, the story—determining and illustrating it at the same time. Charged with philosophical implications, this kind of novel presupposes the necessity of the "long story"; there is no foreshortening, and depth is achieved through an exhaustive analysis of the characters' motivations. It *was* a new departure in Fitzgerald's fiction. But he did not seem to be satisfied with it and revised and reorganized the novel according to a different structural perspective, which stressed the linear development of the story. In this "final version," published posthumously in 1948, Fitzgerald restored the dramatic quality of the novel at the expense of its pictorial vividness. In this way both its informing idea and its fictional achievement were made clearer and brought closer to his main "line" of fictional development.

The road which leads to this result is as long as it is complex. Before attempting an analysis of the novel, it is necessary to examine the story of its laborious composition, both to establish the legitimacy of the text we are considering as "final" and to detect in the gradual unfolding of its themes the exact meaning or the imperfect realization of some of its possibilities. At the same time we shall reach a better awareness of Fitzgerald's painstaking and tormented method of composition [2] and of his complete involvement in the problems of the craft of fiction.

Gerald Murphy, one of Fitzgerald's closest friends at the time, to whom the novel was finally dedicated, speaks of the existence of eight different drafts of *Tender Is the Night:*

> To my knowledge he made 8 drafts of that [*Tender Is the Night*] and I can't help recalling that my wife and I witnessed his destruction of what we were afraid was going to be the last draft, when he went out in a boat and tore it to pieces and scattered it on the waves of the Mediterranean, and we were so afraid that it would not be rewritten; that was the 7th draft. But the 8th he did, and the 8th we have.[3]

The episode has a faintly Keatsian flavor, and it would be difficult to check its veracity. Matthew J. Bruccoli has recently examined eighteen drafts of the novel from its first inception to the 1934 edition. For our purposes, it is sufficient to speak with some assurance of six different stages of composition corresponding to six main drafts of the novel, including the "final version" posthumously published in 1948. Although some of these drafts are obviously incomplete, and their chronological order cannot always be established with certainty, a brief examination of the changes between one draft and another is extremely revealing.[4]

The very first idea, conceived in the summer of 1925, was to write a novel dealing with "an intellectual murder on the Leopold-Loeb idea," "about Zelda and me and the hysteria of last May and June in Paris." [5] The tentative title was *Our Type.* Right from the start the idea was to make the protagonist representative of an entire social class. Fitzgerald began working on it in the fall of 1925, and he completed one-fourth of it by the next April, when he announced to his agent, Harold Ober, that he would complete twelve chapters by the end of the year. But he had already changed his original concept, and he wrote that the book "will be ... concerning tho this is absolutely confidential such a case as that girl who shot her mother on the Pacific coast last year." [6] The "intellectual murder" has been replaced by a matricide—a murder whose motivation can only be emotional or psychological, and the fact is important for a writer like Fitzgerald, who was more open to the charm and suggestion of emotions than to the stimulus of ideas.

This first draft of the novel, of which we have only four chapters, is known as the "Melarky Case." Francis Melarky, a young Hollywood technician touring Europe with his mother, arrives on the Riviera. He has already been involved in a drunken brawl in Rome, and we learn that he has been dismissed from West Point for insubordination; he has a violent temper, and his inborn dissatisfaction and latent rebellion will be released in the Europe of the expatriates. His father is serving a prison term, and he can hardly suffer his dominating mother; he is caught in an impossible situation, and it is easy to foresee that he will revert to desperate means.[7] Of the two titles that the novel might have taken, the first, *The Boy Who Killed His Mother*, admits of no doubt; the second, *The World's Fair*, emphasizes the importance of the setting and the environment which determine Francis' violent actions, indicating at the same time that he was to be representative of a larger collapse of moral values.

The first chapter shows Francis in Rome, disgusted with himself and the "natives," exasperated by the city which seems "corrupt" to him.[8] At the end of a wild night he is beaten by some taxi drivers and then by the police. This episode will be reworked later to show Dick Diver's final deterioration (*TTN*, IV, 10); at this point, it is Francis' mother who manages to get him out of jail. She has for the first time a clear indication of his exasperation and can assert her moral superiority over him, as Baby Warren will later do in *Tender Is the Night*. It is a dark and gloomy beginning, marked by an atmosphere of violence and disorder. Even the airy landscape of the Riviera, in the second chapter, cannot dispel the gloom. Francis arrives on the Mediterranean beach just as Rosemary does (*TTN*, II, 2 ff.) and is taken up by a group of carefree expatriates led by Seth and Dinah Piper (originally Roreback). The episodes in this second chapter were for the most part retained in the novel, but here Francis, in contrast to Rosemary, is still disgusted and dissatisfied: life in France seems to him as "empty and stale" as it was in Rome, and there is a premonition of disaster when he tells his mother: "I thought I could go to pieces better if we had a car." His meeting with the Pipers (a first incarnation of Dick and Nicole Diver), however, seems at first to give a certain order to his life and to stimulate his willingness to work: "He wanted desperately to get back into pictures."

In the third chapter (*TTN*, II, 7 ff.), during a party in the villa of the Pipers, Francis gives way to the temptation to make love to Dinah. This ill-advised behavior only heightens his state of inner tension, and he is driven to thoughtless and irresponsible acts which

speed his ruin. He acts, for instance, as second in a duel between
Gabriel Brugerol and Albert McKisco and shows his willingness to
take part in the duel—to give or receive the *coup de grace*—when he
is not concerned in the quarrel: "All right"—he says—"but this time
it's me. And eight paces." He is prevented by the bystanders; but
when he misses the chance of going back to work for an American
film company in France, owing to his mother's opposition and to his
indecision, it becomes clear that his destiny is marked. Faced with
the possibility of leaving and thus saving himself, he remains instead
entangled in the dubious and dangerous game of the expatriates, and
when Seth goes to see him, he gets the impression that "he looks
exactly like a man planning a murder." Francis accepts the invitation
to go to Paris with the Pipers to see Abe Grant off to America (*TTN,*
III, 2 ff.), and there he flirts with Dinah (Chapter four) as they take
long taxi rides through the city. His behavior becomes more and more
irresponsible: he goes to a homosexual hangout, attacks a Negro and
beats him, despising himself at once for his weakness, and then throws
himself into a disastrous escapade with a girl named Wanda Breasted,
who turns out to be a lesbian and attempts suicide.[9]

The "Melarky Case" stops at this point, although Fitzgerald at
various times wrote his friends and his agent that he had "nearly
finished" the novel; and it stops at the very point when Francis
realizes that he is disgusted and disillusioned by every woman he has
met: "God damn these women!" is his final comment, and his mother
seems to be included in his curse. There is no indication of how he was
to murder his mother, but it is worth noting that one of the characteristics of *Tender Is the Night* is already present: an insistent imagery
of corruption and sexual disorder, of uncontrollable violence and
crude realism—which is at the same time the background and a
reflection of the protagonist's decay. The writer's interest, however,
wavered between the two elements. The interplay between Francis'
dissipation and the corrupted world around him is not clearly defined.
The motivation of Francis' behavior seems to lie only in his pathological predisposition to violence and disorder. He figures, furthermore, as the only protagonist; the Pipers remain in the background,
and although they hasten his deterioration, they remain marginal and
external.

The story, narrated in the third person, is built on rapid dramatic
scenes, but in a later revision some of the scenes are told in the first
person by Francis. The action is therefore filtered through the eyes of

an observer-narrator, and this is perhaps a sign of the way in which Francis (or Rosemary after him) will turn from protagonist to a spectator involved only laterally in the story. If this will be Rosemary's position in the novel, the origin of her character will account for the excessive importance she retains in the plot of the novel and for her constant and overwhelming presence in the central part of it ("Rosemary's Angle," originally Part I in the 1934 edition). Many of the features of Francis will be also transferred to Dick Diver. But springing directly from Francis, Rosemary will have a greater role in the novel than she would be entitled to if we have to consider her merely as a "catalytic agent" of the main plot.

The transformation of Francis into Rosemary begins to take shape in the second draft, known as the "Rosemary Version," or as the "Kelly-shipboard Version," of which only a single chapter and fragments of the second remain. The action begins here at an earlier stage and is set on a liner bound for Europe. Fitzgerald wrote Perkins in 1929 that he was working night and day on the novel "from a new angle," and as the second draft has points in common with both "The Rough Crossing" and "One Trip Abroad," it is safe to infer that Fitzgerald worked at it for a short time in 1929–30. The general concept of the breakdown of the protagonist in contact with Europe remains unchanged, but the relationships between the various characters undergo a definite modification.

A brilliant young movie director and his wife, Lewellen and Nicole Kelly, move gradually into the foreground. He is leaving America for Europe because he feels drained and must take a vacation. A symptomatic episode takes place at the very beginning: a young American named Curly jumps overboard to meet the challenge of two college girls and to perform a gratuitous act of protest "out of weariness with it all." Although he is rescued, his plunge into the abyss can be taken as a symbol of an abdication from life as it will be later exemplified in the novel. It is significant that Kelly is attracted by him, going to the extent of providing him with liquor after the captain has expressly forbidden it. This detail might suggest that he is ready for "experimenting"; and it means that he will not refrain from any temptation that Rosemary might offer him. Rosemary is here a young actress whose mother gets her to sneak from tourist class into first class to meet Kelly and extract, if possible, a contract from him. She is introduced to Kelly, but Kelly is "sick with everything" as much as Francis was; he is weary of his neurotic wife, who is given to drinking, just as Francis was weary of his mother. Going to Europe, he is running away from impotence and decay, and probably trying to run away from himself as well: "He didn't know what relation he bore to Nicole or to the world," we are told. And it can be expected that in Rosemary he will find a factor that will hasten his process of deterioration.

This draft is interrupted before any actual development of the story. But we can see that the general atmosphere evoked in this brief fragment is again one of moral disorder and corruption, and it is important to perceive that the role of protagonists is taken up by the married couple, while Francis-Rosemary is relegated to a secondary position. The draft represents an unmistakable transitional stage toward the completed novel; Kelly himself prefigures Dick (his name, originally Francis, shows Francis' link with Dick, too), while Rosemary and Nicole will gradually develop into the characters of the novel, even if Rosemary's dubious behavior will be toned down. But the whole conception of the novel underwent a radical change in 1931–32 after Fitzgerald's own collapse and his wife's hospitalization. The idea of a compact, dramatic novel gave way to the idea of "a double decker novel," which would rely more and more for subject matter on his personal experiences and for form on the "pictorial" method. Presumably, in 1932 he sketched a "General Plan" for it, which is the first step leading to the third draft, the complete "Dick Diver Version":

> The novel should do this. Show a man who is a natural idealist, a spoiled priest, giving in for various causes to the ideas of the haute Bourgeoisie, and in his rise to the top of the social world losing his idealism, his talent and turning to drink and dissipation. Background one in which the leisure class is at their truly most brilliant & glamorous such as Murphys.[10]

The hero is described as one who "has all the gifts and goes through Yale almost succeeding but not quite"—"a superman in possibilities ... from a bourgeoise point of view," "a moralist in revolt" with socialist tendencies. The plan develops his story more or less along the line it will take in *Tender Is the Night*, but to a rather strange conclusion, according to which the "spoiled priest" after losing hold on his wife and himself

> sends his neglected son into Soviet Russia to educate him and comes back to America to be a quack thus having accomplished both his bourgeoise sentimental idea in the case of his

wife and his ideals in the case of his son, & now being himself only a shell to which nothing matters but survival as long as possible with the old order.

It seems a partial victory won *in extremis* and a vicarious form of salvation. But this illogical and unsatisfactory conclusion (even in the years of infatuation with Russian socialism) is almost immediately given up in favor of a consistently tragic ending, according to which there is no possible recovery for the hero and his ruin is motivated by an interplay of tragic factors. In a "Further Sketch" we read:

> *The Drunkard's Holiday* will be a novel of our time show-
> ing the break-up of a fine personality. Unlike *The Beautiful
> and Damned* the break-up will be caused not by flabbiness but
> really tragic forces such as the inner conflicts of the idealist and
> the compromises forced upon him by circumstances.

Fitzgerald estimated that he would write fourteen chapters divided into three parts ("Part I From outside mostly. II Nicole and Dick. III Dick"), but he wrote the whole story in twelve chapters, and this third version brings us to the very threshold of *Tender Is the Night*. The two working titles which Fitzgerald had adopted were both discarded: *Doctor Diver's Holiday* because he found the refer- ence to Dick's profession depressing, *The Drunkard's Holiday* because it gave away most of the contents. This version is therefore best known as the "Dick Diver Version," both because it is centered on Dick's story and because the method of presentation tends to focus as much as possible on Dick, who was to be called Dick ("the gentle- man of leisure," as M. J. Bruccoli rightly suggests) in the first part, Dr. Diver in the second ("husband and physician"), and Diver in the third ("the emotional bankrupt and spoiled doctor"). Of the two suggested titles, however, the second would be more to the point, because in this version the protagonist's disposition to drinking plays an all-important and prepossessing role.

The informing idea of the natural idealist corrupted by the *haute bourgeoisie* remains latent in the background, while Dick's ruin is brought about by his pathetic weakness and by his drunken dispo- sition. Here Dick does not seem properly a victim of "the compromises forced upon him by circumstances" but rather a victim of his very "flabbiness," of his lack of "tensile strength," and of his "secret drink- ing," which he had begun during the war.[11] It is a substantial dif- ference from *Tender Is the Night* because the outer forces are less destructive here than they will be in the published novel.

The main line of the plot is already that of *Tender Is the Night* as it was published in 1934. It opens with the arrival of Rosemary on the Riviera and her meeting with Dick and Nicole; the duel between Barban and McKisco (this time due to Barban's wish to keep Nicole's secret hidden) follows, and then the trip to Paris to see Abe off, with the beginning of Dick's love for Rosemary and Nicole's collapse.[12] Next is a retrospective chapter (the fifth), as foreseen in Fitzgerald's notes for the "General Plan," which reveals Dick's and Nicole's past, Dick's flight in search of Rosemary and of himself, his trip to America for the death of his father, his drunken brawl in Rome, his encounter with Rosemary, ending in complete breakdown and in his failure as a man and as a psychiatrist, and his final separation from Nicole, who has become Barban's mistress. The order of the main episodes is the same as in the published version, even if this version has a few marginal episodes that will be cut or compressed in the novel. But the general tone and significance of the story—on account of a number of minor details—are substantially different.

To begin with, Dick is not the *brilliant* scientist that he is in the novel, although his personal charm is unquestionable and he is willing to risk his career for Nicole. His first book, for instance, is published at his own expense: "his book which upon consideration of $150.00 help from Dr. Diver, Messrs. etc. etc. were to present this autumn to the German speaking psychiatric world." From the very start his desire to be loved and admired is accompanied by a kind of sentimental weakness and emotional complacency, and he has begun drinking, we remember, "during the war." During his flight from Nicole (Chapter VIII) he is attracted by quite a number of women. He dreams of the girl-friends of his youth, flirts without a moment's hesitation with an "undifferentiated" girl, indulges in a thoughtless adventure with a woman whom he takes for a governess and who is in fact the mistress of his friend; on the ship on which he returns from America after his father's funeral he spends afternoons in the cabin of a lady, and when he finally meets Rosemary in Rome his efforts are clearly directed to the egotistical purpose of seducing her ("to make her," as we read in this text). His moral deterioration is clearly defined in sexual terms and indicated by his urge to pick up women as soon as he sees them. He seduces Rosemary in a rather detached way, realizing immediately that she means very little to him; he does not abandon himself to the illusion, at least, of redeeming and refreshing love. It is not yet a question of achieving "poetic justice," as in the novel, and Rosemary is not seen as the girl "that crowns the other girls with meaning"—she is simply one more conquest, and it is Dick himself who manages with skeptical cynicism to get rid of her after the short-lived affair: "She would have come up to him but he pretended to be tying his tie." There is no sign here of his emotional involvement, and very little suffering on his part, at least as far as Rosemary's destiny is concerned; and the lack of a moral, dramatic dilemma on his part disqualifies him in our eyes.

Just as Kelly had done, Dick finds it natural in this version to sympathize with Curly, the young man who has jumped overboard, and to give him liquor; the episode marks his growing disinterest as a psychiatrist in a case which is apparently neurotic. His only reaction to incumbent ruin is to take more and more to drinking, and this congenital weakness becomes the most important determining factor of his deterioration, if it is true that the external pressures are less active here than in the novel. Nicole, in fact—and this is another very important feature of this version—does not so much act on him as a disrupting force as assist him in an attempt to strengthen his resistance and to preserve his integrity. Nevertheless, her repeated attempts at reconciliation are met by Dick with coldness and disinterest, or even with needless accusations and abuse; and it is Dick that almost drives her to adultery with his detached and insufferable behavior. A single example will emphasize this fact. In the scene at the barber's, when Nicole and Dick discuss their separation, this is Nicole's reaction in the "Dick Diver Version":

> . . .—she felt a little cheated that there had been so little drama; she felt a little hurt at realizing that from the moment of the jar of camphor-rub Dick had planned out everything to this point. (Chapter XII.)

Dick *had planned out everything:* he has managed to come to that point out of his own free will and has even arranged the solution according to a specific *plan.* It is significant that in a "Summary of Part III" we read: "Dick is still in control of the situation and thinks of the matter practically." In *Tender Is the Night,* a change in the verb (from *planned out* to *anticipated*) is sufficient to show that Dick has submitted to events and has foreseen, but not so much planned, his own destiny:

> So it had happened—and with a minimum of drama; Nicole felt outguessed, realizing that from the episode of the

camphor-rub, Dick had anticipated everything. (*TTN*, V, 11, p. 329.)

In the book, Nicole feels at once "happy and excited"; here she suffers for her husband's ruin and is more sympathetic and understanding toward him, eager to prevent somehow the complete break-down of his personality. When Dick, completely drunk, teeters dangerously on the terrace of the hotel and blesses the beach before leaving, Nicole's first impulse in this version is to run to his aid, and she is actually prevented by her sister Baby, whose cynical comment on Dick makes her indignant.[13] In the published novel she is restrained by Tommy, but she does not enjoy the sympathy of her friends as she does here; Dick himself, in the novel, does not have so many reasons for self-pity as he seems to have in this early draft of the episode.

Summing up all these scattered details, we can see that Dick's story was presented in a particular light in this version. The abyss beneath his feet is opened by his obstinate refusal of any moderation, by his contempt for moral and social values, even by his ill-nature— all of them aggravated by his immoderate drinking. And if he falls pathetically into the abyss, he is not pushed into it by a concurrence of inexorable tragic forces. Responsible for his predicament to a great extent, he has not the justification of having been crushed by the weight of a psychological and social conflict which he could not escape. Fitzgerald's statement of purpose, therefore, is only partly carried out. The difference from *The Beautiful and Damned* is not so marked as he would have it. Only in the fourth and notably in the fifth version was this imperfection of focus gradually eliminated and the balance between the external factors and Dick's inborn weakness reestablished according to the original plan.

In the fourth version, published serially in four numbers of the *Scribner's Magazine* (January–April 1934), some stylistic and structural modifications begin to bring the story back to the right track. Some cuts were probably due to a moralistic concern with the possible reactions of the magazine's readers—Fitzgerald omitted for instance Warren's confession of his incestuous relation with Nicole, Dick's interview with the Chilean homosexual, and smaller details. But he also omitted Dick's conversation with Mary on the terrace after his "dismissal" from the beach, which has nothing to do with sexual matters but only serves to stress Dick's self-pity at his failure. This cut clearly had the effect of quickening the pace of the narration and thus might have been suggested by structural reasons. In fact, the writer now was trying to attain a kind of dramatic intensity in the single scenes by tightening the episodes as much as possible. But this cut has also the effect of presenting Dick in a slightly different light by removing at least one pathetic aspect of his final surrender.

This process is continued in the fifth version, which appeared in book form in the same year. The scenes cut for moralistic purposes were reintegrated into the text, but a number of different scenes were cut from the serial, with the result of hastening the pace of the story, of placing the pathetic aspect of Dick's failure in the background, and of stressing the determining value of the social pressures at work to destroy him. Working feverishly on the galley proofs, which had eventually to be reset for the most part, Fitzgerald cut out six scenes: two dealing with Abe North at the Ritz bar, the episode of Dick's involvement with the governess at Innsbruck, his affair with the woman on the ship, the episode of the boy who jumps overboard, and finally Nicole's calling with Tommy Barban at the retired bootlegger's at the end of the book. He also inserted some new material and revised carefully, from a structural and stylistic point of view, the whole texture of the book.

According to M. J. Bruccoli,[14] there is no great difference between the emotional and thematic content of these two versions, but I would stress Bruccoli's own admission that all these revisions had a "cumulative effect" not only on the texture but on the thematic significance of the story, which was somehow brought closer to the original intention. Dick's deterioration is presented here with more equanimity (his sexual disorder is toned down and his drinking is not so much insisted on), while part of the blame is transferred to his wife Nicole and, above all, to the world of careless corruption that she represents and personifies. Dick's plight is seen from a more sympathetic point of view, and the corruption of the *haute bourgeoisie* becomes not only a catalytic agent, but a determining factor of his individual ruin. Through an elaborate interplay of psychological and social conflicts, clearly defined in the book version, the story can develop on the double level of Dick's personal *épuisement* and of his defeat "forced upon him by circumstances." These two levels are strictly interrelated and interdependent, since Dick's *épuisement* is determined by his devotion to Nicole, who is herself part and parcel of the *haute bourgeoisie,* and since the defeat of the idealist is prepared by his psychological condition of *épuisement.*

The implications of this central point of the book will be examined later. We have now to consider the fact that in the 1934 edition of *Tender Is the Night* the structural balance of the story, and hence its precise significance, is brought through to the reader with some difficulty. The novel is organized in three structural units. Part One opens on the colorful Riviera scene and brings together Rosemary, Dick, Nicole, and their friends, who then move on to Paris, where Nicole has a collapse and Rosemary finally perceives the evil hidden beneath the brilliant surface of Dick and Nicole's marriage. Part Two (the retrospective section) tells the story of their meeting and of their marriage and reveals the secret of their behavior. At this point, the flashback is welded to the present story, and Part Three tells of Dick's gradual deterioration, of Nicole's emancipation, and of their final separation. The structure follows Conrad's principle of the "chronological muddlement," beginning with a strong impression and then working backward and forward to the "dying fall." But the fault of the book, if any, lies exactly in this elaborate construction; as there can be no distinction, except empirical and temporary, between the material presented and the manner of presentation—between form and content, story and structure, action and plot—this structural contrivance may confuse the actual meaning of the story and our proper apprehension of it.

It is undeniable that the opening is brilliant and sustained, with its ample perspective and its crowd of characters, its "pictorial" quality and its perceptive and impressionistic style. An element of mystery is gradually suggested under the brilliant façade, some kind of uneasiness is transmitted to the reader, and the suspense is heightened. When it begins to be spasmodic, after 148 pages of tense narrative, the mystery is slowly revealed. But Rosemary in the meantime has been not only the focus but the center of the story, and one might say that it takes more than 200 pages (half the book, that is) to realize that the real protagonists are Dick and Nicole. As has been often noted the book seems to break into two separate units, and the second to move with a new perspective. Furthermore, the brilliant opening engenders the impression that the novel's whole point will be the description of a definite locale, the drawing of a "pictorial" fresco or at most the study of a particular social environment. Only at the middle of the book is the true intention made clear: too late, one might say, when the story seems to be already headed in another direction. Kenneth Burke, in his effective (when not too intricate) terminology might speak of "a failure to fulfil a categorical expectancy."

This "fault," Kenneth Burke would again say, is a fault of "strategy": and so it seemed to Fitzgerald himself, when he reconsidered his novel after its relatively small success. This limited success, one should note at once, was mainly due to a coincidence of external factors. In a period of strong socialist feelings, the book appeared by and large as a stubborn and anachronistic echo of the Jazz Age, as one more story about the expatriates and the very rich, which refused to face the more pressing problems of the times. In fact, Fitzgerald was well aware of those problems, and he was adhering fully to the stimuli of the new age, as we shall shortly see.[15] But if he was worried about the "failure" of his novel and accepted humbly most of the censures, he went to look for his "fault" not in the subject matter but in his treatment of it, not in the story itself but in the manner of presentation. In 1936, in a letter to Bennett Cerf, he envisaged the possibility of "a certain new alignment of scenes" with "sudden stops and part headings which would be to some extent explanatory," and he mentioned "a plan" which he thought was in Baltimore. He did not want, apparently, "to change anything in the book but sometimes by a single word change one can throw a new emphasis or give a new value to the exact same scene or setting." It is a perfect description of the method he had used painstakingly in his earlier drafts of the novel. Two years later, in a letter to Maxwell Perkins, he wrote of *Tender Is the Night* that

> its great fault is that the *true* beginning—the young psychiatrist in Switzerland—is tucked away in the middle of the book. If pages 151–212 were taken from the present place and put at the start, the improvement in appeal would be enormous. In fact the mistake was noted and suggested by a dozen reviewers.[16]

Presumably about this same time, Fitzgerald in a note delineated structurally the material according to the same principle, dividing the novel into five books instead of three and proposing to eliminate two more episodes:

> Analysis of *Tender*:
> I Case History 151–212 61 pps. (change moon) p. 212
> II Rosemary's Angle 3–104 101 pps. P. 3
> III Casualties 104–148, 213–224 55 pps. (− 2) (120 & 121)

He reordered the pages in his personal copy of the book and proceeded to a stylistic revision of the *true* beginning. On the inside front cover of the book he wrote in pencil: "This is the *final version* of the book as I would like it."

On account of these indications and statements of purpose, Malcolm Cowley edited the *"final version"* in 1948. Not everyone accepts it as legitimate or useful, but there can be no doubt as to Fitzgerald's intentions regarding his book. Whoever sees Fitzgerald's own copy feels that Malcolm Cowley followed to the letter his intention. As a working text, moreover, this "sixth" version *is* extremely useful: by toning down the brilliancy and the suspense of the 1934 edition, and by developing the story in a linear way without the possibility of misunderstandings as to its real purport, it gives further consistency, unity, and symmetry to the book. It enhances its dramatic quality at the expense of its pictorial value and thus brings it closer to the main "line" of Fitzgerald's fiction.

2

The title of the book, taken from Keats's "Ode to a Nightingale," bears a vague hint of dissolution and death, a foreboding of the protagonist's gradual sinking into darkness and oblivion. *Tender Is the Night* opens thus on a tranquil and subdued tone in Book One ("Case History: 1917–1919"). It is against the background of isolation and weariness in a secluded Switzerland that the promising young psychiatrist Dick Diver commits himself to the exacting task that will poison his life and his career. Nicole, a young schizophrenic girl who suffers from a persecution complex because of her incestuous relation with her father, falls in love with the doctor and attaches herself to him as to her only hope of recovery. At first Dick is interested only professionally, but he soon realizes that his emotions are involved as well. His first attempt is to run away, but when he meets his patient outside the oppressive atmosphere of the clinic his need for love (his first flaw) and his altruism drive him to marry her. He takes up the double task of being a husband and a doctor at the same time. Nicole's problem becomes his problem and her illness will be gradually transposed to him.

In Book Two ("Rosemary's Angle: 1919–1925") a long stream-of-consciousness passage takes us through six years. The marriage

seems successful, but Nicole, as we learn gradually, has gone through
two or three collapses, and her great wealth has somewhat compromised Dick's scientific career. He no longer signs himself "Dr.
Diver" and has come to identify his life with hers. They have moved
into a big villa on the Riviera, and their social activity has become a
preponderant feature of their existence. In the eyes of Rosemary
Hoyt, the young actress who now arrives on the scene, their life
together seems perfect and enviable. She lets herself be taken in by
the enthusiasm and sympathy that seems to surround them in their
set of chosen and fashionable friends, and she has no suspicion of
the inner tension that threatens to break up their union.[18] The harsh
crudeness with which Barban challenges McKisco to a duel and some
revealing observations of Dick's ("'It is not a bad time,' said Dick
Diver. 'It's not one of the worst times of the day.'") might have
opened her eyes, but until the last minute she remains "unaware of
[the Divers'] complexity and lack of innocence." Her perception is
obviously obscured by her growing love for Dick, who seems to her
to combine charming manners with a depth of human interest, an
unselfish concern for the happiness of his wife with an intellectual
and emotional superiority over his friends. Rosemary indulges in her
youthful dream of love and follows Dick and Nicole to Paris (Book
Three: "Casualties: 1925"), without realizing that her very presence
will act as a catalyst in an already very unstable situation.

Weary of the psychological tension imposed on him by his
double task of husband and doctor, Dick lets himself be drawn by the
allurement of youthful and uncorrupted love—although he knows
when to stop (Chapter 3). But when Nicole, at the end of a night of
wild disorder, has a new hysterical collapse, Dick's loyalty and
resistance are already on the wane: "As an indifference, cherished or
left to atrophy, becomes an emptiness, to this extent he had learned
to become empty of Nicole, serving her against his will with negations
and emotional neglect."

With her eyes finally opened to the reality, Rosemary goes
away. For Dick, however, she has become his only hope for rebirth
and liberation. The psychological effort required by Nicole tells on
his work ("His work became confused with Nicole's problems"), and
her growing wealth minimizes and mocks the value and the necessity of his work: "In multiplying ways he was constantly inundated by
a trickling of goods and money." Facing failure as a scientist ("Not
without desperation he had long felt the ethics of his profession

dissolving into a lifeless mass," V, 3) Dick feels himself to be at the very limits of resistance as a man. Hence his desperate attempt to escape his plight (Book Four: "Escape: 1925–1929"). Nicole has tried to kill him and their children by swerving the car she is driving (Chapter 3), and although Dick has now his own clinic (bought with Nicole's money) his only hope is to leave and go in search of Rosemary.

This search should be his final assertion of vitality, but the remedy is, once more, worse than the evil. Called back to America by his father's death, Dick could regain his hold on himself, thanks to the contact with the native soil and to the recollection of his father's precepts. But he comes back to Europe, and though in Rome he finds Rosemary at last and accomplishes with her the "poetic justice" he has been looking for, the poetic moment is already past irrevocably; Rosemary cannot save him now. Dick gives vent to his feelings of impotence in a symbolic brawl, which leaves him emotionally and physically drained. In addition, the brawl has the effect of putting him more and more in the hands of the Warren family: Nicole's sister, Baby Warren, frees him from jail, and asserts in this way an absurd "moral superiority" over him.

After these tumultuous events, the story takes up again in a slow and subdued tone. In Book Five ("The Way Home: 1929–1930") Dick's parable completes its downward course until he gradually "fades away" [19] from the book, and from life itself. Back at his clinic, Dick finds that his heart "isn't in this project any more," and he lets himself be excluded by his colleague to take refuge on the Riviera, "which was home." His professional failure is accompanied by his social failure as well (as we can see from the episode in the home of Mary Minghetti, Chapter 4). Dick also loses his worldly sensitivity and his charm. Rosemary's reappearance on the scene gives him the last urge toward destruction. Wanting to show off in front of Rosemary (Chapter 7: episode of the aquaplane) he becomes ridiculous and odious in the eyes of Nicole. At this point the slow process of psychological and social collapse reaches the climax of physical decadence (among other things, Dick has taken to drinking heavily). And if Rosemary will pursue her career, Nicole has gradually become independent of him, too, and at his own expense. "'Why, I'm almost complete,' she thought. 'I'm practically standing alone, without him.'" She is no longer frightened and discomposed by the word "father," and she returns to her true self when she becomes Barban's mistress.

The case is finished and Dr. Diver is at liberty, but drained and exhausted both as a scientist and as a man. He has succeeded in his task, but he has been defeated himself; he disappears from the scene, ending in a melancholy provincial anonymity:

> . . . his latest note was postmarked from Hornell, New York, which is some distance from Geneva and a very small town; in any case he is almost certainly in that section of the country, in one town or another.

Everything is developed and concluded in a linear way. We have briefly sketched the plot to make evident how the chronological disposition of the final version contributes to clarifying the progress of the theme. In this final version it becomes apparent that the main theme unifies and combines two motives in a consistent way: the motive of the personal, psychological *épuisement* as a result of a painful transference of vitality, and the motive of the defeat of the idealist trapped in the golden cage of the *haute bourgeoisie*.

The pivot around which the theme revolves is provided by the principle of the transference of vitality, which had already been stated in the "General Plan," where Fitzgerald had written of Nicole that "only her transference to him saves her." The principle and the term itself—only partly related to psychoanalysis—had already been exploited for literary purposes. Henry James, for instance, had often used the principle, particularly for his experimental novel *The Sacred Fount* (1901). In this novel it had been used mainly as a pretext for exploring the mental processes of an inquisitive "narrator," who might even pass for an artist *manqué*. A transference of vitality—both physical and spiritual—seems to take place between two pairs of characters, and the Narrator is obsessed by an absorbing desire to discover whether it takes place or not. Whether this form of "vampirism" actually occurs or whether it is simply the product of his imagination is never made clear, because all his attempts to find the truth are baffled in the end. The principle of "the sacred fount" from which one character can draw youth or intelligence at the expense of another was actually exploited by James as a means of examining two contrasting ways of mental reaction to the immediate data of experience. If the Narrator is apt to connect these data and to weave them together into a pattern by force of imagination, it is because his immediate perceptions seem to have no value for him, unless an "application of intelligence" establishes or creates a system of relationships—and therefore a "story." On the other hand, his antagonist,

Mrs. Brissenden, refuses to organize her perceptions into a system of relationships. The Narrator's clumsy attempts at "finding the truth" are clearly a result of his euristic obsession. Mrs. Brissenden's attitude, if not the result of an interested wish to conceal the truth, might be considered the contrary reaction of someone who accepts the data of experience, however inexplicable or mysterious, without imposing a logical or an "artistic" order on them. The book seems, in other words, a kind of fascinating investigation into the operation and the possibilities of the mind, or into the very possibilities of the *novel* itself. But the motive of the transference of vitality looms large in the background, and if it does not provide the main theme or the informing idea of the book, it is still present in all its force and interest.[20]

In *Tender Is the Night* this principle is central to the development of the theme. As Fitzgerald was later to write to Edmund Wilson,[21] he thought of Dick, in reconsideration, "as an 'homme épuisé,' not only an 'homme manqué.'" And he was *épuisé* because in the double role of doctor and husband that he assumed his spiritual and physical vitality went to fill the void in his wife's personality. The schizophrenia that he cures in Nicole is transferred to him: "He takes up the marriage as a man divided in himself," we read in the "General Plan," and in the "Summary of Part III" we are told that "it seems as if the completion of his ruination will be the fact that cures her— almost mystically"; and when "his hold is broken, the transference is broken." The double obligation that Dick assumes because "he wanted to be good, he wanted to be kind, he wanted to be brave and wise, ... He wanted to be loved too, if that could fit in," brings him to a choice that will mean spiritual death and ruin for him, since "he had made his choice, chosen Ophelia, chosen the sweet poison and drunk it." For Nicole, who "sought in them [the people she liked] the vitality that had made them independent or creative or rugged," and who continues to the very end "her dry sucking at his lean chest," Dick restores her universe, and this task ends by shaking his balance and by depriving him of every resource he had once had. We are told that he lacks "tensile strength," but Dick's spiritual vitality, in spite of his sanguine weakness, is not entirely lost. Its gradual draining restores Nicole's broken universe and fills her spiritual emptiness, and she draws from him the strength necessary to act independently. When the transference is completed, the pathological case is concluded and Dick's pathetic destiny reaches its climax.[22] Becoming self-confident and independent of him, Nicole is ready to abandon him for Tommy Barban—the Latin barbarian, the rugged man of vitalistic strength who in contrast to Dick, an intellectual idealist, has no need for "interpretations" or "qualifications." In the change Nicole loses her grace and charming fragility and reverts to her true nature.[23] From Dick she has borrowed, as it were, only the life force, not his spiritual power or his former mental superiority, even if *his* sacrifice is bound to be complete, because other pressures are added to his psychological depletion.

Since Dick is gradually drained of his force and becomes spiritually *épuisé*, his resistance to the external conflicts is also diminished, and thus he becomes an "homme manqué" as well. By marrying Nicole, the promising scientist enters the world of the *haute bourgeoisie*, which he had observed until that time only from the outside, as a psychiatrist. And by that world, which hides under its economic power selfishness and moral insensibility, corruption, and carelessness, Dick unwarily lets himself be "swallowed"—to the point of becoming a simple tool in the hands of his potential enemies. "He had been swallowed up like a *gigolo* and had somehow permitted his arsenal to be locked up in the Warren safety-deposit vaults," [24] the writer says explicitly. Instead of imposing his way of life on Nicole, Dick lets himself be drawn into her orbit and into the Warren family, and so he blunts his weapons and compromises his strength and professional capacity—his only way of asserting himself—by acceptance of Nicole's way of life and of her money. When he moves to the Riviera, his abdication becomes irreversible, and he realizes too late that he has become a mere instrument in a game. When he is no longer valuable as such, the *haute bourgeoisie* has no scruples in rejecting him ("That's what he was educated for," is Baby Warren's cynical comment).

In this way Dick is also guilty: not only because he drinks but because his "social climbing" predisposes and exposes him to Nicole's exploitation. "The product of much ingenuity and toil," member of a "ducal" family whose "very name, written in a hotel register, signed to an introduction, used in a difficult situation, caused a psychological metamorphosis in people," Nicole exploits—perhaps without being aware of it at the beginning—Dick's compliance and his "psychological metamorphosis." In this way it is typical and perfectly logical that at the end she reverts to Tommy Barban—"a wild man," "who hates all sham and pretense," "one who would lead tribesmen or communists—utterly aristocratic, unbourgeoise king or nothing," just back from a fighting experience in the French foreign legion. We learn from the "General Plan" that Barban's French training prevents him from being a revolutionary, in spite of his destructive tendencies, and "his mind is not quite as good as the hero's." He is basically a Fascist anarchist, finding his outlet in action. His values and his cynicism are those of the social strata from which he springs and to which he belongs, and they can easily be identified with Nicole's. When they join forces, there is nothing more for Dick—their victim but all the same responsible for his defeat (*manqué* that is, and not only *épuisé*) by not having realized the danger of "intrusion" into a world not his own.

In the complex interplay of psychological and social conflicts that determines Dick's defeat, Rosemary plays her part as well. The young actress has the role and the function of a "catalytic agent." [25] Properly introduced at the crucial moment of the story, when Dick is on the verge of depletion, she can precipitate the action and hasten the progress of the events. "Things were never the same after Rosemary"; but if she breaks down his precarious balance once and for all, she might also have been for him a possible way to salvation. "She differs from most actresses"—we read once more in the "General Plan"—"by being a lady, simply reeking of vitality, health, sensuality," and if "she is rather gross as compared to the heroine" the youthful freshness of her love, so different from the tormenting and demanding love of Nicole, might have saved Dick.

On the psychological level she might again bring peace and serenity to Dick; on the social and ethical level she could have brought him back to his own world and to his own true nature. She is a working girl who is building a position for herself with her dedication to her work—a girl "who spent money she had earned—she was here in Europe because she had gone in the pool six times that January day with her temperature roving from 99° in the early morning to 103°." It is true that the world of the movies is not the best field in which to acquire a moral standard or social status, but Rosemary works in it with the awareness of being a wheel in the mechanism of a big industry, and if she is a temporary expatriate she is not in the least an escapist. In her initial position, therefore, she is very close to Dick's original idealism. It is significant that she is the only person who asks Dick why he does not "practice" any more, and if she is enchanted by his social charm, she is also interested by his intellectual superiority. Rosemary might become his ally in the daily struggle, but

Dick seizes at this possibility only when it is too late and the "spear had been blunted." In his flight after Rosemary he "flees with himself," bringing with him the burden of all his past attachments and compromises. When he finds her again his state of deterioration is too far advanced. Instead of saving him, Rosemary can only worsen his desperate and helpless impotence.

"*Tecum fugis,*" Seneca had said. But Dick carries with him the germ of awareness as well, and it is for this reason too that he attains a tragic stature. As Karl Jaspers has remarked,[26] the tragic conscience is not in the mere inclination to pain and failure, but in meeting the danger and in the inevitability of guilt, "in the ruin that follows our concrete action and our realization." There is no tragedy in the simple alternative "succeeding or failing," but in the sharpened thought of someone who sees the real failure in the happiest success. If we want to use Jaspers' definition, we can see that Dick succeeds very well in curing Nicole: and his ruin follows his "concrete action," his realization. His failure is in his happiest success; he meets the danger with an "inevitable guilt," and he comes to a full awareness of his predicament, of his weakness, and of the reasons for his defeat.

Dick's defeat, furthermore, is brought about by a concurrence of psychological and social pressures; the novel, therefore, comes close to the conditions of tragedy. It is not only Dick's awareness that accounts for his tragic plight, it is the situation itself that has an objective element of tragedy in it. It is not tragedy in the Aristotelian sense but in a more domestic and modern sense—in the sense which Karl Jaspers attributes to the word, or in the sense in which F. O. Matthiessen uses it in *American Renaissance*, and which is so often reechoed by Arthur Miller in the notes to his plays. According to Matthiessen, modern tragedy

> demands of its author a mature understanding of the relation of the individual to society, and more especially, of the nature of good and evil. He must have a coherent grasp of social forces, or, at least, of man as a social being; otherwise he will possess no frame of reference within which to make actual his dramatic conflict. For the hero of tragedy is never merely an individual, he is a man in action, in conflict with other individuals in a definite social order.[27]

Fitzgerald reached a coherent grasp of social forces in *Tender Is the Night,* and he clearly defined a frame of reference in which to make actual Dick's dramatic conflict. He saw and represented him as a man in action and in conflict in a definite social order, not as a mere individual but as a social being, and Dick succumbs exactly as a "social being." It is his initial idealism that drives him to act as a social being in his profession and in his marriage. If the frame of reference is provided by the conflict between the *haute bourgeoisie* and Dick's sentimental form of idealism, his dramatic situation comes as near as possible to the condition of tragedy as described by Matthiessen. We might even say that the entire novel, in its formulation and general lines, is an attempt to illustrate and comment on a fundamental dramatic conflict of the ethical and sociological order. The single characters stand for definite social and moral positions and exemplify in their conflicts a contrast of wider social implications and of larger moral and symbolic significance.

Rosemary's vitality is representative of the vitality of a growing and dynamic industry. She is "the product of her mother's loving care . . . embodying all the immaturity of the race, cutting a new cardboard paper doll to pass before its empty harlot's mind"; but as Fitzgerald clearly states, the people in the movie business "were people of bravery and industry: they were risen to a position of prominence in a nation that for a decade had wanted only to be entertained." Nicole's illness is a reflection of the corruption and of the spiritual instability of a whole social class—the *haute bourgeoisie* corrupted and made dangerous because of its economic power. Fitzgerald makes it clear that she is the product of a series of exploitations and abuses, the "prototype" of an abdication from moral values:

> Nicole was the product of much ingenuity and toil. For her sake trains began their run at Chicago and traversed the round belly of the continent to California; chicle factories fumed and link belts grew link by link in factories; men mixed toothpaste in vats and drew mouthwash out of copper hogsheads; girls canned tomatoes quickly in August or worked rudely at the Five-and-Tens on Christmas Eve; half-breed Indians toiled on Brazilian coffee plantations and dreamers were muscled out of patent rights in new tractors—these were some of the people who gave a tithe to Nicole and, as the whole system swayed and thundered onward, it lent a feverish bloom to such processes of hers as wholesale buying . . . (*TTN*, pp. 113–14.)

Moment by moment all that Dick had taught her fell away and she was ever nearer to what she had been in the

beginning, prototype of that obscure yielding up of swords that
was going on in the world about her. (*TTN*, p. 316.)

Behind her and close to her stand her incestuous father, her
sister Baby Warren (who has "something wooden and onanistic
about her"), Mary Minghetti and Luis Campion, Abe North (a victim
of dissipation in Europe and violence in America), McKisco with his
bourgeois view of literature and his mean wife, Tommy Barban
with his typical bourgeois contempt of the bourgeoisie, and a host of
characters [28] representing every facet of "that obscure yielding up of
swords"—of that moral confusion which followed the heroic period
of the war and which the *haute bourgeoisie* has erected into a system
of behavior. In Nicole the "original sin" is explicit from the very
start—incest. The psychiatric clinic is her original home, and not
merely in a metaphoric sense; to Dick, who would like to separate her
from that world with his own love, she seems symptomatically to
embody "the essence of a continent"; "now there was this scarcely
saved waif of disaster bringing him the essence of a continent."

The symbolic extension is here too wide, since that continent has
in fact produced Dick, too. And it produced him, as it were, by con-
centrating on him all the gifts that Nicole cannot have, or that her
world has refused and denied. Just as Nicole is, so Dick too is the
product and representative of a whole social class. When he sets out
on his adventure, he carries with him the illusions and weaknesses of
a whole nation:

> —the illusions of eternal strength and health, and of the essen-
> tial goodness of people— . . . the illusions of a nation, the lies
> of generations of frontier mothers who had to croon falsely that
> there were no wolves outside the cabin door. (*TTN*, p. 5.)

Courting the danger as a pioneer (we might recall here Gatsby's
link with the pioneers), Dick has met the wolves "outside the cabin
door"—the Warrens and their ducal family, their world of hidden
perfidy and irresponsible carelessness. In this way his adventure
epitomizes the doom of all idealists, of all the "innocent" Americans
who played, like him, "too close to the line" only to be wrecked on
the beaches of Europe and to return beaten to their "cabins." East
and West once more, seen and represented as ethical poles or social
positions in conflict; even Europe and America, maybe (if it is true that
Nicole is half-European and chooses Tommy Barban, as we have
seen) in a typically Jamesian contrast; and once more the significance

of the novel transcends the literal statement to become "philosophic" and to foreshadow a complex parable as in *The Great Gatsby*—but with a basic difference of fictional methods in this case.

In the previous novel the symbolic implications sprang from the inner core of single dramatic moments; they were suggested and projected with a technique of rapid allusions, meaningful hints, sudden realizations in a foreshortened perspective. In *Tender Is the Night* they are conveyed to the reader through an extensive elucidation, insisted upon with scrupulous documentation and explicit comments, explained in undisguised "statements of purpose" inside the novel. These were perhaps the "new canons" of "the philosophical, now called psychological, novel" of which Fitzgerald wrote in a letter to John Peale Bishop. Fitzgerald acknowledged that Bishop had been the first to feel that the intention in *Gatsby* and that in *Tender Is the Night* were "entirely different" and admitted that his new novel "was shooting at something like *Vanity Fair.*" This meant substituting a *"tour de force"* with a "confession of faith," "a sonnet sequence with an epic":

> There were moments all through the book where I could have pointed up dramatic scenes, and I *deliberately* refrained from doing so because the material itself was so harrowing and highly charged that I did not want to subject the reader to a series of nervous shocks. . . .

In *Gatsby* he had not been "afraid of heightening and melo-dramatizing any scenes"; in this case, on the contrary, the material itself required a less tense and less nervous treatment, a kind of "epic" extension and grandeur, an abundance of qualifications and a phil-osophical as well as psychological build-up.[29] The pace was to be slower and the rhythm less compressed or syncopated; instead of a series of dramatic scenes we are given the subdued unfolding of the story in all its richness of psychological, social, and "philosophical" elements. There are no sudden starts or elusive and allusive passages, but a gradual development of the main theme together with a wealth of qualifying and illustrative episodes. Nothing seems to be left for the reader to guess or surmise, everything is made explicit and dealt with at length, so that the "pictorial" quality of the book is enhanced at the expense of its dramatic compression.

The subject matter is woven into recurrent patterns, embroi-dered as it were on the counterpoint of thematic motives, exhausted in all its implications by a detailed documentation and an underlying comment. It was, as suggested, and as Fitzgerald himself wanted to make clear, a typical nineteenth-century tradition that he had in mind, a shifting from the dramatic convention to the pictorial ideal. There are, therefore, no "marginal" episodes in the book, if practically all of them serve to illustrate a widespread condition of moral disorder and social corruption, for the most part represented in sexual terms: Nicole's incest, Baby Warren's uncleanliness, the ghostlike reappearance of their father at the end, Collin Clay naked and drunk in bed before Baby Warren, the homosexuals in the clinic, the girls who greet the sailors with their panties from the room where Nicole has given herself to Barban, the disgusting reappearance of Mary Minghetti with Lady Caroline shut up in jail for having picked up girls, and so on. If Dick's sexual exploits are remarkably toned down in the last versions of the novel, even Rosemary seems to be tainted by this prevailing atmosphere: not only because of her adventure in the train with her young friend, but because she cannot give herself to Dick in Rome since, as she puts it, "those things are rhythmic." Abe North's deterioration or McKisco's cheapness are none the less revealing for not being strictly related to sexual matters.

We are confronted with a wealth of details and episodes which make up the "pictorial" background and are at the same time strictly functional from a thematic point of view. The imagery is overwhelmingly sexual or woven in with suggestions of violence and disorder: Barban's exploits as a military leader or as a lover, the Negroes in Paris, the murder at the station, Nicole's homicidal tendency, the brawl in Rome, and so on. The wolves are present everywhere, roving undisturbed through Europe. Rosemary has a passing contact with them, and she might still save herself. But if the idealists like Dick succumb to such an array of disrupting forces, it is because the times themselves are "out of joint." And this thematic implication is made clear in the novel exactly because its pictorial quality allows the writer an extensive documentation.

In his way, therefore, Fitzgerald complied with the precepts of the Thirties.[30] The danger for him was that the "tempo" of the narration, "so harrowing and highly charged," might also be "out of joint." This danger was still present in the 1934 edition of the book; and one might claim that the new chronological disposition of the "final version" helped quite a bit to remove it, or at least to obscure it as much as possible. In this new disposition everything seems to find its proper place and to harmonize with the general trend of the story. All the motives gradually introduced in the first book are resolved in the last, and the tone of the narration is made uniform; what is lost in brilliance is gained in clarity and simplicity.

The first book is written on the key of Nicole's psychic disorder, in an atmosphere of postwar dissolution which might recall Thomas Mann's *The Magic Mountain* or *Death in Venice*. The fifth book is written on the key of Dick's psychic and moral *épuisement*. In the first the action is chiefly seen through the sane and steady eyes of Dick and filtered through his conscience as he scrutinizes Nicole's illness and his own involvement. In the fifth book the action is filtered through Nicole's restored sensibility, to which Dick's breakdown is gradually revealed.[31] If in the first book Dick stands up "like Grant in Galena, waiting to be called to an intricate destiny," in the fifth he is shown in the same attitude, "biding his time again like Grant in Galena." If in the first book the movement slowly rises toward the climax of the wedding, in the last it ends its downward course, which had already begun at the end of the second book, with a dizzy descent. In the second book the action is seen "from without," filtered through Rosemary's eyes, and the young girl, dazzled by her love for Dick and by the brilliance of the Divers cannot see the horror that lies behind the fascinating façade of their life on the Riviera. The movement is for awhile suspended, almost as if in a dance or ballet, until it gradually resumes speed and precipitates to the conclusion. In the third book the rhythm becomes broken and nervous; the unity of the point of view is lost, as though the events themselves were no longer under control, while the movement begins its downward course until it becomes precipitous and fractured in the fourth book. The last book marks then the completion of the waning parable until it reaches a disconsolate conclusion "not with a bang but a whimper," as T. S. Eliot had prophesied. "You felt—Fitzgerald had written to Hemingway—that the true line of a work of fiction was to take a reader up to an emotional pitch but then let him down or ease him off. You gave no aesthetic reason for this—nevertheless, you convinced me." [32] He had more than learned a lesson: he had mastered his technical means in a perfect way.

One might even maintain that the dramatic "canons" of *The Great Gatsby* had not been completely forgotten, though they were resolved in a wider perspective and varied for the new requirements of symmetry and full illustration. "ACTION IS CHARACTER," Fitzgerald

was to write in a note for *The Last Tycoon,* but the discovery had
already been made in *Gatsby.* Although in *Tender Is the Night* the
psychological analyses of the characters have the upper hand, it is
always in action that their true natures are revealed. The interplay
between incident and character (in the Jamesian sense) is more
complex and even tortuous; if we want to draw a comparison, we
must revert to James's "second manner" and no longer to Conrad's
"magic suggestiveness." But the line of development from *Gatsby* to
The Last Tycoon is unbroken and goes through the highly original
experience of *Tender Is the Night.* The "valley of ashes" in *The Great
Gatsby* is still present in the background of the Riviera, and it will
reappear along the desolate beaches of California, where Monroe
Stahr will meet his destiny in the next novel. And if Fitzgerald, when
he thought of rearranging *Tender Is the Night,* had a bitter exchange
of letters with Thomas Wolfe in which he maintained the validity of
the "novel of selected incident," [33] the same concern with selection
and structural symmetry was brought to bear in the "final version" as
in the two other novels. Viewed in this light, *Tender Is the Night,* as
we read it now, is much more Jamesian in quality than one would
think at first—not only in its structure but in its texture.

James's "second manner" is well-known for its complexity of
style, for the breadth and largeness of its prose, and sometimes even
for its complicated and involved language. In *Tender Is the Night*
Fitzgerald's language is maturer and more complex, syntactically
more elaborate. Less nervous and evocative, less syncopated and
colored than in *Gatsby,* it spreads out in descriptions and analyses, in
considerations and comments; it is more diffuse and full-bodied in its
diction. Its pattern is here given by the long paragraph; its flow is
discursive and spreading; it presupposes the "long time" and the calm
development from sentence to sentence, from period to period. It is
difficult to give a single specimen of it, because it is the extension of its
rhythm, not the intensity of it, that counts. But see with what delicacy,
both descriptive and introspective, this language can convey Rosemary's melancholy reaction at Dick's refusal to "take her":

> She looked up at him as he took a step toward the door; she
> looked at him without the slightest idea as to what was in his
> head, she saw him take another step in slow motion, turn and
> look at her again, and she wanted for a moment to hold him
> and devour him, wanted his mouth, his ears, his coat collar,
> wanted to surround him and engulf him; she saw his hand fall

on the doorknob. Then she gave up and sank back on the bed. When the door closed she got up and went to the mirror, where she began brushing her hair, sniffling a little. One hundred and fifty strokes Rosemary gave it, as usual, then a hundred and fifty more. She brushed it until her arm ached, then she changed arms and went on brushing. (*TTN*, p. 127.)

The sense of her dejection is conveyed through little specific details, and the whole scene is beheld as it gradually develops its purport to Rosemary. The urge of her feeling is checked by her sudden perception of Dick with his hand on the doorknob, and it is released when the door closes; then Rosemary moves to the mirror, and we are left with the final image, full of James-like grace, of the girl brushing her hair. The repetition of the number of strokes slows down the pace of the narration; it was her "usual" number of strokes, but now she goes on, as if to blunt with her physical ache her inner pain. Or one could take the beautiful scene of their first kiss, the brilliant scenes on the Riviera and in Paris, the magnificent episode on the forlorn and forgotten battlefield. In each Fitzgerald's stylistic mastery appears in his slow and measured beginnings, which are worked out to the climax of the scene and then carefully brought to their conclusion, usually with a "dying fall" or a "fading away."

A literary masterpiece, as Valéry once stated, is never "finished"—it is only abandoned. *Tender Is the Night,* after so many years of revision and reworking, was somehow "abandoned" by Fitzgerald; he was prevented from "finishing" it either by weariness or by his early death. But the reasons for its greatness and for its validity are unimpaired; one might even say that the writer stopped reworking it at the right moment.

CHAPTER VII

The Drama of Existence

> *... at three o'clock in the morning,*
> *a forgotten package has the same*
> *tragic importance as a death*
> *sentence, and the cure doesn't*
> *work—in a real dark night of the*
> *soul it is always three o'clock in*
> *the morning, day after day.*
>
> CU, p. 75.

1

The comparative failure of *Tender Is the Night* created a gap between Fitzgerald and his public. It isolated him in what, to many, appeared to be the position of a survivor from another age. The failure of his marriage, by this time beyond repair, made his crisis even more acute. Fitzgerald felt alienated from his contemporaries and extraneous to the times, which had taken an unpredicted course and had relegated him to a marginal role.

Overwhelmed by this sense of neglect and isolation (to which a number of letters to Maxwell Perkins bear witness), Fitzgerald moved to Hollywood. Here his physical and nervous resistance gave way unexpectedly. And yet it was in this atmosphere, which seemed so repulsive and histrionic to him, that he succeeded in the desperate attempt to pull himself together for a short while, to acquire a kind of psychological and emotional balance, and to give a genuine, original impulse to his fiction. To the poetic—and we might even say personal—catharsis of *The Last Tycoon,* Fitzgerald came only when it was too late. But that does not change the fact that the road he traveled shows all the signs of a deep renewal, which becomes all the more significant when we realize the handicaps he had to overcome. Between *Tender Is the Night* and the fragment of the new novel which astonished even his enemies when it appeared in 1941, and which officially reopened the Fitzgerald "case," there was a long period of readjustment. To reach the stylistic bareness of *The Last Ty-*

coon Fitzgerald had to undergo an artistic involution of the darkest kind and the most ruthless confession of his crisis; but from these experiences, however negative they seemed, he derived the strength for the last achievement. Both these experiences will be examined here, not only for obvious reasons of completeness, but also to illustrate once more how Fitzgerald's new achievement did not flower of a sudden in a void, but came as a result of precise antecedents after a slow preparation.

Relegated, as we have said, to the relics of a former time, in what he defined as "a dark night of the soul," Fitzgerald seemed at first to justify the prophets of his decline. Soon after the publication of *Tender Is the Night* he began writing a strange novel that bears all the marks of a clear artistic involution. It was to be a romance set in France at the time when feudalism replaced the chaos in the social structure that had followed the fall of the Roman Empire. It would be difficult to imagine an idea farther from Fitzgerald's actual possibilities, and in fact he gave it up at an early stage of composition. But he abandoned the project only after completing four chapters and having worked on it for almost two years, and even later he was to insist on the artistic value and the intrinsic possibilities of his attempt. By choosing that subject, it might be maintained, Fitzgerald took refuge unconsciously among the specters and puppets of an age in which the fabric of history and society offered an "objective correlative" to the conditions of chaos and darkness of his soul; and at least in intention, he was trying to conform to the fashions and the precepts of an age—the Thirties—when, according to Maxwell Perkins, there would be a demand for historical novels. Significantly enough, the novel was to be called *The Kingdom of the Dark;* and in his desire for success and popularity Fitzgerald went even further, allowing that the evocation of that medieval period (880 to 950) "simply vibrant with change" would offer him the possibility of a fictional development in which the social element was to play a large and important part, "in view of . . . the new Marxian interpretation." [1]

It was nothing more than a trick on his part, because he was unable to escape the attraction of the present: the model of the protagonist was to be no other than his friend and rival Ernest Hemingway, while the aim of the novel was to represent "the real modern man." [2] It was a confusion of categories of time and space, and a notable confusion, therefore, of concept and intent. All that could come out of this was a confused and shapeless patchwork, where the artistic decline is emphasized by a language that shows at every moment the signs of an unresolved dualism of inspiration.

Three of the four completed chapters appeared in *The Redbook* in 1934–35, while the fourth was printed in the same magazine only after Fitzgerald's death.[3] But the original conception of the novel— as it appears from Fitzgerald's manuscript notes—was considerably larger. The story was to have followed the vicissitudes of a knight, Philippe, during his entire lifetime. Divided into three parts, it was to deal with his youth in the first (six "stories" or chapters), with his maturity in the second (three "stories"), and with his old age in the third (two "great episodes"). The main thread was to have been supplied by Philippe, but the interest would have been divided between his story and the whole historical fresco of an era of great instability, to which Philippe would bring the new gospel of feudal order, hierarchical organization, iron discipline, and efficient work.

It is difficult to see how the figure of Philippe—reminding us in so many ways of Tommy Barban, though on a different level of elaboration, and of his brutal energy and violence (Barban too was a Latin "knight" seen as a "barbarian")—could help the writer in his approach to the Marxian ideology. Nor can it be easily understood just what relationship he wanted to establish between the ninth- and tenth-century France and the depression that was troubling America. If this was his way of conforming to the new socialistic ideologies, the result could not fail to be one of even further misconceptions. Every consistency of historical reconstruction was wrecked among the ambiguities of the pasteboard background that was to have exhibited, who knows why, the "modern" man. Fitzgerald had prepared himself with wide, but not too profound, reading. As he recorded in a note, he had read (or at least seen) Gibbon's *Decline and Fall of the Roman Empire* (but only the fifth volume), Jessie Weston's *From Ritual to Romance*, Margaret Murray's *Witch Cult in Western Europe,* various histories of France, and many articles in the *Encyclopedia Britannica.* But in the last analysis, the erudition that stole into the work did not prevent Philippe's story from remaining in the foreground; and Philippe himself was represented as an equivocal figure, a mixture of gangster and hero, of *condottiere* and robber, with Byronic attitudes and the vulgar slang of many of Hemingway's characters.

A mere outline of his adventures would serve to justify the total oblivion into which the work has fallen, because Fitzgerald's creativity is here at its lowest point. But it can also illustrate how he was able to rise from the deepest involution in only a few years, and in view of this, even an uncharitable curiosity or an insistence on the critic's part becomes legitimate. In the first "story" (or chapter) of the novel—"In the Darkest Hour"—Philippe returns to Villefranche after a captivity in Spain at the hands of the Moors. Finding only famine and disorder in his lands, he begins his mission as "leader." By defeating a local usurper, he wins the support of his first "vassal," Jacques; and when he is confronted with the diffidence of the abbot who rules the region, a discontented monk, Brian, provides him with a following of men and gives him the blessing of the Church. Philippe foils a Norman attack and obtains oaths of allegiance from them, thus providing himself with an armed guard; he then makes a treaty with the abbot. He builds his first camp and at the end, of course, a woman appears—the wife of the dead Norman lord, who offers herself to the victor. Philippe receives her, and when his first task is accomplished, like Amory or Stephen Dedalus before him, he feels that he is "embodying in himself the future of his race," and like them too, he dallies and strolls under the starry sky.

Up to this point there has been some progression. In the second "story," however, which is called "The Count of Darkness," Philippe has to come to terms with the woman he has taken on, and in this case ludicrous echoes of Shakespeare's *Henry V* are mixed with the kind of language that one of Hemingway's "toughs" might have used:

"What do you want little chicken?" he asked.

"I wanted to see you. I could only see you a little from the tent, and . . ."

"Don't grovel in the dirt, for God's sake! Get up from your knees!"

"I'm not a man." She stood and faced him. "And how do *I* know about your habits for gals?"

"There *are* no habits—I *make* the habits."

His eyes became covetous as he looked at her. "How would you like to be one of my habits?"

"Oh, sire, I would be so glad to be yours—"

"What's your name, little baggage?"

"Letgarde."

"Who gave it to you? That Norman?"

"It was my christened name."

"Come you and see what you taste like." [4]

The episode continues along these lines. If the leader has found his woman, his followers must find their own women, and this is accomplished with a new version of the Rape of the Sabines. Letgarde escapes with a minstrel, and Philippe recovers from this defeat by obtaining a regular toll from some merchants, whom he has surprised while fording the river and spared, so that the community may profit from their tolls in the future. Having now a regular income, Philippe builds a palisade round the camp, thus giving the men a sense of stability, he sets up rules of vassalage and allegiance, institutes rights and duties for his subjects, gives the first lessons in hunting and fishing. Letgarde is found again, but drowned in the river, like a new Ophelia; Philippe's suffering is here described in the same absurd sentences that were used to describe his love ("'I guess I must be pretty much of a tough,' he thought"). He becomes adjusted to his loss by adopting an orphan.

A new heroine appears in the third "story"—"The Kingdom of the Dark"— and she is nothing less than the former mistress of Louis, king of France, who is fleeing from him. After the arrival of Griselda, the king appears on the scene with his knights. Philippe hides Griselda and welcomes the weak king with all honors, giving him for the first time in the course of his travels a sense of security. Louis refuses, however, to attack the Normans who are devastating and raiding the region, and discovering the white palfrey of Griselda he leaves in the middle of the night after burning the camp.

Alone with Griselda—who is petulant and bourgeoise [5]—Philippe rebuilds his little "kingdom." In the fourth "story"—"Gods of the Darkness"—the scene is even more agitated; it resembles a kind of medieval pageant, at once sacred and profane. To the motives of love and war are added the themes of religious conflict and witchcraft and the persistent attraction of paganism. When he decides to marry Griselda, Philippe discovers that many of his followers are still pagan, and only by agreeing that they perform a magic rite can he rout the attack of a powerful duke. Griselda herself has participated in the rite (she had admitted, almost by chance, that she had been "*dépucellée par Satan ille mesme*") and the rite has married her to Jacques. Philippe's rage and murderous threats are of no avail. He has won the promised victory for his people, but he has to pay for it by losing his promised wife, and he can find consolation only with his little orphan. The abbot writes a Latin motto for him: *Cum aliqui relinquant incapiturus sum.* But there is no new beginning for him, because Fitzgerald broke off his story before the great undertakings that were to have made Philippe's name famous in history.

In fact the fragment (although almost a third of the novel which had been planned), could not have lasted for long. Any adequate support of the imagination is missing, and there is no possible unity of vision or an informing idea. There is nothing more than a series of episodes, often repetitious and never too significant, which are conditioned only by the figure of the protagonist and never developed in a synthetic way. They only follow the linear progression of the events; Philippe never changes from beginning to end. The people around him are mere puppets or marionettes, who are sometimes given a role to perform (and not always the right one) and who parade for a brief moment according to the length of the strings. Then they stop and vanish, leaving no trace, fallen back into the shadows of history or of Fitzgerald's artistic conception.

Separated from his own reality, transported into a too distant and inconsistent past, Fitzgerald seems to court evasion and flight, and he can only fail. In this escape, he brings with him the burden of his past and the earnest preoccupations of his present, and he unloads his burden and his preoccupations in confused chatter. Philippe, in sum, was to have represented "the real modern man" only because he spoke with the authoritative tone of a Robert Jordan, or because his brusque manners were those of the college students and "philosophers" of the Jazz Age. In the same way the physical, moral, and religious independence of Griselda would be simply a medieval counterpart of the "freedom" of so many later "flappers." But history cannot be troubled for such slight ends. If it were really necessary to give some idea of the tremendous historical and social upheavals of the tenth century it would have been better to forget Stendhal, Ernest Hemingway, and the superficialities of the Jazz Age.

There is further evidence of this momentary decline of Fitzgerald's creative powers in the stories published in this period. "The Fiend," [6] for instance, also goes back for its setting to a past epoch—the end of the nineteenth century. It deals with the motive of cold and calculating hate that has its punishment in itself (a typically Hawthornian motive), but it only states the theme and develops it in a routine and superficial way, in the manner of a literary exercise. Like Chillingworth in *The Scarlet Letter,* the protagonist of this story, Cranshaw (whose name itself seems to be derived from the name of Hawthorne's first hero: Fanshawe) accomplishes a cold, protracted revenge on the killer of his wife—tormenting him for thirty years in prison with continual visits which are only meant to remind him of his crime. When the man dies, however, Cranshaw discovers that he has lost the only human relationship he has ever had, because his victim was his only friend. Guilty of the "unpardonable sin," in Hawthorne's terms—the lack of love, the cold intellectualism, the pitiless use of ratiocination for a kind of cruel vampirism—Cranshaw has his own punishment in his solitude. His sterile demonism shows nothing of the profundity nor the grandeur of its models in Hawthorne and loses all its strength as it becomes an end in itself. The only "vampirism" from which Fitzgerald could draw inspiration was the domestic kind of Nicole's; in "The Fiend" one gets the impression of an intellectual elaboration of a badly realized theme.

The same is true, though in a different way, of "The Night at Chancellorsville," [7] a sketch in the first person set in the time of the Civil War. Fitzgerald was apparently trying to write a popular story on the adventures of two thoughtless girls who have gone with a convoy toward the South, where they watch a battle, flee from the "rebels," and return home in a fright. All his efforts, however, seem to be devoted to a kind of naturalistic transcription of the soft and singing Southern dialect; there is no elaboration, nor any technical build-up of the material, nor any attempt at stylistic resolution. Everything is told in haste, with weariness under the burden of writing.

We are truly at the lowest point of a literary career, if in addition to the unfinished novel, the same considerations apply to an entire group of stories.[8] But the positive aspect of the situation lies in the fact that the writer gradually became aware of his decline and of his waning power and realized that desperate ills demand desperate remedies, or at least drastic measures. The dark night of the soul is not eluded by the balm and palliative of looking elsewhere: Fitzgerald then, with obstinate will power and with the lucid grasp of an artist, set out on the task of analyzing to the bitter end the crisis from which he suffered and of looking for his own salvation among his own ghosts. Repeating the perennial story of the man who has to pass through a season in hell before coming out *"a riveder le stelle,"* Fitzgerald found in the realization of his crack-up the liberation from his ills and in the representation of the hell itself the germ of an artistic rebirth.

2

In the three essays commonly known under the title *The Crack-up*— "The Crack-up," "Handle with Care," "Pasting it Together" [9]—the final and open confession of a personal state of *épuisement* and of an artistic bankruptcy or impotence was offered to Fitzgerald's enemies and detractors. Fitzgerald admitted a complete collapse—the apparent inability to get out of a blind alley into which he had slid little by little. And if he himself let it be known, what other proof was necessary? In truth, these articles disappointed and embarrassed even his closest friends and admirers, from Hemingway who resented Fitzgerald's making public his troubles, to Thomas Wolfe who recognized in the essays a clear sign of weakness, and to John Dos Passos who hurled an impassioned condemnation against his friend.[10] Edmund Wilson kept silent about his disapproval and did not condemn him. This attitude of protest against Fitzgerald's confession was based, perhaps, on love—or self-satisfaction in feeling stronger and healthier than he was. Now that time has passed, however, it is apparent that a little objectivity or a better insight would have been sufficient to see how Fitzgerald gave a supreme proof of courage with his essays and how he was able to create thereby, quite unexpectedly, a small masterpiece of psychological introspection and poetic release. At the same time, while exorcising his ills, he was rising in perfect self-awareness to evaluate and judge a general crisis of which his own personal crisis was merely a reflection.

The first interest of the three essays is essentially biographical, but their value is not exhausted by a simple application of their statements to the author's own life. In an earlier essay entitled "Sleeping and Waking," [11] Fitzgerald had already described the beginnings of a condition of restlessness and anguish of which insomnia was a concrete and tangible manifestation. "The *real* night, the darkest hour, has begun," he had written then; and the light tone of the writing, almost humorous, deceived no one. In the three essays that followed, he brought all his attention to the description of that "dark night of the soul" in which "it is always three o'clock in the morning," and every small incident, even a forgotten package, has a tragic importance. The analysis of his crack-up made no mystery of the most intimate details; it tried to assume a light tone and to rely on surprise, but the disenchanted attitude made the process of self-realization all the more terrible. Using the image of a cracked plate, Fitzgerald worked out the simile to convey to the reader the sense of his intimate breakdown. He did not refrain from personal recollections and in his desire for orderliness he even added the list of the conclusions he had reached.[12] He did not make any great discovery, but in the third essay, devoted to the attempt of shoring up the fragments of his ruin, he ended with a ruthless affirmation of cynicism which was also an affirmation of artistic vitality. "I must continue to be a writer because that was my only way of life, but I would cease any attempts to be a person.... There was to be no more giving of myself—all giving was to be outlawed henceforth under a new name, and that name was Waste." And he continued:

> If you are young and you should write asking to see me and learn how to be a sombre literary man writing pieces upon the state of emotional exhaustion that often overtakes writers in their prime—if you should be so young and fatuous as to do this, I would not do so much as acknowledge your letter, unless you were related to someone very rich and important indeed.[13]

With these sentences, Fitzgerald was indeed verging on self-denigration, or at least he took a position antithetical to Dick's. But he broke with the past and its self-complacency and in his ruthless denunciation he reached, as Lionel Trilling rightly remarked, a sort of "heroic awareness" and a dignified "heroic quality." [14] In this view, far from being a mere exercise in self-pity, these essays offer the example of a painful attempt at definition; far from being a "subtle form of rebellion" or a hysterical cry (as has been maintained), they become the means, the very instrument for a search for truth, a firm point in a process of enlightment. By rejecting half measures, they prefer the cruel truth of the facts to any childish form of illusion—to the mistaken idea that "all's well with the world."

"The very meaning of expertness"—Henry James had written in his Preface to *Roderick Hudson*—"is acquired courage to brace one's self for the cruel crisis from the moment one sees it grimly loom." Fitzgerald was a bit late, then, and his courage might well have been the courage of desperation; but he was able to throw light on his crisis and by that very fact to prepare himself for a radical change of life and interests. As he wrote later to an unknown correspondent who had written for advice:

> I don't know whether those articles of mine in *Esquire*—that "Crack-Up" series—represented a real nervous breakdown. In retrospect it seems more of a spiritual "change of life"—and a most unwilling one—it was a protest against a new set of conditions which I would have to face and a protest of my mind at having to make the psychological adjustments which would suit this new set of circumstances. (*Letters*, p. 589.)

He did make the psychological adjustment, and he was able to change his life. Some of his remarks, moreover, served as a comment on the fictional crisis of his character Dick in *Tender Is the Night*.[15] But there was something more, and much more important. In his own crisis Fitzgerald found unawares the underlying reasons of the collapse of a whole age. This was obviously colored with the reflection of his private suffering, which served to put into relief as never before all the tragic experiences of the time in which he lived, and whose collapse he shared. "I have spoken in these pages of how an exceptionally optimistic young man experienced a crack-up of all values," Fitzgerald wrote, but he added in conclusion: "My recent experience parallels the wave of despair that swept the nation when the Boom was over." More than merely paralleling it, his experience *expressed* it, as Mark Schorer has aptly remarked in his essay "Fitzgerald's Tragic Sense," in which he proceeded to show with notable insight the exact range and value of these writings:

> The *Crack-up*, like almost everything else Fitzgerald wrote, is excellent in the degree by which it transcends mere pathos. This comes in part from his writing itself, which is marked by a colloquial ease that persistently achieves genuine poetic effects. But these effects, in turn, depend on his capacity to hit upon details which invoke an atmosphere much larger. . . .[16]

The self-immolation of which Fitzgerald speaks is, by his own admission, the same as that of many of his contemporaries. The denunciation of individual ills reveals therefore a historical and universal dimension; the confession betrays the intent, or perhaps the possibility of an independent artistic creation. The three essays are among his best achievements; speaking of himself, he ended by writing "a haunting footnote to the inner history of America and of American writing in our time," according to Alfred Kazin's definition. The artistic achievement lies in the perfect balance between the individual and the representative, the biographical interest and the historical implications or connotations. Avoiding the dangers of being pathetic, Fitzgerald succeeded in representing all the details that suggested or connoted a wider context and a more general purpose. And he succeeded, we must here repeat with Mark Schorer, thanks to the particular quality of his writing. His language is here simple and flowing, discursive and easy; by reducing the expressive means to the level of conversation, he achieves unexpected results. Expressing with everyday words his inner crisis, Fitzgerald detached himself, as it were, from his person, and he stood by to contemplate and record. He did color his exposition with emotional participation, but from the introspective and diary-like manner of his essay he gradually moved on to the tone of the essay on manners, of the social denunciation, and finally of a quite autonomous fictional achievement. His experience of pain and suffering is purified by an internal fire that removes from the language any sentimental weakness, any concession to polemics or to self-pity; his confession thus is similar in tone, purport, and development to so many highly personal analyses of Montaigne in his *Essays*.

After the three essays, whose purely aesthetic achievement cannot be overestimated, there followed other personal writings or meditations. Here the historical implications are lacking, and we can detect a significant return to objective narration. They are short, occasional pieces, half-way between stories and essays or confessions; sketches written in a rapid and apparently colloquial prose, broken up in frequent dialogues, which already foreshadow Fitzgerald's "second manner" in style. The language is bare and concise in the highest degree, and almost feverish in its intensity—far from the flowing fullness of the language of *Tender Is the Night* or the balanced harmony of style reached in *The Great Gatsby*. It is a kind of language that in *The Last Tycoon* will seem to postulate an absolute adherence to objects, things, the living voices of people.

In this writing, the plot is reduced to a minimum; it is the tension of the emotions evoked, as Arthur Mizener has remarked,[17] that is substituted for proper action, or that enlivens it when it is present. Whether or not Fitzgerald was aware of it or wanted to acknowledge it, whether or not he welcomed it, this seems to be his first step toward a narrative that was to adopt some of Hemingway's stylistic features. Three of these sketches exemplify to perfection this development, and all of them have in their titles the word that betrays their half-biographical and half-fictional characteristic: "An Author's Mother," "Afternoon of an Author," and "Author's House." [18] A kind of sentimental reminiscence prevails in the first of these; but in the second there is a clear indication of the new development. Fitzgerald presents with incomparable simplicity the small details that fill the afternoon of an author suffering from overwork and creative weariness. In a colorless, third-person narration all his gestures and insignificant actions are given: the effort required to work on a story, some recollections from the past, a ride around the town, a stop at the barber's, the return home. There is nothing more in the story, but it lives because of its interplay between irony and participation, detachment and involvement, precision of detail and simplicity of diction. The third sketch is even more concise and scanty in its subject: the author shows his house to a hypothetical visitor. In each room he evokes or remembers an episode that has happened in it, or he tells of his life as an author. The dialogue absorbs in itself almost every movement of the narration, and yet that house, so similar to many others, acquires a distinct identity and becomes almost a living projection of the author. The narrative approach is the same as in some sketches by Hawthorne ("The Celestial Railroad," for instance), and even reminiscent of the latest "discoveries" of the French *nouvelle vague,* with its poetics of the object minutely observed, its insistence on the photographic reproduction of the smallest details, and its assurance that the only field for the writer lies in the most ordinary and least poetic aspects of reality. Fitzgerald, it goes without saying, was soon to reintroduce warmth of feeling and personal participation into his stories. But in these sketches—incisive in their dialogues, rapid in their diction, direct in presentation—he found a rewarding formula for the fictional attempts that were soon to lead him to the barren intensity of his last stories and of his last, unfinished novel.

This is the period, moveover, in which Fitzgerald felt that he had to rebuke Thomas Wolfe for his lack of detachment and conscious artistry, and to invite him "to cultivate an alter ego," to use his material sparingly, to accept the inner measure of the "novel of selected incident." Fitzgerald had never been much of an admirer of Thomas Wolfe's "sprawling novels," and his short letter to Wolfe was received as "a bouquet . . . smelling sweetly of roses but cunningly concealing several large-sized brick-bats." Wolfe was violent in defense of his own narrative method, and it would be out of place here to examine his argument.[19] What is interesting and significant, however, is the fact that in his letter from Hollywood (July 1937) Fitzgerald seemed to express again the need for formal control and artistic detachment in terms that are clearly Jamesian, at least in their origin. He went even further than James—guilty himself of a questionable fullness in his later novels—in his advocacy of a Flaubert-like essentiality. Fitzgerald was perhaps remembering his own experience in *Gatsby* and wanted to turn back for inspiration to that novel; but now the "selection" that he advocated could easily do without any

ornament or stylistic device and reduce everything to its bare substance. In *The Great Gatsby* he had left some material out on purpose,
but he thought that he had concealed the gap with "blankets of
excellent prose." Now he could do without his excellent prose, and a
feverish and naked intensity [20] is the outstanding feature of his latest
stories and of *The Last Tycoon*. In these the new narrative form with
which he had experimented in the sketches was combined with an
intensity of human insight that found in existence itself a wealth of
dramatic implications or even drama in its purest form.

3

"An Alcoholic Case," [21] is a domestic drama in which the protagonist
is a direct projection of Fitzgerald himself. And yet the story is
resolved objectively through an effective detachment of vision, since
the few events are seen and interpreted by the nurse, entrusted with
the "case." It is the nurse who tells of her difficulties with the patient—
at first with scientific coolness, and then by degrees with a deeper form
of sympathy. When she decides to remain with her impossible patient,
although she has lost all hope of a cure, she betrays that she has been
involved in the case, and we are made to understand that the core of
the story and of its artistic interest lies in the representation of that
suffering pair of human beings who find the motivation and the sense
of their existence in their indissoluble relationship. "The Long Way
Out" [22] was also inspired by an autobiographical reminiscence. The
protagonist of the story is a schizophrenic woman who hopes to leave
her asylum and to be reunited with her husband. Gradually she falls
back into "the dark night of the soul" after her husband has died in a
car accident. Without being told of the accident, Mrs. King waits day
after day for the liberation that will never come, and for years she
repeats the painful comedy of getting ready to leave the hospital and
then going back to her room. Either she does not realize what has
happened, or she does not want to accept the evidence; or, better still,
she prefers her fiction to the crude rules of reality. In any case her
long wait becomes in the end the effective symbol of a condition that
can again be defined as "existential." Life—and this seems to be the
informing idea of the story—is nothing but waiting and silent suffering, so it is sufficient for the writer to represent the endless routine of
a meaningless act to convey his sense of the drama of existence.

   In the best cases, life is made up of ironic surprises, as in
"Financing Finnegan," [23] where Fitzgerald split himself, as it were,

into two characters and more than ever before relied on his gift of the "double vision." The protagonist, a successful writer, is in debt and insolvent, as well as momentarily forgotten. He never appears directly on the scene, although he is constantly present by means of letters and telegrams; and his legendary figure acquires substance and weight as it is reflected in the admiration, mixed with impotent envy, of a second, mediocre writer—the narrator of the story, who tells of the moves of Finnegan. Fitzgerald loaned some of his traits to both Finnegan and his poor and helpless rival, but in this fictional division nothing human was lost, because the narrator and the famous writer offer two facets of a single reality—that of the difficult and insecure world of writers. Together they give a single image of a troubled life. After a fantastic—and symbolic—disappearance at the North Pole, when everyone believes that he is dead and the narrator thinks that he now has his revenge over Finnegan's agent and publisher, Finnegan turns out to be still alive. And if he comes back to life asking once more for advances, this humorous conclusion does not lessen the seriousness of the story—a melancholy appeal for understanding and mutual sympathy among those who have made writing their profession, or their damnation. In fact, under the veil of a disenchanted *divertissement*, Fitzgerald was able to express two of his most personal feelings: the sad awareness of being relegated to the background or to the past, and his need to reaffirm, against every sign to the contrary, his literary capacities.

For a short while, the real is not apprehended or represented as essentially dramatic. But in "Design in Plaster," [24] a story which is almost a study in the progress of jealousy, the human predicament is again in the foreground. Bedridden in a plaster cast, Martin has ruined by excessive jealousy his chances of being reconciled with his estranged wife. She might have come to an accord with him, but when he follows her home and then falls on the stairs she withdraws from him in horror and suddenly feels a need for the previously rejected suitor. Martin's desperate attempt is unsuccessful because his morbid attachment and even his run-down image are bound to alienate his wife from him. There is irony in this conclusion, too, but this time it is a kind of dramatic irony: destiny is indifferent or hostile to the plans of men, and human existence is in itself absurd and mocking. There is no way out of the "existential predicament"—a predicament which prevents the solution of inner conflicts or determines it according to the whim of destiny.

We are confronted by two stories in which Fitzgerald succeeded in finding and expressing an "objective correlative" of his own predicament and of the human plight in general, and in which he was able to contemplate and to resolve them through the objective detachment of a cold and impersonal narration. He attained and expressed "a wise and tragic sense of life," [25] and he was able to convey it to the reader by combining once more "the innocence of complete involvement with an almost scientific coolness of observation." Arthur Mizener's definition is again perfectly adequate to characterize these stories, and it was a precious achievement—even in view of the novel on which he was working—which has a particular significance in these last years of Fitzgerald literary activity. Even more openly than in the Basil stories, his double vision here redeemed his fictional escapes into the past and provided him with a perfect means for coming to terms with the present. The protagonist of "Three Hours Between Planes," [26] meeting his childhood love, has the momentary illusion of being able to "repeat" the past, but he is soon brought to realize that the past itself was far from idyllic. The girl has taken him for someone else—which means that the past is now marked with the same doubts, the same misunderstandings, the same disappointments with which the present is so prodigal. His discovery is an actual "shock of recognition," conveyed to the reader with the matter-of-fact tone of an obvious, although painful, statement. The same barrenness of diction is also the distinctive characteristic of "The Lost Decade" (a sketch that compresses into few pages the guiding theme of "Babylon Revisited") and of "News of Paris—Fifteen Years Ago," [27] which represents a thematic reversion to the Jazz Age.

In "The Lost Decade" a survivor from the past walks like a ghost in New York; his shock of recognition brings him to the realization that he has been "drunk for ten years," and in this disconsolate, conclusive sentence is all the lesson of his brief pilgrimage. There seems to be no possible escape or redemption for him: lost in the struggle for life, he has exhausted all possibilities of resistance. His existential predicament has reduced him to the state of a straw man. In "News of Paris—Fifteen Years Ago," the protagonist Henry is about to begin a new life, and he is on the point of leaving romantic Europe for America. "He had been romantic four years ago"; and although he leads a frivolous life—he has a short flirtation with one of his friends, goes to a wedding, and begins an affair with a girl he has met by chance—he is gradually becoming aware of the inconsistency and meaninglessness of his life. He begins to realize that he is nothing more than "a contemptible drone," and in the end he turns back for consolation to his adopted daughter. One perceives that his former world is being undermined by his self-consciousness, which reveals its poverty and inconsistency, its worn-out thread. What was fascinating in former years has lost its glamor, and each moment or aspect of life is now as dramatic as any other. The concise and almost broken style is intense in its bare diction, in dialogue for the most part, as if in a film script.

In this, we reach the extreme of stylistic compression and essentiality, which, whether one likes it or not, has a great deal in common with the fashionable style of Hemingway, especially in his *Forty-Nine Stories* (collected in 1938). While avoiding imitation of his "infectious style," Fitzgerald showed that he had learned and absorbed the lesson of economy and precision inherent in Hemingway's stories and in most of his writings. "News of Paris" provides a clear example of it, for instance, in the description (if it can really be called a description) of the meeting of Henry with Bessie, his chance acquaintance: he is waiting for a taxi and in his haste he gets into the cab that has stopped for her:

> "Oh, look," begged Henry. "You're not by any chance going near the Bois?"
> He was getting into the cab as he spoke. His morning coat was a sort of introduction. She nodded.
> "I'm lunching there."
> "I'm Henry Dell," he said, lifting his hat.
> "Oh, it's you—at last," she said eagerly. "I'm Bessie Wing—born Leighton. I know all your cousins."
> "Isn't this nice," he exclaimed and she agreed.
> "I'm breaking my engagement at luncheon," she said. "And I'll name you."
> "Really breaking your engagement?"
> "At the Café Dauphine—from one to two."
> "I'll be there—from time to time I'll look at you."
> "What I want to know is—does he take me home afterward. I'm not Emily Posted."
> On impulse he said:
> "No, I do. You may be faint or something. I'll keep an eye on you."
> She shook her head.

"No—it wouldn't be reverend this afternoon," she said. "But I'll be here weeks."

"This afternoon," he said. "You see, there's a boat coming in." (AA, pp. 222–23.)

One is reminded of a stenographic report. The narrative parts are minimal, the sentences are short and broken, extremely rapid in their succession. The tone is half serious, half humorous, but the dialogue attains an effectiveness which is beyond question. There is no superfluous word, no intervention to ease or interrupt the urgency of the narration. Everything is governed by the necessity for rapid progression, by the exigency to express only the meaningful nucleus, the core, "the stress and passion" within each moment or revealing fact. Fitzgerald's stylistic economy seems to avoid even the brief suspension of the question mark ("... does he take me home afterward."), to rush from one statement to the next with no intermission ("... I'll be here weeks." "This afternoon," he said). The tempo and the rhythm of the passage are broken and jolted, the language expresses in rapid succession only the bare facts without any delicacy of development. The people in this passage are obviously in a hurry. But Fitzgerald is not a victim of a "pathetic fallacy"—he has reached and perfected a new style, which in its immediacy and rapidity compresses and intensifies the narrative pattern.

This new need for brevity and compression was perhaps determined—if only marginally—by the fact that most of these stories and sketches were written for the magazine *Esquire* and were therefore conditioned from the very start by the limited number of pages available and by the comparatively small amount of money that Fitzgerald received for them. Undoubtedly, however—as is clearly demonstrated by *The Last Tycoon*—Fitzgerald found his new "measure" by himself and did not submit to any particular requirements of the magazine. In *The Pat Hobby Stories*, the series of sketches with which he ended his career as a story writer, and which appeared in seventeen consecutive numbers of *Esquire*,[28] Fitzgerald's new measure permitted him to cut the abundant material into short pieces, into so many rhythmical episodes, which gain in intensity and clearness (although with some repetitions) on account of their very brevity. A new subject matter, drawn from his Hollywood experiences, found here its first trials and, progressively, its focus. This series brings us to the threshold, and into the setting itself, of *The Last Tycoon,* but it is thanks to the drastic foreshortening of the single episodes or of the single characters that it reaches a narrative liveliness of considerable efficacy.

The setting (the underworld of Hollywood, as it were) is new and original; the figure of the protagonist has, on the other hand, much in common with previous "survivors from the past." But as a result of the environment which conditions him, Pat Hobby, the unsuccessful scriptwriter, acquires an entirely new individuality and a human personality—human in so far as it is linked to an objective condition of pathetic frustration. Pat Hobby has been pushed aside by the advent of the sound movies; his former creative vein (if he had any to start with) seems completely drained, and step by step he loses all his dignity as a result of an endless series of compromises. Relegated to the "misfits" by his own weakness and by the ruthless laws of the commercial world, he is represented as trying desperately to regain a position, to be reintegrated among the "Big" by any means and at all cost, to have a new chance of reasserting his abilities. All his efforts, however, are doomed to fail in a hostile world; he goes from one humiliation to another, each time rejected by the "Big" whom he worships with exaggerated respect.

In Pat Hobby, one might say, Fitzgerald wanted to give once and for all an epitome of the mediocre in its human dimension. He describes Pat Hobby as a "complete rat," who unhesitatingly betrays his friends or passes himself off for what he is not, who pretends to be much more important than he is, who insists on his former (and unproved) "glory" and is basically dishonest. And yet Pat Hobby is not a downright villain; he is human and even humane, and, in spite of his equivocal traits, he is represented as a victim of external circumstances that almost compel him to be dishonest or to resort to questionable means of survival. He is dishonest because in the world of Hollywood, where money is law and the abuse of power is accepted and recognized, he *has* to accept the rules and behave accordingly, he *has* to avail himself of the means used by his opponents and "superiors." There is no moral stature or revulsion in his nature, but he is also the victim of a technical revolution (the shift from the simple craft of movie-making to the big industrial process of the entertainment business) which brings with it a revolution in manners and morals. There is a kind of strength and validity in his struggle, even if the struggle is often damnable in the way in which it is conducted, because his attempt to break his isolation has all the dignity of a struggle to survive. At his age—forty-nine—it is not easy to recover a lost position, and even his questionable expedients, inferiority complex, sense of awe in the presence of the "Big," and despicable servility are at least partly redeemed by his exclusion.

His story is not a parable of the defeat of the "villain," but it shows the precarious balance and the sad compromises to which man is exposed in his daily struggle wherever the "Big" impose their laws and where life is dominated by the rules of economic power. Fitzgerald seems really to provide us with an example of a subdued and low kind of moral realism, without violent flashes of dramatic conflicts or passions (as in *The Last Tycoon*), in which the human dimension is constantly the measure and the pattern of the portrayal. Pat Hobby never takes a critical stand against the movie world; he merely lives there. He accepts and conforms to some of its less pleasing laws (such as the need for predominance: see how he protects, in a humorous episode, the coveted table of the "Big" from a false intruder), and he too dreams of becoming a big fish able to swallow the little ones. But if all his attempts fail, his human predicament becomes only more painful and "existential" in its irreversibility.

In this figure, Fitzgerald projected perhaps his never-quieted nightmare of complete deterioration and failure and exorcised at the same time his own ghost. And yet he managed to avoid any direct identification with his character and to represent Pat Hobby in an objective light. In this way he was able to criticize him by endowing him with the most disconcerting weaknesses, without making him, on the other hand, a stiff, mechanical, or grotesque character. He mitigated the ridicule and the condemnation with a touch of light irony. The story of Pat Hobby takes place in an atmosphere in which any over-harsh judgment is suspended; it does not mock the misdirected efforts of human frailty nor make light of the human contradictions, but shows them with gentle comprehension. Without heavy moralizing, the irony makes it possible for the drama to touch the personal note, to develop in a subdued manner, in a low voice, avoiding big words and severe attitudes. It is no longer—we must remember—the easy irony of the superman or the aesthete who contemplates in complete detachment the absurdities of life, but rather an irony that betrays sympathy and involvement—the irony of one who has learned to smile sadly at the weaknesses and faults of mankind. It is an irony, among other things, which is clearly reflected in the style and confers a lightness of touch to the narration.

Fitzgerald's fiction had to reach this point to destroy the legend of uniformity and to reveal its deeply felt components of human sympathy and understanding, its essentiality and intensity of style. The Pat Hobby stories must be seen, therefore, as one of his final achievements, as a definite phase of his narrative development. They cannot be forgotten nor considered as a minor exercise in satire or as momentary concessions to a taste for the grotesque. They represent a form of recognition of everyday reality and a search for human truth, and they can be regarded as a calm and tentative introduction to the world of *The Last Tycoon*.[29] An analysis of the single episodes would not add much to the general picture which we can draw from them. There is no narrative development from one moment to another, but rather a repetition of a few basic actions, similar in substance and often predictable, in a limited context of different situations. A few indications will suffice: in the first episode ("Pat Hobby's Christmas Wish") he is desperately trying to "get back" into the pictures, but he can only show that he is a talentless relic from the past; in the second ("A Man in the Way") we have a first inkling of the unpassable barrier that "shuts him out," while in the third (" 'Boil Some Water— Lots of It' ") he becomes a ridiculous defender of the acquired rights by keeping an intruder, who is in a fact a "big" writer, from the Big Table. In the fourth episode ("Teamed with Genius") Pat Hobby tries to get the upper hand over his collaborator, who completes a "swell script" without his assistance; in "Pat Hobby and Orson Welles" he can only manage to "draw another ten bucks," which he spends as usual in the bar, and in "Pat Hobby's Secret" he manages to forget his valuable secret—an idea, stolen from another writer, worth one thousand dollars. In "The Homes of the Stars" (the eighth episode) he is reduced to the undignified and unauthorized role of showing the homes of the stars to tourists, and he hardly escapes being caught at it; he "does his bit" in the next, which means lying on the ground for a car to "drive slowly across his middle," and he is forgotten in the excitement, when the car turns over before touching him and the big actor breaks his leg. In "Pat Hobby's Preview" he is admitted with his girl to the preview of a picture only when the big writer with whom he has "collaborated" withdraws his name from the picture; in "No Harm Trying" he launches on an ambitious project of an independent production, but he chooses an actress who does not know English, a director who is an irresponsible alcoholic, and even his film script has been stolen—he can only get "another month at two-fifty." In "A

Patriotic Short" Pat Hobby dreams of his happy past, and in the next episode he is called upon to provide a title; in "Two Old-Timers" he emerges, at the expense of another old-timer, but in "Mightier than the Sword" he is completely excluded from the picture world, and in the final episode ("Pat Hobby's College Days") his humiliations seem to reach the lowest point.

As one can easily see, there is no actual conclusion to the series, and there could not be, since the story of Pat Hobby continues uninterrupted to its bitter end. He is the prisoner of an "existential" situation without realizing it, and there is no possible escape from the predicament of existence for him, as for so many of his predecessors in Fitzgerald's mature fiction. From the dark night of the Middle Ages Fitzgerald passes on to the immediacy of the turbid world of Hollywood, and we have the first glimpse of the sunny beaches of California from which Pat Hobby is so ruthlessly excluded. An involuted style has given way to the lightness of one that is spoken, rapid, and staccato; in *The Pat Hobby Stories* the bareness and quickness of the dialogue is of paramount importance for artistic achievement. Like the artist envisaged by Joyce in the *Portrait*, Fitzgerald succeeded in assuming the passive indifference of the author who watches from above the movements of his characters and no longer intervenes to correct or determine them. In *The Last Tycoon* his imagination flares up, does violence to reality itself, colors it with expressionistic touches: but the writer can afford it because he has now renounced the ornate word for the effective one, turned the musical sentences into terse and direct statements, reduced the full narration to the scantiness of effects of a movie script.

CHAPTER VIII

The Wise and Tragic
Sense of Life

*Once one is caught up into the
material world, not one person in
ten thousand finds the time to
form . . . what, for lack of a better
phrase, I might call the wise and
tragic sense of life.*

Letters, p. 96.

1

The Last Tycoon has much in common with *The Great Gatsby* and
with *Tender Is the Night,* and yet it represents a notable turning point
in Fitzgerald's fiction. Like *Gatsby* it is a tightly knit and well-
constructed novel—even in its unfinished state—based on the skillful
juxtaposition of "dramatic scenes" filtered through the eyes of a narrator involved in the story. Its affinity with *Tender Is the Night* is in
the informing idea, if it is true that the story concerns a "superman in
possibilities," almost an artist and a creator, who finds his defeat in a
psychological and emotional *épuisement* and at the same time is
crushed by adverse circumstances. But in comparison with Gatsby the
protagonist of *The Last Tycoon* is more extensively defined, both on
the psychological and on the social and ethical level of his conflict,
while in comparison with Dick in *Tender Is the Night* his predicament
is more deeply rooted in a context of external circumstances and his
struggle is less passive and more virile.[1] Moreover, the adventure of
Monroe Stahr is presented in a fairly realistic way, and Fitzgerald was
availing himself of a quite different type of diction—a diction which
came as close as possible to the ideal of immediacy and concreteness
that is present in Hemingway's fiction. This is why *The Last Tycoon,*
although basically in line with the motives and methods developed in

his previous works, is an original achievement which shows the degree of renewal that Fitzgerald could reach without denying himself or his past. While remaining faithful to his inner convictions and "traditions," the writer was not prevented from asserting himself with a final *tour de force* that might have radically changed his line of development.

The incompleteness of the novel does not allow any excessive speculation on the entity and the eventual future bearing of such a change, and it is safer to consider the novel in its relationship with the preceding works. But it will be necessary, from time to time, to stress the differences, and even if we have to suspend final judgment because of its incompleteness, it would be amiss to neglect its unsuspected potentiality of new motives and new techniques.

Checked in the "game of life," Fitzgerald was also betrayed by his luck. He was betrayed by his weakened physical condition, which prevented him from gathering the reward of his assiduous effort under adverse conditions, and as in no other case death came at the wrong moment. Of this novel that should have marked his triumphant return among the leading authors of the Forties, Fitzgerald was able to complete only five chapters out of nine. We are left with little more than half a novel, even considering the scattered notes, outlines, and fragments that remain. It is probably too little for us to speak of a "novel," especially since Fitzgerald used to rework his novels even when he had completed them (*Tender Is the Night* is typical in this sense). Nevertheless, *The Last Tycoon* belongs to the canon of Fitzgerald's fiction, and it must be considered as an important part of it. For Dos Passos, who cannot be suspected of any tenderness toward Fitzgerald, it represents "one of those literary fragments that from time to time appear in the stream of a culture and profoundly influence the course of future events." [2] If this is an exaggerated and questionable statement, the fact remains that this fragment has all the intensity, the effectiveness, and the significance of a final outburst of artistic vitality.

The first idea of a new novel was conceived by the writer three or four years before his sudden death. "This has been in my mind for three years," he wrote in a note, and his first idea was to write a love story set in Hollywood. The protagonist was to be a brilliant producer, possessing many of the qualities and limitations of the producer Irving Thalberg whom Fitzgerald had met as far back as 1927. From the very start he committed himself to an objective rendering, since for this character he could not use his own traits and personal experiences as such, but had to embody them in a character seen from the outside, who would lead his own independent life. According to a first outline of the plot, the brilliant producer would have been ruined by his love for a woman whose resemblance to his wife would stir him to a longing for a new home, a new affection, and a new form of life. Realizing that in this way he would break the prospect of a happy marriage for the woman, the producer was to have left her, only to find himself alone in his daily struggle for survival and preeminence in the movie world. Physically worn out, emotionally disappointed and persecuted for his attempt to continue his relations with the woman after her marriage, he was to break down like Dick Diver. An accident in an airplane during his "flight" would have sealed his ruin.[3] The theme had much in common with the theme in the first drafts of *Tender Is the Night:* Stahr's tragic flaw appears to be mainly his need for love, while it is his blind dedication to the woman that determines more than anything else his *épuisement* and his collapse.

There is no indication, at this point, of how Fitzgerald intended to handle the difficult problem of the point of view. In other notes, however, he faced the problem and ended by making the narrator a girl, Cecilia, daughter of Stahr's fellow-producer and rival; Cecilia's unrequited love for Stahr was to have colored the whole story with an intense participation, while at the same time objectifying it through the detachment of a limited point of view. In two detailed plans the story is then delineated and divided into eight chapters, subdivided into thirty-one episodes. In these plans the story was still described as a love story (the working title was quite revealing in this respect: *The Love of the Last Tycoon*), but it was already determined and conditioned by other, more realistic elements. The story of Stahr's love for Thalia made up the largest part of the episodes and was followed for a rather long span of time, although it was not marked by the breathless rapidity that characterizes it in the novel. There was also to be a conflict of interests between Stahr and Bradogue (Cecilia's father), which would push the former, after a hard struggle, to eventual defeat in a framework of conflicting social and economical forces. Stahr did not give in or fly as in the first outline, and even the plane crash was to happen when his defeat had been already determined. The two themes, however, were separately developed, and the inner and the outer conflicts remained independent of one another, without really coinciding or being structurally combined.

Fitzgerald's difficulty in freeing himself from the limitations of a pathetic love story and in dealing consistently with the theme of a more realistic conflict is evident in the second outline of the plot, which he sent to his publisher and to the editor of *Collier's*.[4] Many of the definitions and statements of purpose in this outline clarify the purport or at least the intention of the story that he had in mind after the first attempts. Fitzgerald discussed at length the figure and the function of the narrator, the nature and the characteristics of Stahr and Thalia; he attempted a definition of the conflict that opposes Stahr to Bradogue and to the writers' union; he alluded to a struggle for the control of Stahr's company—but he insisted all the same that "the love affair *was* the meat of the book." Unexpectedly, the tragic end is here represented as an ironical twist of fate, since Stahr was to die when he had not only regained the love of Thalia, but was flying to New York to clinch his victory over his rival.[5] In addition, a penultimate chapter would have represented a boy who would find in the wreckage of the airplane a "moral heritage" by simply reading Stahr's papers.[6]

If the love story was to have been "the meat of the book" and was to end in reconciliation, it is difficult to see how the writer could have sustained it through a turbulent conflict of interests, which was also to work out favorably for Stahr, and then end it in an incongruous plane crash. There is no link of cause and effect among the various elements, between their development and their conclusion, especially if we consider that the love affair, far from precipitating the conflict of interests and deriving from it a dramatic tension as in the novel, has no apparent obstacle to overcome. It is compromised by Stahr's own indecision and particular form of mind, by his psychological and aesthetic requirements only. There is no other man in Thalia's life and nothing would prevent her from staying with Stahr. All the difficulties are in him: in his dream of an emotional as well as social superiority Stahr is unable to accept such a girl as Thalia, who has a poor background and humble appearance. It is he who alienates Thalia without realizing that she is much more important to him than he thinks, that she is in fact necessary to him. The motivation that Fitzgerald had envisaged is quite revealing. "Previously his [Stahr's] name had been associated with this or that well-known actress or society personality, and Thalia is poor, unfortunate, and tagged with a middle-class exterior which doesn't fit in with the grandeur Stahr demands of life." Everything seems to be the result of an excessive squeamishness on the part of Stahr; his hamartia is really a form of pathetic weakness—an incapacity to accept reality, a little like the early Dick, or Gatsby himself, not to speak of Anthony. If Fitzgerald had developed his story along these lines he would have run the risk of repeating himself, and it is significant that he defined the book as "an escape into a lavish, romantic past that perhaps will not come again into our time."

In the third diagram of the story, which seems to be connected with the previous outline,[7] and which is divided into ten chapters and twenty-three episodes, the love affair is still the dominant theme of the book. A good four chapters (II, III, IV, and VII) are devoted to the meetings of Stahr and Thalia, while only two deal with the same material in the novel. The seduction is accomplished in Chapter VII (Chapter V in the novel) and the conflict of interests with Bradogue begins to take shape only in the eighth chapter, when the story is already turning to its logical conclusion. From this moment the story seems to be centered on this conflict, and the love affair seems to be almost forgotten. The two motives, therefore, are not only separated in this diagram, but they seem actually to offer two separate possibilities, as if the second might at a certain point take the place of the first. It is Stahr again who seems to refuse the possibility of marrying Thalia, and Thalia herself, as is apparent in a first version of the second chapter based on this diagram,[8] is represented without the elusive and slightly mysterious charm that she will have in the novel. Stahr saves her from the flood in the set, and in this immediate contact the girl not only loses every mysterious fascination, but in fact appears to him as " 'common' . . . ready for anything—a wench, a free-booter, an outsider." Cecilia, though with the irritation of a rival in love, later describes her as "that wretched trollop." If Thalia had been developed according to these premises, there is little doubt that the story would have never come to a logical formulation.

Fortunately, the story was reshaped in a fourth diagram, and when it was written down in an extended narrative the two main motives were blended and fused in a functional way. The story was developed in a tightened structure of episodes in which the elements found their proper place in the close relationship and interdependence of the two informing ideas. Stahr's love story preserves its necessary importance and its dramatic quality (the girl is about to marry another man and does so despite meeting the producer), but it is unfolded in close connection with the conflict that opposes Stahr to Bradogue for the control of the movie company and to the writers' union, over which he wants to maintain his paternalistic predominance. The *épuisement* of the impossible relation with Thalia undermines Stahr's chances of affirming himself in the double struggle and offers to both enemies the occasion for a frontal attack, while the straits of his material interests prevent him from finding in his love the evasion from or the solution to his problems.

In a fine example of *discordia concors*, *The Last Tycoon* has all the premises and many of the qualities of a highly dramatic story, complex in motivation, realistic in context and statement, rapid, immediate, and intense in diction. By following it step by step we can attain a clear idea of its nature and significance and establish both its relations to *Tender Is the Night* and *Gatsby*, and its intrinsic novelty in comparison with these two novels.

2

Like *The Great Gatsby*, *The Last Tycoon* opens with a careful characterization of the narrator and then introduces some of the secondary characters whose function is to bring us near the protagonist; Stahr is already caught sight of toward the end of the first chapter,[9] but he is still detached. Like Nick Carraway, Cecilia is given all the qualities of a perfect narrator, including the ability to imagine certain episodes at which she was not present or which could not be related to her. "She is *of* the movies but not *in* them," as the writer warns us, and detached chronologically from the facts, which she reconstructs after five years have elapsed.[10] Intelligent and observant, she is involved in the action and is a product of the social environment, but with a certain measure of disenchanted cynicism. Like Nick, she presents herself directly at the beginning, and if she declares that she accepts Hollywood "with the resignation of a ghost assigned to a haunted house," she proclaims nevertheless her capacity to be "obstinately unhorrified." Cecilia can be perturbed by the movie world (like the nun who wanted to study a script), but she does not question it. She takes it for granted, and to understand it she suggests that it is sufficient "to understand one of those men." She is flying back to this world from the East, but the haunting atmosphere of Hollywood is already present on the plane, and we are given a clear warning as to its possible destructive effects when the plane lands in Nashville during a thunderstorm. When she goes to the Hermitage of Andrew Jackson in the night, Cecilia can

neither enter nor properly contemplate the sanctuary of the uncorrupted American faith in progress and democracy. And on its thresh-
hold Schwartz, a Hollywood cast-off whom Cecilia has met on the
plane, commits suicide.

He has killed himself because Stahr has turned against him, but
he has warned Stahr of a mysterious danger that threatens him. Wylie,
the script writer who is a friend of Cecilia and works for Stahr, also
vaguely hints at a possible danger to the producer, even if he predicts
his victory over his rival.[11] When Stahr, traveling incognito on the
plane, first chats with Cecilia and then holds a brief soliloquy in the
pilot's cabin, his charm and his energy are still dominant. Cecilia discovers that she is childishly falling in love with him, and she sees only
strength and amiable manhood in his personality; and as Stahr sits in
the pilot's cabin to contemplate Los Angeles from the sky, all the
writer's abilities are brought into play to give us a sense of enlightened grandeur. Fitzgerald attached an important symbolic significance to this episode, so much so that he prepared a longer version
of it in which his intentions are made even more obvious.[12] By sitting
with the pilot, Stahr comes to identify himself with him: like the pilot
he is a "leader" of men, aware of his responsibilities, quick and
resolute in his decisions, somewhat isolated from the rest of the people
and relying only on his intuition when it becomes a question of life
or death. He too operates "on a high level"—far from the ground—
master of his own destiny and of all who are with him. And when in
the course of the story he is compelled to "come down to earth" and
to measure himself with others on their own level, he will be bound to
face his ruin; even the plane's landing acquires a symbolic meaning.
It is significant that Stahr sees in the approaching lights of Los Angeles
a sign of his passion for activity, and he returns to the city with the
pleasure of an empire builder, of an artistic creator, almost, who is
interested in it not because he possesses it, but because he has *created*
it. Yet, his going down "into the warm darkness" [13] will soon turn into
a crash against a hostile ground. The lights go out, and his activity will
languish, blighted by its own worm, wrecked by contrasting tensions;
even his descent might be taken as a thematic forewarning of his
fatal destiny, when he will crash in another plane into the snowy
mountains.

In Hollywood the action moves on in a second, very brief
chapter.[14] Brady makes his first appearance on the scene, and during
an earthquake, which is both functional and symbolic in the story,

Stahr sees for the first time an unknown and mysterious woman who closely resembles his dead wife. The convulsive rhythm of the chapter, which was meant perhaps to convey an idea of the sudden illumination that was to strike Stahr, is smoothed and quieted in the two successive chapters,[15] whose main purpose is to acquaint us with Stahr in an almost analytic way. Unable to forget Stahr, Cecilia tells us of his working day by reconstructing a broken series of episodes, a sequel of dramatic scenes which gives an idea of his character and his nature while also illustrating the Hollywood background. To believe that Stahr is "a marker in industry like Edison and Lumière and Griffith and Chaplin," we must see him at work to appreciate his qualities as a man and leader. He can show his humanity toward a cameraman who has attempted suicide, and thus restore him to his work and happiness; he can teach a presumptuous English writer what amount of imaginative power is needed to make a film; he can solve the personal crisis of an actor (even if he has to keep important people waiting); he is stubborn and dictatorial at the rushes, but always with competence and success. And when he joins the other producers at the commissary, he is willing to sustain the production of a quality picture even if it means losing money. Brady is already opposed to this idea, but Stahr turns a deaf ear to any opposition, without ceremony, and with almost too much precision [16] gets rid of a director who is unequal to his job, and is not afraid to deal at cross purposes with the script writers. His only reward after a long, tiring day is his attempt to find the unknown girl he has seen on the set after the earthquake.

When the setting has been established and the nature of the various characters has been illustrated, the action begins to take shape. In the fifth chapter,[17] which is described as the "dead middle" of the book, the various threads begin to be drawn together. A little like Rosemary—and using almost the same words ("Undertake me," she says to Stahr)—Cecilia tries to interest the tycoon, who is, however, deeply involved in his dream of repeating the past with Kathleen. Allusions at this point indicate that his health is not of the best, and Stahr attaches himself to Kathleen as a way out of his isolation and overwork. To meet her on a sad, long Sunday he neglects his work for the first time. This might be the beginning of a new life for him, but his affair with Kathleen worsens his inner conflict. If it is true that they meet "as strangers in an unfamiliar country," not even the closest intimacy will bring them really together and that country will never appear familiar to them. Kathleen recounts her past to Stahr, tells him of her impoverished childhood and of her humiliations, culminating in an impossible and weary relationship with a king.[18] Her background is as artificial and incomplete as the house on the beach where the tycoon takes the girl on their first day together. The skeletal house, suggestive of a movie set and somehow constituting a symbol of the desolation of Stahr's unstable life, is where their bodies are united. It is a breathless union—almost in the open, without any shelter—that will never turn into a harmonious life.

Four times Stahr drives with Kathleen on the road that joins Hollywood with Malibu. Each time the tone and the atmosphere vary, in keeping with the state of mind of the two characters. The first trip is full of expectancy and uncertainty, the second (their first return to Hollywood) is sad and marked with dissatisfaction, the third is lively with expectancy and impatience—after a dreary dinner in a drugstore Stahr and Kathleen have decided to go back to the house, under the pressure of their emotions and the urgency of their senses. The act of love is accomplished in the unfinished house, and it is "immediate, dynamic, unusual, physical" as Fitzgerald had said in his letter, almost too quick in its urgency (there is only a broken piece of dialogue between them: " 'Wait,' she said."). For a time the atmosphere becomes idyllic, in the twilight on the beach, where they meet an old Negro awaiting the arrival of the grunion. During their fourth trip back to Hollywood the enchantment seems broken, and Stahr has a feeling that nothing has been achieved. The final blow comes when he learns that Kathleen is going to be married; only the pile of film scripts will be waiting for him at home.

Such a cruel disappointment needs silence, and in the meantime the other motive of the book is developed with the reappearance of Brady in the foreground—as he is surprised by his daughter with a nude secretary hidden in a closet. This is the vulgar and cheap counterpart of the previous love scene between Stahr and Kathleen, and it is easy to foresee that between these two opposing poles of behavior and sensitivity there will not be a lasting truce. Stahr, however, has still a chance of dissuading Kathleen from getting married, but his disappointment is too deep and he can no longer deal with her with his customary decision. Kathleen is attracted by him, and a word from him at this time would have been perhaps sufficient to win her back. But Stahr is unable to utter it, since his pride and his boundless egotism have been hurt. Like Gatsby, he is unable to accept a compromise or to bargain for the thing he wants, and being unable to accept Kathleen as she is, he is almost guilty himself of losing her. In this way his destiny is marked: "the dam breaks" in the sixth chapter,[19] of which only the first part has been written. Disturbed to the point of getting drunk by the idea of Kathleen's marrying another, Stahr for the first time lets himself be taken "off guard" when he has the greatest need for all his strength. He is overcome in a discussion with the leftist union leader Brimmer, and even physically hurt, since in his impotence Stahr can think of nothing better than trying to strike the man. From then on we can assume that his decline was to be steady and inescapable, but the novel was cut off here by Fitzgerald's death.

The turning point, however, has been reached, and it is fairly clear from the scattered notes and the diagram that he left how he intended to end the story. Stahr's health was to decline rapidly, and he was to visit Washington in the summer,[20] without being able in the empty city to make any contact with the traditional values of America. Crossed by Brady, who has imposed a wage cut during his absence, Stahr opposes the union also, with the result that "the Reds see him now as a conservative—Wall Street as a Red." Heedless of everything Stahr leaves Cecilia, whom he has accepted as a substitute for Kathleen, and Cecilia tells her father of Stahr's secret love for Kathleen, thus furnishing Brady with the possibility of blackmailing Stahr. Stahr blackmails Brady in his turn, argues with Wylie, and his affair with Kathleen becomes instrumental in his ruin. In the eighth chapter,[21] Brady was to resort to Kathleen's husband, an active union leader, who would seize the chance of suing Stahr. According to Fitzgerald's first conception, he was to murder the producer; in either case, Stahr was to be saved by Peter Zavras, the cameraman whom he himself had saved at the beginning of the story. Under the pressure of all these tensions, however, Stahr is on the verge of collapse. Suspecting that Brady wants to murder him he resorts to Brady's own means and hires gangsters to kill Brady. The murder is to be accomplished while Stahr is flying to New York. On the flight he is disgusted with himself for having stooped to Brady's methods and determines to stop the gangsters as soon as the plane lands. But the plane crashes and Brady is murdered.[22] Stahr's funeral, an orgy of servility and hypocrisy, was to have ended the book with a bitter and ironic touch: a cast-off actor, invited by mistake to be one of the pallbearers, is immediately reinstated. The future of the movie industry was to be foreshadowed in the grim figure of Fleishacker, the unscrupulous and opportunistic company lawyer. Finally, having separated from her husband, Kathleen comes back to gaze from the outside on the studios in which she has never set foot, while Cecilia, overwhelmed by the events, has a nervous breakdown after she has given herself for spite to a man she does not love (Wylie or Fleishacker); she relates the story from the hospital where she has been confined.

It is clear enough that in the unfinished novel we are confronted with only part of this story. As Edmund Wilson has warned, "This draft of *The Last Tycoon* . . . represents that point in the artist's work where he has assembled and organized his material and acquired a firm grasp of the theme, but has not yet brought it finally into focus." [23] This warning should be constantly borne in mind. Nevertheless, the part that was written, the many indications as to its conclusion, and the notes that Fitzgerald left allow us to define the nature and the significance of the unfinished book.

In a certain way *Tender Is the Night* could also be interpreted as a novel dealing with the tragedy of the creative artist. Dick Diver could be seen as an intellectual, whose main motivation has much in common with the creative motivations of a scientist or, by extension, of an artist. He creates or recreates an organism which is dependent on him (Nicole) and succeeds in giving life and consistency to what did not exist and was shapeless before his intervention. His problem and his tragedy would then become identified with those of any other creator who, when his work is completed, finds that he has exhausted all his energy for its benefit and is therefore depleted, defeated, and overcome by his own creation.[24] James's fiction abounds in similar representations, not only in obvious examples such as "The Figure in the Carpet," "The Lesson of the Master," and "The Middle Years," but also in works less openly focused on the theme of the artist. In his "major" works, characters like Lambert Strether, Milly Theale, or Maggie Verver are represented as obsessed by the need of imposing an order on their emotions, experiences, and behaviors, while in *The Sacred Fount* the role of the artist is explored in his extreme commitment to the task of reordering the world. In most of James's works, as R. P. Blackmur has remarked, "The fate of the artist is somehow the test of society," [25] and the same definition might apply to *Tender Is the Night*, if we bear in mind that Dick's defeat implied a more general surrender of the idealistic and creative impulse to the organized forces of a hostile society.

In *Tender Is the Night,* although implicit rather than explicit, there seems to be a clear thematic and stylistic derivation from James; in *The Last Tycoon* it would be difficult to find a precise link with James. Yet, in this novel, Fitzgerald offered a particular treatment of the theme of the artist which has a typically Jamesian flavor in its general outline. Stahr is, of course, a "limited" type of artist, but he also finds the test of society hostile to his attempts and is snared by the social context into an inglorious defeat. In *The Last Tycoon,* moreover, the protagonist meets his ruin both on the psychological and emotional level of his *épuisement,* and on the social level of a conflict of interests; and this is a clear link with *Tender Is the Night,* where the defeat of the "artist" had been dealt with precisely on those two levels.

Writing of *The Last Tycoon,* Fitzgerald had made a point of noting the differences between his new novel and the preceding one: "Unlike *Tender Is the Night,* this novel is not a story of deterioration— it is neither depressing nor morbid, in spite of the tragic ending." [26] He was partly right, of course, because the new novel avoided the canons of the "philosophical novel" and aimed at a "compression" in many ways similar to the compression of *The Great Gatsby.* But art, like nature, does not take jumps, and Fitzgerald remained faithful to the "ideal line" of *Gatsby* without denying the experience of *Tender Is the Night,* even if he was bound to surpass both experiences in a new form of achievement. It is from the point of view of continuity of motives (if no longer of techniques) that we are best able to appreciate the purport of *The Last Tycoon.* The mechanics of the situation are quite familiar, although his new story was developed in a rather different way.

That Monroe Stahr is basically an artist is made clear in various places in the book and in the notes. He lives and works in Hollywood because it is an empire that he has created, not because he wants to make money, as Brady does. All his energies are directed to raising the movie industry to an artistic level, and the passion and competence with which he works qualify him for the role of leader. He gives *unity* to the movies that he produces, "he takes the gloom out of a picture and gives it style" (as we find written in a note). He is able to direct the energies of his script writers and to sustain them in the effort until he gets the best out of them. He has a gift of seeing "below the surface into reality"; after him, the movie industry will gradually decline. Lastly, as we have noted, he is not afraid of sustaining a quality production even if it will lose money—and all these details contribute to qualify the artistic role that Stahr is at least potentially supposed to play in the novel. As an artist he has the typical awareness of his limitations, and his character is made credible and mature since, like Gatsby, his greatness is only partial and he carries within himself the germ of destruction.

Like Gatsby, who did not cut the pages of the books in his library, Stahr has no time to read, and his culture is superficial. He reads synopses—whether of the Bible or of the *Communist Manifesto*—and he values literature from a utilitarian point of view. His potential artistic nature finds an outlet in his efficient organization, and bows to the slightly presumptuous ideal of the tycoon. The practical results, to be obtained at any price, make any means legitimate in the end, and in consequence the creative impulse becomes an exaggerated form of paternalistic individualism. Egotistical and self-centered, Stahr carries all his qualities to an excess. With his domineering character, he tends to become a despot; an enlightened tyrant, he mistakes himself for an oracle. An efficient leader, he ends by relying only on his own strength and ideas; he underrates his enemies and does not grasp the natural evolution of the times. He has good cause to stand up against Brady, but he shows as much hostility to the writers' union. On the human level he can be generous and altruistic to Zavras, but he is so enraged with Brimmer that he has to resort to physical violence, and as we have seen, he stoops to Brady's methods when he feels threatened.

Great in a partial way, a character who cannot "give himself entirely" to others (not even to Kathleen) ends by compromising the greatness of his efforts. "Note also in the epilogue that I want to show that Stahr left certain harm behind him just as he left good behind him," Fitzgerald had remarked. And it is this undoubted negative touch that makes the defeat of Stahr less lamentable, though more "realistic" in the ordinary sense, almost more existential, than the defeat of Dick. Stahr's defeat is made more concrete in a specifically social frame of reference, and his struggle is more virile than Dick's. He is "more of a men's man than a ladies' man"; he likes combat ("he was Napoleonic and actually liked combat"), even if he is described by Zavras as the Aeschylus and the Euripides of the movie world. Stahr has enough in his life to struggle against; but his struggle is only partly legitimate or justifiable, and it is disproportionate to his forces. In this way, Stahr is a victim of Brady's ruthlessness, but also of the just opposition of the unions, and of his own weaknesses, disguised under an exaggeration of his own strength. He is above all victim of himself and of his own "artistic" creation. "Stahr didn't die of overwork—he died of a certain number of forces allied against him," Fitzgerald had stated. His overwork is a result, more than a cause, of his unbalance; yet, among Stahr's worst enemies, is the less noble aspect of his character, and the external forces allied against him find an easy access into his home front—the weakened home front of his inner contradictions, of his unhappy and irregular love affair, of his waning strength.

Brady is the natural opponent of Stahr—the typical, mean merchant, interested only in making money, whose motivations are dictated by "Wall Street" ethics. Stahr's friend as long as Stahr is "productive," Brady begins to turn against him when he realizes the artistic and idealistic sides of his character, and his opposition becomes greater when he discovers that Stahr is honest and considerate to his workers. Brady neither respects Stahr nor understands his enlightened motives. On the other hand, the union leaders do respect Stahr's efficiency and understand, perhaps, his fair play and his sense of responsibility to his men. But they are bound to oppose his methods and his despotic individualism, while Stahr opposes the union not so much out of personal interest as out of principle, fearing in a way that in a Hollywood where the social structure is changed his preeminence would no longer be possible. He cannot ally himself with Brady, nor compromise with the union, and as a result he is torn between these two forces when they join to attack him on his vulnerable home front.

Stahr has already been defeated in this respect, owing to his contradictions. As Rosemary was for Dick Diver, Kathleen might represent a way out for Stahr, or at least an anchor for him in his loneliness; she might still bring order and affection into his existence.[27] It is for her that Stahr does not work on Sunday for the first time, that he breaks the iron rules of his long working hours. With Kathleen he might start a new life. But confronted with the possibility of a normal life, it is Stahr himself who withdraws: Kathleen is a modest woman, a bit too old perhaps for him, and she lacks "grandeur." To have her for himself, Stahr should ask her not to marry, take her from another, submit somehow to a compromise. And not knowing how to stoop to conquer, he lets her marry another, forfeiting all his chances of renewal. Kathleen attracts him because she does *not* belong to the movie world; yet for this very reason Stahr is unable to accept her completely. When he resumes the affair after she has married, everything is compromised, and he is bound to end up in *épuisement* and consequent ruin. When Brady learns of the affair and goes to the union leader, Stahr's home front, already weakened, collapses. The outer conflicts find the softened ground of an inner conflict to work on; as in *Tender Is the Night* the objective tensions break the resistance of a protagonist already weakened by his inner tensions.

Dick Diver had made his dangerous choice and had succumbed to it, betraying his real mission. There is no *trahison des clercs* in Stahr, who fights his battle to the bitter end in *his* world and with his own weapons, as long as he has any. When he has no more, he capitulates, but his spear has not been "blunted" and his capacities have not been "locked up" by a hostile social class as in Dick's case. He has been defeated in an open struggle which leaves him no escape. He has not moved from one milieu to another or from one profession to another: he has stayed in *his* world, and the poison has grown as it were in his hands, when the creature to which he has given life revolts against him. Dick was responsible for his initial choice; Stahr is guilty for the way in which he reacts to a situation and to a world where he is at home and which he should know better. There is actually no other choice for him, and therefore his end is less melancholy than Dick's, but perhaps more painful and inevitable. The whimper of Dick becomes here—not only in a metaphorical sense— the bang of a man who strikes against the reality of his own natural surroundings.

This realistic frame of reference is made more concrete and visible in *The Last Tycoon* than in *Tender Is the Night*. In the earlier novel, the psychological and social conflict was basically between two moral attitudes and two universal aspects of human nature—between the idealism of Dick and the corruption of the bourgeoisie. Here the social and moral conflict is rooted in a local framework of contrasting attitudes and activities which are typical of a precise and well-known social milieu. Hollywood is an equivocal milieu, where the artistic impulse is blighted and frustrated by an industrial organization. In that milieu the artist—any kind of artist—has to face a dilemma every day, and the tragic potentialities are inherent in its nature. Stahr sets them in motion, and his story, while perfectly in keeping with the milieu, is an illustration of its intrinsic nature. The novel, as Fitzgerald had warned, was not to be *about* Hollywood; [28] and yet Hollywood is indispensable in the whole design, and it becomes an overwhelming presence, like the sea in *Moby Dick*. Hollywood is the *sine qua non* condition for the book to develop along its lines, and it is in the book not for documentary but for purely artistic purposes of consistency and effectiveness. Without that framework the novel would not be possible. Fitzgerald gave a picture of that world in all its minutest details, in its mechanics and in its essence, representing it, moreover, in a particular period of its development—the social crisis of 1935, when the writers' union was in fact constituted. It was a particular moment in which the consequences of the depression were still badly felt, and it is significant that Stahr's defeat was to have had all these social as well as economical connotations in its unfolding.

At this point the novel begins to draw away noticeably from *Tender Is the Night* and *The Great Gatsby*. Fitzgerald's use of Hollywood as a setting is proof of his mature seriousness and of his unsuspected capacity for a realistic rendering. For the first time Fitzgerald chose to represent a business world, which he then defined in all its functions and represented with a rigorous adherence to its secret motivations. The field of action is no longer that of the expatriates, of the college students, or of the outsiders like Gatsby, but rather of people who work for a living, who build and produce and create. Quite rightly, in the third and fourth chapters, Stahr is represented, in every sense of the word, at work. The characters are no longer romantic projections of the author, adolescents or flappers; they are people caught and revealed in the sphere of adult and responsible action. Parties, so important in *Gatsby* and in *Tender Is the Night*, are here only marginal and of small importance; there is only one, at the beginning of Chapter V, and it does not counterbalance the long hours that Stahr spends in his office, in the projection rooms, on the sets.

Thus, Fitzgerald seems really to have confronted an experience which imposed on him the task of a realistic and objective rendering. The love scenes themselves, which were at first surrounded by a dreamy halo of idyllic sentimentalism, are finally represented in a direct, immediate, and dynamic way. Fitzgerald responded to the exacting requirements of his subject matter by adopting a bare, unadorned style, perfectly in keeping with the crude reality it had to express. One might speak of dramatic realism, although not in the sense that the term realism is applied, let us say, to the works of W. D. Howells or J. T. Farrell. Its connotations are much more complex here.

Like Melville, Fitzgerald seized upon a well-defined framework of reality and immediately distorted it with the urgency of his imagination, colored it with nightmarish hues and shades, violated its surface, and corrugated it to make it a vehicle for larger meanings. Melville built on his realism the myth of the chase of the white whale; on a lower level, Fitzgerald extracted from his glimpses of reality a more human legend, strengthening the sinews of his narrative with concretions and distortions of a clearly symbolic nature. One might even speak of expressionism, but it would be better to say that Fitzgerald followed the traditional pattern of American fiction, which finds in the balanced fusion of realism and symbolism the typical mark of its identity.[29] Nothing that serves to characterize the Hollywood milieu and the figure of Stahr is neglected in *The Last Tycoon*. In this manner, we are given a representation of life and even a *tranche de vie*. The symbolic method, however, comes in to modify and distort the picture, enlarging and enhancing its representational significance. The initial flight from East to West is clearly symbolical—both of Stahr's leadership and of his final descent "into the warm darkness." The emergency landing shows that Stahr will have to face a more painful descent: like Alice in the rabbit hole, Stahr will sink into the ambiguities of his soul and see the Gorgon-like reflection of human experience. Isolated in the bridal suite or in the pilot's cabin, he will also be isolated in his life. Schwartz and Wylie—Cecilia herself—find that the gates of the Hermitage are closed, and Stahr will wander in a deserted Washington. The story is set in motion by the gushing forth of volcanic water: the earthquake and the flood, as the author says, set Stahr in front of his destiny and they "seem to release something in him." The unfinished seaside house recalls the movie set ("odd effect of the place like a set," we find in the notes), and it is clearly an indication of Stahr's unstable equilibrium. It is impossible for him to hear the President in that house—he can only hear the grotesque gibberish of a monkey. Against the idyllic background of the beach at night, the Negro who is waiting for the grunion and is in communion with nature refuses to give credit to the tycoon's activities. "The dam breaks" in the sixth chapter, and the beginning of the downfall is subtly represented by the symbolic battle with pingpong balls, among which Stahr ironically falls in the end. The detail seems ordinary and banal, but the turning point of the action revolves around this objective correlative of Stahr's final collapse.

The action was to end with the fatal return of the plane to New

York, interrupted before its arrival there. The thematic correspondence with the beginning is evident, and it is just as clear that Fitzgerald wanted to convey the idea that Stahr was surrendering himself to the world of the East. In fact, if we bear in mind all these details, it becomes clear that in *The Last Tycoon*, as in *Gatsby*, the symbolic conflict is once more between the two moral and geographical poles of East and West. Brady, Stahr's antagonist, is basically linked with the world of the East, with the world of money and ruthless business, the world of Wall Street and competitive acquisition, of brutal and corrupt force. Stahr, on the other hand, tries to give life to his creation—which permits at times the flowering of art, humanity, and idealism—in the West. In this case, the West is not ruined by its contact with the East, but the East pushes its tentacles toward and into the West, cracking and corrupting it from the inside. Stahr ends by accepting it as a component of his world and of his life. If he is thrilled by the lights of Los Angeles when he flies back to Hollywood at the beginning, he will find the Eastern corruption flourishing there, and he will have to surrender to its overwhelming pressure. Between East and West—in Nashville, Tennessee, or Washington, D.C.—are the traditional and genuine virtues of the country. But here the doors are closed; there is no communion with the men and women who have been tainted by the Eastern corruption.

Within this symbolical frame of reference, the "artist" finds that his own creation has turned against him and that the "test" of society has forced him to a moral compromise and eventually to defeat. It has brought to the surface the less noble aspects of his characters and has directed its attack against the tycoon in a subtle way—by making him instrumental in his own ruin. The "merchant" wins an easy battle, and Wall Street denies the potential flowering of a civilization that might have stood against its commercial predominance. And all this Fitzgerald recorded with an "unshakable moral attitude towards the world we live in and towards its temporary standards, that is the basic essential of any powerful work of the imagination," if we want to use again the words of John Dos Passos.[30] There is perhaps some exaggeration in this statement, but it really seems that here Fitzgerald was attaining that "wise and tragic sense of life" which he proclaimed to be the ultimate achievement of the writer. Henry James had stressed "the perfect dependence of the 'moral' sense of a work of art on the amount of felt life concerned in producing it." In *The Last Tycoon* the amount of felt life concerned in producing the novel is such that its aesthetic significance coincides with the apprehension of a specific "moral" sense. It is an advance over *Tender Is the Night* and *The Great Gatsby* as well, and all the more so as the extensive analysis gives way here to a rapid and vivid foreshortening, and the elegiac tone of the "tragic pastoral" is substituted by an intense urgency of feeling and emotion. The style of this novel vibrates with immediate intensity, is compressed and, as it were, contracted, so that the magic suggestiveness of *Gatsby* and the analytic fullness of *Tender Is the Night* are left along the way. Although starting from the same thematic awareness of the two previous novels, *The Last Tycoon* aims at a typical form of modern essentiality both in its technique and in its diction.

3

In its structure, *The Last Tycoon* is basically in line with *The Great Gatsby*, but in its texture (if we want to adopt John Crowe Ransom's distinction) it is considerably different. Fitzgerald stated that "if one book could ever be 'like' another, I should say that it [*The Last Tycoon*] is more 'like' *The Great Gatsby* than any other of my books," and he had stressed the fact that his new novel was "as detached from *him* as *Gatsby* was, in intent, anyhow." But he also wrote to Edmund Wilson that he had written it with great difficulty and that it was "completely upstream in mood." [31] These statements are a good starting point to determine to what extent *The Last Tycoon* is both similar to and different from the earlier novel.

The detachment of vision is achieved through the use of a narrator. But Cecilia is more involved in the action than Nick Carraway, and she is even responsible for the turning point of the story—when she tells her father of Stahr's secret affair with Kathleen. Of course, Cecilia's main role is to give the story a center of interest, in the Jamesian sense, and a unity of structure. As in the case of *The Great Gatsby*, the "greatness" of the protagonist is emphasized here by the sympathy and the love of the narrator, and it is thanks to her emotional reactions that Stahr attains an almost fabulous dimension as a character. Cecilia writes down with impartiality (and therefore with some kind of objectivity) the main events of the story, but she also colors them with the warmth of her intense participation, going so far as to interpret the facts and to convey to the reader their moral significance. Moreover, with her gift of imagining the events at which she has not been present, she can register those details that are meaningful and symbolic in the story and emphasize in this way the symbolic aspect of her realistic tale. "By making . . . Cecilia an intelligent and observant woman"—Fitzgerald had written—"I shall grant myself the privilege, as Conrad did, of letting her imagine the actions of the characters. Thus, I hope to get the verisimilitude of the first person narrative, combined with a Godlike knowledge of all events that happen to my characters." This compromise, far from breaking the unity of the limited point of view, allows the "omniscient" narrator to give a personal and subjective twist to the story. Cecilia can record the events at which she has not been present with the objectivity of a reporter (especially in Chapters III, IV, and V), but when she takes part in the action (notably in Chapters I, II, and in some episodes of Chapters V and VI) her report becomes less documentary; it is full of passion and participation and vibrates with undisguised emotion. Thus, Cecilia introduces us to Stahr and reveals the baseness of her father, and it is quite natural that she should bring Brimmer and Stahr together in their confrontation. But when she is not in the foreground, she gives a chronicle of Stahr's working day with dramatic precision and absolute detachment, and this fictional device of her alternating absence and presence makes it possible for the book to shift from a purely realistic notation of the events to an intensely emotional presentation of the story.

With her good *ficelles* (a device clearly derived from James), Cecilia, like Nick in *Gatsby*, breaks down the action into dramatic scenes, and if she gathers information from Wylie, Robinson, and Prince Agge, she knows very well when and where to introduce it. But it is at this point that the method used in *Gatsby* becomes "upstream in mood," more and more distorted in order to emphasize the symbolic possibilities. Having learned a lesson from the negative example of a certain heaviness in *Tender Is the Night,* where the predominance of the analytic method had compromised the natural development of the action and excluded the necessary relief of the dialogues, in *The Last Tycoon* Fitzgerald had decided to resolve the characterization *exclusively* in the action and to stress the *essential* nucleus of each incident, to the extent of depending almost completely on the dramatic intensity of the dialogues. In his notes there are clear indications of the method that he proposed to follow, and this method is adopted in the parts of the novel that he was able to write. "This chapter must not develop into merely a piece of character analysis. Each statement that I make about him [Stahr] must contain at the end of every few hundred words some pointed anecdote or story to keep it alive . . . I want it to have . . . drama throughout." [32] In characterizing Stahr he followed this method precisely, and to characterize Brady and Brimmer he used two highly dramatic incidents: Cecilia's discovery of her father with the nude secretary in the closet, and Brimmer's fight with Stahr. Kathleen is gradually developed as a character through her successive meetings with the tycoon, and only through their dialogues do we catch a glimpse of Wylie's and Robinson's characters. The action never slows down or stops to allow a reconsideration of the events, as in *Gatsby*. And if we want to resort once more to James's concept of the relationship between character and incident, we should say that here every possible consideration is given to the incident and that the character is subservient to it in the highest degree. In *The Great Gatsby* these two theoretical terms of reference had been balanced in the rendering; here the scales are weighed in favor of the dramatic incident, which, furthermore, is represented only in its intense *final* moment and is compressed by an extreme form of foreshortening.

The reader finds himself confronted with an incident when it is usually turning to its conclusion, and he must go back from that point to the antecedents of the situation, reconstruct its premises, imagine its slow preparation and its gradual development. The author gives the impression that he has no time or willingness to give us the facts in their unfolding, that he is too pressed by the urgency of the events, and that he can only give us the conclusion, the significant result of the facts. He seems to compress the full purport of any incident into the last few acts or words of the characters. In contrast to *The Great Gatsby*, it is not the connotative suggestion that indicates the meaning of each single moment of the story, but rather a violent illumination at the very end of each significant moment that sends us back to reconsider the possible purport of the episode. The narration moves in a rapid and impetuous way, with the bouncing momentum of a cataract, not with the full ease of an abundant stream or the precision of a narrow brook. At each bounce, one might say, the previous stretch is gathered in a single knot of meaningful suggestions, which must be unraveled backward at great speed so as to be prepared for the next. This is why the story is really upstream in mood and in movement. Each dramatic incident, at the very moment when it has given a new turn to the action, must be explained and as it were completed by a consideration of what has made it possible, of what has determined it, of what has in fact prepared it.

The ideal of essentiality, that is, is pursued in two ways. *The Last Tycoon* contains only those episodes which are strictly functional to a consequent development of the plot, have a definite thematic meaning, and give impulse to the action; in the compass of the single episodes only the culminating moment is represented in a dramatic way, to the exclusion of both the beginning and the outcome. For this double reason (and the role of Cecilia is of only secondary importance here) the story is really reduced to its essentials and moves with sudden leaps and daring elliptical transitions, without any continuity in the narrative pattern. The action proceeds from one intense nucleus to another, from one meaningful point to another, and these points are really flashes of intuition which throw light only on the essential part of each incident until the subject matter is reduced to its barest essence. The action develops at a speedy and breathless pace: the plane stops in Nashville and is soon off again, and there has already been a suicide; in Hollywood there is an earthquake. Stahr rushes from one activity to another without intermission. When he finally meets Kathleen "he remains breathless," and after four convulsive trips to and from the beach there is the sudden blow of Kathleen's marriage, and immediately after the fight with Brimmer. . . . The staccato (no longer the fading away) is almost compulsory here, and the same technical principle of an extreme form of staccato operates within the economy of the single scenes.

One single example should be sufficient to illustrate the point. When he put down some notes for the episode of the airplane crash, Fitzgerald made it clear that the episode should be as much as possible represented in a foreshortened and compressed way. "Consider carefully"—he had written—"whether if possible by some technical trick it might not be advisable to conceal from the reader that the plane fell until the moment when the children find it . . . the dramatic effect . . . might be more effective if he did not find at the beginning of the chapter that the plane fell." Far from "describing the fall of the plane," he wanted to hint at this crucial point only in a passing paragraph which was to be as "evasive" as possible, in order to move on immediately to the effect of the crash, to its consequences—that is to say to the situation of the three children who pick up the "moral heritage" of the people killed in the crash. If the whole passage is analyzed, it will become clear that we are confronted with the extreme development of a fictional technique which aims at the maximum degree of dramatic concision, even to the point of neglecting the gradual unfolding of the episodes. These episodes are not described or represented in the usual sense of the word—they are compressed in sudden and unexpected flashes which compel the reader to move backward in order to understand the "upstream mood" of the narration.

Most, if not all, of the episodes in the book are dealt with in the same manner, and the book as a whole is constructed on the same principle, since Stahr is presented only at the crucial point of his long career. Kathleen makes up her story through a disconnected series of hints and suggestions, Brady is characterized in a single incident, and the other characters appear only to point out the significant changes of the story. Cecilia herself is present only at crucial points. A particular kind of foreshortening and a restricted angle of vision allow the writer to illuminate with flashes only a few dramatic scenes, which consequently acquire an unforgettable relief and cannot be dealt with in a descriptive way. There are no shades or hues of color in the canvas—only a heightened quality of chiaroscuro and a hallucinatory reflection of violent flashes of light. This is the exact contrary of a "rounded-off" narration, and the foreshortening is here much more drastic than it was in Gatsby. In that novel the dramatic scenes were suspended at times to allow for reconsiderations or elegiac intermissions. Here everything is dramatic—the general framework,[33] the single scenes, and whatever portions of the single scenes Fitzgerald chose to represent in his urgency to get at the core of each significant moment. Such is the concision and the essentiality of the actions which *are* represented, that the diction itself is influenced by this urgency to the extent of being reduced to the bareness of an outline of a film script.

After all, we are in the world and in the atmosphere of the movies. Though the incompleteness of the novel might partly account for a certain rapidity of statement and the quick transitions from one episode to another,[34] we must still recognize the mark of inner development in the use of this highly concise form of diction. The language is here constantly breaking into dialogue, and if we bear in mind that a similar phenomenon was recognizable in Fitzgerald's latest stories, it becomes clear that we are confronted with a real stylistic development. If the structure of the novel is reduced to essentials, so is the texture; and this is a new departure, unfortunately broken off at its inception, in Fitzgerald's fiction. If the single scenes or incidents are not represented in their gradual unfolding, but rather compressed into significant moments and sudden flashes, in the same way the sentences are compressed and reduced to simple statements. They follow one another in quick succession and find their natural measure in the broken rhythm of the dialogue. In *The Last Tycoon* the language seems to avoid any syntactical subordination and is entirely dependent for its effectiveness on the simplicity of the direct statement, which is immediately ended by a period. Adjectives and adverbs are seldom used in a context of isolated and barren enunciations, whose main purport is conveyed to the reader by the kinetic force of the verbs. "About *adjectives:* all fine prose is based on the verbs carrying the sentences. They make sentences move," Fitzgerald had written, taking his cue from a line of Keats.[35] And in *The Last Tycoon* he adhered to this principle and to this ideal, because he wanted his sentences to move as quickly as possible and to be carried forward at a quickened pace by the urgency of the verbs. In this way, too, he developed a staccato form of diction, a clear-cut simplicity of sentences, avoiding the harmonious fullness of the paragraph or the soft musicality of the evocation.

Converging into the mainstream of twentieth-century literature, like Eliot and Pound, Sherwood Anderson and Hemingway, Montale and Valéry, to name only a few, Fitzgerald found and asserted in his desire for a bare language the sense of his modernity. Like Yeats and Juan Ramon Jiménez he came to realize that "there's more enterprise / In walking naked," in renouncing the ideal of an adorned style and accepting the bare facts of what Jiménez had called *"poesía nuda."* In his own field and in his own way, he had eventually achieved this ideal: the language that he perfected in *The Last Tycoon* justifies a reconsideration of Fitzgerald on the level of twentieth-century adherence to the common yearning of poetry and fiction toward the concrete, the concise, and the essential. It is sufficient to give a single example, chosen from a number of passages that would equally bear out the point, because it deals with the subject—a love embrace—on which the author had previously exercised his skill in a different way. Stahr and Kathleen have gone back for the second time to the house on the beach:

> Immediately she spoke to him coarsely and provocatively, and pulled his face down to hers. Then, with her knees she struggled out of something, still standing up and holding him with one arm, and kicked it off beside the coat. He was not trembling now and he held her again, as they knelt down together and slid to the raincoat on the floor. (*LT,* p. 87.)

The urgency of their emotions transfers itself to the action and is reflected in the broken movement of the sentences. Everything in this passage seems to be in motion and the sense of movement is emphasized by Fitzgerald's insistence on the verbs (... *spoke ... pulled ... struggled ... holding ... kicked ... trembling ... held ... knelt ... slid ...*). There are a few nouns in the context (five in all) and no adjectives to slow down or qualify the kinetic rhythm; there are three adverbs which define not the situation but the action (*immediately ... coarsely ... provocatively*) and the personal pronouns (which in English are actually *part* of the verb in the sense that they absorb the function of the lost terminations, but would not be necessary in some other languages). For the rest, the passage is completely dependent on the urge of the verbs, most of which are renderd still more effective and urgent by the prepositions or verbal adverbs that follow (*to him ... down to hers ... out of something ... standing up ... kicked it off ... knelt down ... to the floor*). In this case Fitzgerald was really able to express "the stress and passion at the core of each convincing moment" with the utmost bareness of language and diction. If there is poetry in this scene, in which Fitzgerald gave us for the first time a dramatic presentation of physical love, it is poetry achieved and expressed through the immediacy of the simple statement. The same is true of other episodes, and in particular of the episode in which Stahr is hit by Brimmer:

> Then Stahr came close, his hands going up. It seemed to me that Brimmer held him off with his left arm a minute, and then I looked away—I couldn't bear to watch.
> When I looked back, Stahr was out of sight below the level of the table, and Brimmer was looking down at him.
> "Please go home," I said to Brimmer.
> "All right." He stood looking down at Stahr as I came around the table.
> "I always wanted to hit ten million dollars, but I didn't know it would be like this."
> Stahr lay motionless.
> "Please go," I said.
> "I'm sorry. Can I help—"
> "No. Please go. I understand." (*LT*, p. 127.)

The "stress and passion" of this episode are expressed in a series of brief notations of heightened intensity, with a bare and feverish language, elliptical in the extreme, that aims at conveying the effect of the action, not at describing it. The few notations are sufficient to give the sense of what has happened even if Cecilia "cannot bear to watch"; the effectiveness of this kind of language, to express it in linguistic terms, is dependent on the prevalence of the morphemes—the words that express relationships, the verbs of action, the dialogue reduced to stichomythia—over the other linguistic functions.

One is tempted to see here a direct influence of Hemingway's style, and a certain similarity of manner is unquestionable. In an independent way, according to his own sensitivities, Fitzgerald recreated certain stylistic features typical of Hemingway's style: the hardness and precision of diction, the taste for the essential and the concrete, the predominance of the dialogue, the directness of statement, a refinement of language disguised as simplicity. One is reminded here of "Up in Michigan," among the *First Forty-Nine Stories,* or of the dialogue in *The Sun Also Rises* or, better still, of *To Have and Have Not* (1937), a novel that Fitzgerald seemed particularly to admire.[36] In this novel Hemingway's imagination had been engaged in the realistic rendering of a situation that presupposed a definite framework of social and economic relationships. The story was concerned with the struggle of an individualist against the "organized worlds" of the leisure class and the gangsters, and his inevitable defeat had been represented in a rapid sequence of dramatic scenes, according to the principle of a violent compression (and even distortion) of foreshortened episodes. Even there the language, clear-cut and concise, elliptical and allusive, was based essentially on the verbs of action and reduced to the measure of the direct statement. Hemingway, of course, had something else in mind and was "tougher" than Fitzgerald would ever become in his general outlook on life and in his style, both of which if closely analyzed, reveal profound differences from Fitzgerald's. For our purposes it is sufficient to mention a momentary convergence, to indicate how Fitzgerald was nearing, if not actually meeting, a form of diction which might have had much in common with Hemingway's. It would be an idle speculation to carry the investigation too far, but even this assumption can give us an idea of the direction in which Fitzgerald seemed to be naturally evolving. The ultimate result might have been, quite logically, a kind of conscious expressionism: the potentialities are evident in *The Last Tycoon.*

While remaining true to himself, to his inner motives, and to his fictional "tradition," Fitzgerald was able to start (if not to accomplish, owing to his early death) a clear revolution in his narrative. He left us with a premature and unexpected gift of his rising artistic vitality. When it was published, *The Last Tycoon* was hailed as a little miracle. It was in fact an achievement and a personal conquest, linked with the past experiences of the author and yet open to new forms of artistic development. It finds its place next to *The Great Gatsby* and *Tender Is the Night* for the maturity of its conception and the intensity of its form. Together with *The Crack-up* and the last stories, these three novels must be seen as his lasting contribution to twentieth-century fiction. In the convulsed pages of *The Last Tycoon* there is a single, bizarre poetic quotation, taken from Gautier's *Emaux et camées*. We are no longer confronted with the "mysterious" (and in fact quite familiar) Thomas Parke D'Invilliers, or with the bitter irony of Anthony Patch, or with a recognizable allusion to Keats. We are confronted with a clear statement of the ideal that had inspired both Pound and Eliot—the ideal of a hard and "robust" type of artistic achievement:

> *Tout passe.—L'art robuste*
> *Seul a l'éternité.*

Fitzgerald's fiction seems in retrospect to be much more robust than we were (or still are) inclined to believe. Life is short—as James had complained with Chaucer and Horace—and Art is long; and it is always risky to speak of "eternity." In a world of relative values, however, only a lack of love or a deeply rooted prejudice can regard as of secondary value an artistic achievement that possesses all the marks of genuine identity and that can remain so fruitful for so long.

CHAPTER IX

The Wider Context: Fitzgerald and American Fiction

From a little distance one can perceive an order in what at the time seemed confusion.

CU, p. 233.

1

It was only in the early Fifties that critical reconsideration transformed the Fitzgerald "legend" into a literary reputation. The assessments made during those years revised many previously held critical positions.

In the Twenties, following the great success of his first novel, Fitzgerald had appealed to the public more for the charm of his personality and his alleged role of spokesman for a generation than for his artistic achievement. Praised as the creator of a disenchanted, but at the same time sentimental, attitude toward experience he was overwhelmingly present in the public's mind and in the gossip columns, but at the expense of seeing his work misunderstood or obscured by his personal legend.[1] In the Thirties, the fallacious reasons for which he had been admired in the previous decade offered the pretext for an almost general condemnation. What had at first appeared as representative of an age was overturned by the failure and collapse of that age, and for a good span of time the writer appeared as a lonely survivor from a period that had wrecked American society with its irresponsible attitude. Relegated into the background by a wave of puritanical prudery and socialist feelings,[2] Fitzgerald died a bitter and early death without completing the novel that was to redeem him in the eyes of the public. It was with the unfinished *The Last Tycoon* that a reevaluation of his fiction began in the Forties.[3] The publication of *The Crack-up* and the reprinting of

The Great Gatsby with a perceptive introduction by Lionel Trilling in 1945 officially reopened the "Fitzgerald case." An immediate proliferation of specialized critical essays concerning marginal aspects of his fiction [4] finally led to the pubication of Arthur Mizener's well-known critical biography, *The Far Side of Paradise,* followed in 1951 by a collection of critical essays edited by Alfred Kazin. These two books restated the "Fitzgerald case" in critical terms and led to some kind of comparative agreement as to the respective value and artistic quality of Fitzgerald's novels. Exactly at this point, however, the critic was confronted with the task or with the necessity of placing his fiction in the wider context of American fiction in the twentieth century. It was, and still is, a difficult task and an obvious necessity. If it is true, as T. S. Elliot maintains in a well-known passage, that

> no poet, no artist of any art, has his complete meaning alone. His significance, his appreciation is the appreciation of his relation to the dead poets and artists. You cannot value him alone; you must set him, for contrast and comparison, among the dead. I mean this as a principle of aesthetic, not merely historical, criticism,[5]

this problem is important not only for the position in which Fitzgerald can be eventually placed among his contemporaries, but also (if not mainly) for the literary "tradition" to which his fiction can be tied. In his volume *After the Lost Generation* (1951), John Aldridge placed Fitzgerald at the head of a tradition of rebel artists who had flourished in the uncertain years after World War II. In other words, Aldridge shared the commonplace opinion that Fitzgerald was the leader of a revolt against some kind of previous literary form, which had never been properly defined. Arthur Mizener tried to assess Fitzgerald's literary antecedents as early as 1950, but he limited himself to framing Fitzgerald's fiction within the context of the novel of manners. Distinguishing between two tendencies in the novel, one tending to a lyrical achievement and based on the author's own experiences (James Joyce, Virginia Woolf, Compton Mackenzie), the other tending to a documentary and collective representation of reality (Theodore Dreiser, James T. Farrell, H. G. Wells), Mizener saw in Fitzgerald's fiction a compromise between the two possibilities. Mizener's distinction was not very precise, and even as a working definition did not prove very revealing or fruitful, but it allowed him to stress Fitzgerald's superiority over Dos Passos and to link him with

Hemingway and Faulkner for the rounded quality of his artistic achievement. In another essay Mizener, stressing Fitzgerald's peculiar sense of the past, even felt entitled to link him with Marcel Proust. Both definitions were rather tentative; they were, however, a first step toward a critical definition of Fitzgerald's position in the context of American fiction.[6]

Maxwell Geismar, too, had stressed the link between Fitzgerald's fiction and the novel of manners and, in particular, the "well-made novel" as it had flourished in the nineteenth century. But Geismar was guilty of an arbitrary and artificial division of Fitzgerald's fiction into two contrasting blocks,[7] which ended by shattering every possibility of seeing in it a consistent development. In his sociological study *On Native Grounds* (1942) Alfred Kazin had relegated Fitzgerald to the awkward role of an obstinate playboy and a leader of the expatriates, a youngster *"venu trop tard dans un monde trop vieux pour lui,"* according to De Musset's terms. It is surprising to see that this same idea was developed by F. J. Hoffman, who in his ponderous and elaborate *The Twenties* chose *The Great Gatsby* as a textbook for a chapter dealing with "The Very Young." [8] These few examples indicate the early difficulties in arriving at a just evaluation, both aesthetic and historical, of the Fitzgerald case.

In 1957 James E. Miller, Jr. demonstrated in his valuable book *The Fictional Technique of Scott Fitzgerald* how much concern with form Fitzgerald had brought to the writing of his novels and proved, in addition, what precise technical links they revealed with the "saturated" fiction of H. G. Wells and his followers, and then with the highly "selective" fiction of Henry James and his disciples. The examination was restricted to the technical level and limited to a consideration of the first three novels, but it emphasized Fitzgerald's craftsmanship and indicated how his achievement might be strictly related to certain methods of composition which were—in the last analysis— of a Jamesian origin. This was a first, necessary step to a reconsideration of Fitzgerald's literary production in terms of a strictly literary criticism. On this basis—the following year—Wright Morris could venture to place Fitzgerald's fiction above Hemingway's, in an essay devoid of any polemical intention as well as of any biased exaggeration.[9]

By bringing Fitzgerald to the foreground among contemporary writers the way was opened for a reappraisal of his fiction in terms of the American literary tradition, and this is the main critical contribution of Marius Bewley in his *The Eccentric Design* (1958) and of Richard Chase in his *The American Novel and Its Tradition* (1958). In both books the substantially Jamesian derivation of Fitzgerald's fiction is properly emphasized.

Bewley had set out to examine the way in which the American artist had tried to face and to understand his own emotional and spiritual needs as an American artist, and in the case of Fitzgerald he came to the conclusion that he had been the first to be aware of the existence of a social class of Americans that was distinct from the old expatriate group of Henry James. As a result, Bewley saw in Fitzgerald's characters the representatives of a "solid and defined" social group and not, as had been claimed so often, the symbolic expression of American solitude or the two-dimensional types of a "morality." With the possible exception of Gatsby (important for his mythical link with Natty Bumppo and Huck Finn) the youngsters and the rich boys of Fitzgerald seemed to Bewley the only mature examples of treatment of a particular aspect of American society. As such, they seemed to him to be much superior to the "tough guys" of Hemingway for the degree of their human and social definition; and in this sense, again, Bewley saw in Fitzgerald the *last* genuine representative of the American literary tradition:

> I have ended my "tradition" of American novelists with Scott Fitzgerald simply because it seems to me to end with him. I believe Scott Fitzgerald *is* a great American writer, and fully deserves the company I put him in. He deals with "the new American experience" more critically than anyone in this tradition since Cooper, and at times it seems to me that he has a finer sense of the inherent tragedy in the American Experience than any of the others. The alcoholic haze in which he spent so much of his time has obscured for us how intelligent he really was in his best writing. If he had some of the characteristic weaknesses of his decade and his country, he knew them with a rare inwardness, and his writing is not a celebration of them but a judgment on them. His one great figure, Gatsby, is the only symbolic figure in American literature who descends to the depth of the American Dream and comes back to tell us it is a nightmare. (Marius Bewley, *The Eccentric Design*, pp. 290–91.)

The tradition in which Bewley placed Fitzgerald is that of the great novelists of the nineteenth century who had brought about the well-known flowering of the American Renaissance. On the other hand, Richard Chase saw the European or strictly English components of his fiction, which only stress the "typically American" representational qualities of his work. The complexity of the problem would logically demand a wider treatment, but this would fall outside the limits of the present study. We must limit ourselves to hints and suggestions, deal with simple indications and sketchy outlines.[10]

2

In *The American Novel and Its Tradition* Richard Chase saw the tradition of American fiction as characterized by the dialectical interweaving of two tendencies: one aiming at the luxuriant freedom of the romance, the other at the closely-knit structure of the novel. If the romance tends to be fantastic and symbolic, to depend on an unrestrained imaginative freedom and to become the vehicle for metaphysical inquiries, the novel is characterized by the careful observation and by the realistic representation of everyday life. It aims at the comedy of manners rather than at the tragedy of the mind; its frame of reference is limited by the common facts of ordinary reality. Cooper, Hawthorne, and Melville are on one side—Howells, James, and Twain on the other. This is, of course, a crude simplification, and Chase correctly remarked that in the second group of writers—just because they are *American* writers—there is also a strong component of romance: the same kind of "romantic" awareness that permeated even the works of the naturalistic writers from Hamlin Garland to Frank Norris and Theodore Dreiser. Richard Chase's fruitful conclusion was then that the inescapable presence of the element of romance becomes the distinctive trait of the literary tradition he was exploring.

All this is largely true. The novel is eminently European in its tradition, and one has only to think of Jane Austen to see this tradition in its purest form. This was the kind of tradition that F. R. Leavis had in mind when he wrote his influential study *The Great Tradition,* dealing with three "typically English" novelists (George Eliot, Henry James, and Joseph Conrad) who in fact were themselves far from "typically English." It is significant for our purposes, however, that James was regarded as part of that tradition and that Chase himself set out in his study from a discussion of Leavis' book. The novel presupposes a well-defined and stabilized society, and James had gone to Europe to find a crystalized society which was missing in

America. The novel is utterly dependent on the social contrasts, and it must be rooted in a world offering at least some temporary frame of reference, an intrinsic, even hierarchical, order. This same need for a social order had driven another great American expatriate, T. S. Eliot, to live in Europe; but such a need seems to be felt much more by the novelists, and in particular by the novelists of manners, who are by definition bound to depend on a stabilized system of manners and habits.

It is obvious that the romance is also present in Europe and that in America it could only have been derived from Europe. Walter Scott, the Brontë sisters, and the "gothic" writers are at the beginning of a tradition that had its best fruits in America, from Charles Brockden Brown to Hawthorne and Faulkner. And in America this form found its most genial home, continuing down to our times in the late followers of Faulkner, such as Truman Capote, among others.

The distinction between the two kinds of fiction is obviously also one of form. The romance is dependent on an expressive form tending toward the "lyrical" and the rhetorical, the symbolic and the imaginative; the novel tends to a closely knit structural form, controlled in its imagery and in its diction, organic and logical in its developments of plot, aware of the significant qualities of the technical devices. To use the terms with which we started, the romance is "saturated" while the novel is basically "selective." The romance develops in the twentieth century into the kind of fiction that Joseph Warren Beach called "expressionistic" and others "experimental" (James Joyce's *Ulysses,* the works of Gertrude Stein, J. B. Cabell, Dos Passos in his early stage, and Faulkner). The novel remains basically the same in its form, although now the personal quality of the rendering is stressed and its technical devices have been carried to their extreme possibilities by writers such as Joseph Conrad, F. M. Ford, E. M. Forster, Edith Wharton, and Willa Cather. The acknowledged master is always Henry James, and the putative father can be no other than Flaubert. The *mot juste,* the limited point of view and the well-made plot are still the basic tenets of these writers, and the quality of their achievement is typically "English," that is to say rounded-off and self-contained, organic and complete in itself—insular, in a word.

For James, the writer's experience was in his apprehension of what man does as a social being; the main task of the writer was to illustrate relationships and to fix the significant moments in the never-ending flux of life, so as to give a direct impression of life. To do so he needed a precise social context in which to work and from which to draw the subject matter of his illustration or impression. And by choosing to operate in a culturally conscious and difficult environment, he was able to resolve his innate "Americanism" into the wider context of the "international theme," in which he brought to bear both his European culture and his American subject matter. From a technical point of view he ended by rendering the novel the same service that Edgar Allan Poe had rendered to poetry—that is, he made it the conscious result of a rigorous application of ordering intelligence. At his death, in a period of dissatisfaction and uncertainty, the purport of his lesson seemed lost and obscured in the fury for innovation and experimentation. But gradually, in the Twenties and Thirties, a new awareness of James's role in the literary tradition of America was brought to bear in the field of fiction, and James's mark became recognizable in numerous separate endeavors and achievements.

Fitzgerald's fiction finds its place in a position which initially is half-way between the "experimental" writers and the traditional writers of the well-made novel, and then it becomes more and more identified with the latter. His beginnings, under the dominant influence of H. G. Wells and Theodore Dreiser, might have easily taken him another way, but a "conversion" to James through Conrad in *The Great Gatsby* marked the later phase of his fiction in an indisputably clear way. As soon as James's prefaces to his works had been collected and published in 1934, under the title *The Art of the Novel*, Fitzgerald had immediately bought the book, as a way, one might say, of identifying himself more and more with the followers of the traditional, well-made novel.

A few months before his death, in a letter to his daughter, he had stressed the superiority of the innovator and the inventor over the perfecting artist:

> You asked me whether I thought that in the Arts it was greater to originate a new form or to perfect it. The best answer is the one that Picasso made rather bitterly to Gertrude Stein:
>
> "You do something first and then somebody else comes along and does it pretty . . . ."
>
> In the opinion of any real artist, the inventor—which is to say Giotto or Leonardo—is infinitely superior to the finished

Tintoretto, and the original D. H. Lawrences are infinitely greater than the Steinbecks. (*CU*, pp. 293–94; *Letters*, pp. 72–73.)

The references are not really well chosen; and some time later Fitzgerald himself was to write to his daughter that "a good style simply doesn't *form* unless you absorb half a dozen top-flight authors every year." [11] This was in fact a more faithful description of his own method, and it should be clear by now that the type of superiority which pertains to the inventor does not belong to Fitzgerald as a fiction writer. He was working along lines already laid down, though obviously with his own voice, his own personal awareness, and with the possibly new discovery of a theme that Marius Bewley attributed to him. The traditional lines along which he was working link him on one side to the well-made, traditional novel which we have called "English" [12] in contraposition to Chase's "American novel," while on the other side they connect him with a thematic awareness which is typically American. Even in this sense he occupies a middle position, drawing his inspiration from a human and cultural context composite by nature and therefore so much the more modern. If it is not exactly true, as Maxwell Geismar said, that *The Great Gatsby* is "a perfectly *planned* novel . . . in the mathematical sense of a Bach concerto," it is true that Fitzgerald, in his open or latent controversy with Dos Passos, Wolfe, and "the Steinbecks," and in many of his letters, constantly stressed that "the necessity of the artist in every generation has been to give his work permanence by a safe shaping and a constant pruning." [13] This was actually the ideal of the traditional well-made novel transposed into the context of a typically twentieth-century formal awareness—and in this field Fitzgerald's achievement was outstanding and representative at the same time.

The desire for a "safe shaping and a constant pruning" is reflected in Fitzgerald's preoccupation to give order and consistency—consistency *through* order—to his elusive subject matter. Hemingway too had spoken of the "feeling for the house in order"; sought after and achieved with much more difficulty, this desire or feeling developed in Fitzgerald—as it had in James—into a particular type of comedy of manners which often reaches the depth of a tragedy of manners. In the finished product—in the novels or in the stories—his desire for order is an obvious premise and the only means of expression; on the other hand, the comedy of manners *as such* imposed upon him the need for order and fictional consistency. The two terms, if not interchangeable, are interdependent and complementary, and they were so naturally blended in Fitzgerald's fiction that the writer takes his place as the leader and the outstanding figure of this literary trend. He becomes the most important figure operating within that area in the twentieth century in America, and he can easily be regarded as James's best follower in this respect. He dealt with the novel of manners as a major literary form, bestowing on it the same artistic dignity and the same endless care that the Master had given it. It is sufficient to look at the other practitioners of the novel of manners in America after Henry James to see the outstanding quality of Fitzgerald's performance.

Edith Wharton had given a pleasant and pleasing picture of the decline of New York society at the turn of the century; Ann Douglas Sedgwick had repeated the theme of the contrast between Europe and America almost to the point of exhaustion; Willa Cather had used for her novels of manners the human drama of the Nebraska pioneers. Ellen Glasgow had found the material for most of her novels in the historical, human, and social problems of Virginia; Thornton Wilder, with all his subtlety of approach and texture, had remained a little on the outside, somewhat isolated by the sheer sharpness of his intellectual refinement. All these writers in one way or another and in various measure were faithful to the motives and methods of James; their main preoccupation was with form, structural problems of presentation, the harmony of design, and so on. All of them contributed to make up precisely that literary tradition of the novel of manners, the main origin and characteristic of which we have described as "English" in contradistinction to Chase's "American tradition." [14]

Fitzgerald can be seen as a representative of this group also, and he undoubtedly shared most of their concerns. He had in common with James the motive of the "international episode" and the theme of the artist (both in *Tender Is the Night* and in *The Last Tycoon*); he also made use of the geographical and ethical distinction between East and West and accepted James's suggestion of rooting his stories in a well-defined social context. As we have seen, he also adopted most of James's technical devices in his mature fiction. But whereas the lesson of James had been reduced by his other disciples to a form of mildly psychological or moral realism, vaguely sentimental, moderated and genteel, the same lesson was enlivened from the inside and developed by Fitzgerald not only in a personal way, but within the highly crucial context of the American experience at large. Edith Wharton and Willa Cather, Anne Sedgwick and Ellen Glasgow, Thornton Wilder himself had illustrated aspects of that experience with a feminine prudery and moderation, with a typically genteel reticence and a substantial lack of artistic aggressiveness toward their materials. Fitzgerald wrestled, as it were, with his subject matter, brought into it the fire and the distortion of his imagination. His comedy (or tragedy) of manners is never merely marginal, it deals with the core, the very kernel of American reality as such.

The basic suggestions and the manner of presentation are derived from the "Europeanized" James; the formal awareness, the ease and precision of diction belong more to an "English" tradition than to an American literary tradition. In the *Times Literary Supplement* of January 20, 1950, one could read a kind of prophecy that is becoming almost a commonplace today: "If a time should come in which they [writers and readers] turn again to a more English tradition, Scott Fitzgerald would provide a rock on which to build." There is little doubt that this is happening precisely to those writers (or readers) who want to turn to a more English tradition in fiction. And yet, even in this case, one must be careful to qualify or modify the statement as far as the subject matter of Fitzgerald's work is concerned. The experience which is at the root of his fiction and that substantiated it is exclusively and typically American, and it would not be possible, such as it is, on any other native soil. It is basically and consistently "in the American grain"; its themes and motives are strictly connected with and dependent on the American fictional tradition. If Fitzgerald gave them an artistic form through the conscious use of a "Europeanized" technique, this proves the validity—not the limitation—of his achievement.

The comedy of manners, with all its tragic implications, is for Fitzgerald a way of apprehending and realizing the American experience in its various aspects, of getting at the core of it, of expressing it by imposing a formal order on it. By representing an experience based on manners and through manners, Fitzgerald created an artistic reality which transcended the simple question of manners or of behavior. And he did so not only by surpassing James's other disciples, but by getting at the very gist of the matter. In the area of the well-made novel he brought first the freshness of his youthful approach and then the deep insight of his mature years. In either case, for good or bad, he touched upon some key points of the situation of the *homo americanus*. Picturing manners is never an end in itself, but rather a means, in Fitzgerald. The milieu of the fatuous and rich *haute bourgeoisie* is never the object, but rather the pretext of his fictional parables. His realistic rendering allows for the possibility of legend or of symbolic expansion. This fusion is typically American; the motives and themes that are made to serve this purpose are none the less so.

3

Fitzgerald brought two innovations to American fiction, and in the way in which he developed them there is already a mark of his "Americanism." The theme of love is of central interest in his fiction, and it is one of Leslie Fiedler's stimulating paradoxes that no American writer, by definition, is able to deal with adult sexual love with the effectiveness of even a second-rate French author. In fact there is no American novel which can be even distantly related for its theme to *Madame Bovary*, except perhaps *The Scarlet Letter*. It is not so very important, from a literary point of view, that there should be a novel however distantly related to *Madam Bovary*, but the mere juxtaposition of the two titles is all-revealing in this respect. The ambiguity and the complexity of love are never the object of analysis in American fiction, but rather a mere pretext for metaphysical explorations. In Fitzgerald, for the first time, we witness instead a profound interest for the theme as such, and a corresponding intensity of artistic realization: the end of a sentimental delusion in *This Side of Paradise*, its pathetic consequences in *The Beautiful and Damned*, its ruin and tragedy in *Gatsby* and *Tender Is the Night*, its instrumental role in *The Last Tycoon*. The love motive is always at the center of these stories, no longer as a pretext but as a catalytic agent in reality. In Edgar Allan Poe the love passion had been mainly an expedient for self-commiseration, in Melville and Hawthorne it was the starting point for complex "moralities" or for a breathless spiritual adventure, in James a stratagem for the application of intelligence, in the naturalistic writers a means of exposure and denunciation, and in Hemingway himself only a marginal motive—even in *A Farewell to Arms*. In Fitzgerald the experience of love—youthful and deceitful, mature and altruistic, barren and tormented, as the case may be— finds its artistic consecration and is brought to the foreground of the action.

At the same time, Fitzgerald was able to discover another fictional possibility provided by American reality—the possibility of artistic treatment offered by the leisure class and the very rich.[15] As

we have seen, Marius Bewley is willing to stress the absolute origi-
nality of Fitzgerald's awareness and perception in this respect. And
since his love stories are set in that social context, the theme of love is
developed interdependently with the theme of money and wealth.
Fitzgerald seems in fact to be one of the most perceptive and sensitive
interpreters of the interdependence between money and love as
fictional possibilities, and his attitude in this respect is basically in
keeping with the attitude that so many American writers have taken
even in different cultural or social contexts. A fictional connection
between the two themes has quite often been the distinctive mark of
a good number of American writers since the very beginning of
American literature, and it reflects a deeply rooted awareness of the
close links between these two modes of experience. Samuel Sewall,
courting Mrs. Winthrop, brings her half a pound of sugar almonds
and is asked how much they cost; the following conversation
(recorded in his journal) brings together in an awkward mixture
thoughts of love, money, and death:

> Novr. 2 . . . Went to Mrs. Winthrop. Gave her about ½
> pound of Sugar Almonds, cost me 3s. per £. Carried them on
> Monday. She seem'd pleas'd with them and ask'd what they
> cost. Spake of giving her a hundred pounds per annum if I
> dy'd before her. Ask'd what sum she would give me, if she
> should Dy first. Said I would give her time to Consider of it
> [!] . . .

This is not so surprising if we realize that in those days a man
like Cotton Mather, in the well-known chapter "Poetry and Style" in
his *Manoductio ad Ministerium* (1726), could think of indicating the
monetary value of Virgil's *Aeneid:*

> . . . [Vergil's] *Aeneid* . . . may not appear so valuable to
> you that you may think the twenty-seven verses of the part that
> is most finished in it worth one-and-twenty hundred pounds and
> odd money . . .[16]

An "economic conscience" more than anything else is the distinguishing trait of Benjamin Franklin, and it is at the root of his
Autobiography. Thoreau began *Walden* with a chapter on "Economy"
and indulged every so often in careful reckonings. William Dean
Howells sees love and money as opposing but interrelated principles
in his bourgeois and genteel novels; Henry James has heroines and

seducers revolve around fabulous inheritances. From Stephen Crane to Theodore Dreiser, a whole school of naturalistic writers saw money as a corrupting force and love as the only redeeming force. Dos Passos wrote a book on it *(The Big Money)*, and a whole series of proletarian writers with him, from Farrell to Steinbeck, exploited every possibility of the connection. Poe was aware of money as an obstacle to love or life; Pound regarded it as a determining factor of historical decadence and sexual sterility (Canto XLV); even Faulkner had Flem Snopes rise to financial predominance not only by cunning, but by a well-chosen rich partner.

Fitzgerald wove his parables along the same lines, on the two themes of love and money, indissolubly connected. Thus, he linked himself with a traditional experience both human and cultural, but he also colored it with a residue of Puritan morality. Pressed by these two contrasting tensions, it is always the individual conscience that suffers in the dilemma. The aesthetic and literary interest is divided between the illustration of a social and ethical reality characterized by those tensions, and the inner reaction of the individual confronted with that reality. The outer tensions are then internalized: they offer the cue or the starting point for a psychological search, for the probings of conscience, and are in turn seen and represented in terms of that conscience. The same procedure, whether conscious or unconscious, had been adopted once more, although in different context, by Hawthorne and Melville, by James and Poe and most of their predecessors.

The conscience that illustrates or reflects that reality is still the typical conscience of the *homo americanus*, endowed with an unsustainable burden of dreams and illusions and bound to failure in its inevitable collision with experience. The dream is a central motive in Fitzgerald's fiction as it had been a central motive in all the human and cultural experience of the Americans, with its necessary and inescapable corollary and completion in disillusionment and frustration. "Fulfillment destroys the dream," Fitzgerald had written. Both dream and frustrated fulfillment had been present since the very beginning in the American experience.

The dream as a motivating factor and an urge to action, as a dimension of behavior, in fact, was present in the idea of the Cavaliers to build *ex novo* a world of "infinite possibilities"; in the equivocal desire of the Puritans to build "ideal cities"; in the ruthless movement of the pioneers to the West. It inspired the singers and recorders of these events, and imbued the transcendentalism of Emerson and Thoreau, who thought of attaining a communion with the oversoul through the stairway of nature. It turned quite easily into the doctrine of self-reliance and reappeared with brutal violence in Walt Whitman; it determined an all-embracing optimism at midcentury, and a fury of reproach at the turn of the century among the naturalists. The same dream inspired Gertrude Stein when she was dreaming a revolution in words and swirled Pound's mind with impossible aspirations.

Hawthorne and Melville had shown the basic inconsistency of this dream and its catastrophic results. And in respect to the ideals that they professed, both Cavaliers and Puritans had failed, together with the pioneers—marked with the original sin of the Indian massacres and dispossession. Poe was a living epitome of frustration. The transcendentalists ignored at all costs the possibility of failure, but even Walt Whitman, for all his youthful enthusiasm and optimism, turned pessimist in his later years. Mark Twain developed with the years a kind of sceptical disillusionment. Emily Dickinson vindicated in and through her poetry her life of self-denial, while Henry Adams raised the elaborate construction of his *Education* only to tell us that it had been a fruitless attempt toward unity and consistency. From Dreiser to Sinclair Lewis, from Faulkner's degenerates to Hemingway's old man defeated by the sea, the whole tradition is an uninterrupted record of failure and frustration, of big attempts wrecked by a destiny of doom. The unlimited possibilities of mankind, its strength and resistance against the opposing fate provide a constant inducement to song; but there is little doubt that the contingent and repeated failures of that dream are constantly brought into the foreground. Everything seems to head toward an Apocalypse which has nothing in common with the subdued tone of a Götterdämmerung. Fitzgerald has his contribution to make to this general Armaggeddon and joins in with his twilight and subdued manner of exposition; he vibrates on the "frequency" of the tradition.[17] He records failure and frustration while projecting continually on that background a reaffirmation of the purity of the dream of his characters. In an ordinary and everyday dimension he repeats the parable embodying the aspiration and the lament of a whole nation. His "representative" level is not, therefore, limited to the Jazz Age: in his fiction can be found the horror and the glory of American experience at large.

Another trait of the American tradition is that of an "innocent violence"—one need only think of Cavaliers and Puritans, pioneers and Indians, the nineteenth-century "empire builders," the perverse characters of Melville and Hawthorne (Ahab and Chillingworth), the wicked heroines in so much of James's fiction. Peaceful Thoreau cried out for revolt in his *Civil Disobedience*, Emerson admired Napoleon, the naturalists worked the idea of violence into a statement of purpose for their fiction. In this century Hemingway's "tough guys," Steinbeck's "grapes of wrath," the *homo homini lupus* conception of Farrell, and Faulkner's dark melodramas indicate a kind of cult of violence which springs from an "innocent" conception of the world.

Here, Fitzgerald is less at ease and not so much within his domain, and he denies or flees from violence as long as possible. But in *Gatsby* or in *Tender Is the Night* there runs a streak of violence all the more pernicious for its pleasant aspect, and in *The Last Tycoon* there is an open explosion of ruthless violence. In the midst of all this, the conscience is always alert. If the writer has so many links with the American tradition, he has also the gift of an exasperated self-consciousness, of a lucid and relentless self-analysis. This immersion into the dark soul—almost a season in hell—permits him to give the human sense of all these traditional motives, and conditions them by referring them constantly to the self. It had been so for the Puritan preachers with their diaries of introspection, for the gentle Franklin, for Emerson who read into the self by contemplating nature, for Thoreau who mirrored in the lakes and rivers the picture of his own soul, for Poe who turned away horrified from the self, for Ahab or Dimmesdale together with their creators, for James who had been exhilarated and tormented by conscience. Hawthorne had written allegories of the heart, Melville of the insatiate romantic soul, James of psychological behavior. In all of them predominated the self-awareness and the awareness of the self, with all its problems; the same self-awareness was transferred by Fitzgerald into his characters and into his *Notes from Underground*—the "Crack-up" articles. It is apparent in the immature probings of Amory into the mysteries of his psyche, in Anthony's stubborn and discontented cry, in Gatsby's fatal game with his dreams, in the illusion of Dick, in the false titanism of Monroe Stahr.

A "vertical" examination of the origins of American tradition reveals these kinships and these derivations, a continuity of motives and fictional concerns, whereas a "horizontal" analysis divides Fitzgerald from his contemporaries and stresses the "European" component of his fiction. No great damage is done, because the author can sustain these different tensions, and his fiction is enriched by them, at least in a historical sense. Fitzgerald blended a typical set of tendencies of the American soul as such with the suggestions offered by a wider Anglo-Saxon or European tradition. Not many writers of the twentieth century have been so successful, and it is for this reason that Fitzgerald's fiction should be evaluated next to that of Hemingway and Faulkner.

Fitzgerald's stories are now comparable to Hemingway's more fortunate collection of stories: *Gatsby* does not seem to fall short of *The Sun Also Rises,* and there is nothing farfetched in comparing *Tender Is the Night* with *A Farewell to Arms* or *For Whom the Bell Tolls;* the struggle of Stahr is perhaps more human and complex, or better defined anyway, than the struggle of the old man with the sea in Hemingway's last novel. Hemingway has the obvious advantage of being an innovator, an "inventor," whereas Fitzgerald seems to have perfected, more than originated, a new form. Hemingway really renovated in depth, and with the endless elaboration of a pure artist, the language of fiction. He provided a model of stylistic rigor, of flawless representational technique, of subtle counterpoints. He had his link, too, as he himself indirectly acknowledged in *Green Hills of Africa,* with Stephen Crane and Mark Twain, and even with James. But he rendered an undeniable and incomparable service to the cause of flawless writing, of neatness, precision, and concreteness of diction. If he can give at times the impression of being "bound for the museums," as Gertude Stein wrote, his contribution to the art of fiction is of major quality and importance.

Faulkner remains a little isolated in his indisputable greatness, all absorbed in his creation of the vast myth of a legendary, cruel South. In a general survey of twentieth-century fiction, he can only occupy the unique place that greatness occupies at any time—he shares all contemporary concerns, all the contingent and historical elements of his times, but he is also above all this and outside of any classification. Faulkner did rather little—or never cared to do very much—to renew the language and technique of fiction. Usually, he maintained that he had no time for it. He did, on the other hand, a great deal for what was close to his heart—his myth of a titanic and cruel South. In this respect, his historical sense, the amplitude and comprehensiveness of his vision, the deep reach of his human sympathy have made it possible for him to aspire to the greatness of the nineteenth-century novelists, with their wide perspective and preoccupation with history. The general conception of life and its representation reach in Faulkner that degree of intense human participation, historical awareness, and mystic or legendary drive attained by Hawthorne and Melville. If both of them originated a tradition, which can be identified with that of the romance, their greatest disciple today is Faulkner. To both of them, and to the type of romance that they came to represent, Faulkner is linked also by his insistence on baroque imagery, by his taste for expressive form, by his predilection for the basic, existential conflicts with all their human, social, historical, and ultimately metaphysical implications. Through Hawthorne and Melville, Faulkner could also derive inspiration from the great Elizabethan writers who so thoroughly influenced his two predecessors.[18] In this way, although rooted in history and geography, and in a perfectly recognizable and significant literary tradition, Faulkner's fiction is not bound by time or space; it lives in the sphere of the universal (or better, in the sphere of the *concrete* universal, as Hegel demanded).

Faulkner gives at times clear indications of weariness, puzzles with his complacent obscurity, annoys with his tendency to the *grand guignol* style. At times he can be involuted and confused, bombastic— a victim, in fact, of his own creative exuberance. Yet his power is so great that he can afford these luxuries. This is not the case with Fitzgerald. The few luxuries that he thought he could afford in his life or fiction cost him dearly. He does not reach Faulkner's undisputed greatness or Hemingway's perfection of style. But he is redeemed by the poetic quality of his style, the delicacy and naturalness of his diction, his introspective subtleness, his genuine emotion. In this respect, together with Hemingway and Faulkner, he can assert that resistance to time and fashion that very few other American writers can claim in the twentieth century.

Comparisons are always risky. If there is a grain of truth in them, at any rate, one might say that Faulkner stayed with the "classics" of the nineteenth century and that Hemingway made good use of Crane and Mark Twain, only to match and surpass both of them on the level of style and precision. Fitzgerald was content to stay with James and Conrad,[19] but in that line of descent he was able to attain visions and revelations of unexpected clarity and intensity. The line that he chose—and that seems to reveal more and more possibilities of critical reconsideration—led him to achieve a modern tragicomedy of manners which has lost nothing of its flavor and is becoming ever more interesting. Faulkner found a South fertile in motives for high tragedy. Hemingway discovered the outposts of human action, whether the arenas or the trenches, the waters bloodied by the Cuban smugglers or by an old man struggling with the sea, with an ever-fleeting image of reality and conquest. Fitzgerald was content with a much more ordinary reality, the only one that he knew, and was its interpreter and singer with a modesty of approach and an acuteness of insight that speak for his seriousness and dedication. The violence which he, like any other artist, did to his reality is perhaps less apparent and obvious, more subdued and reserved, but none the less effective. His style is also less original, or at least less revolutionary. Thus, while Faulkner surprised readers and critics and appealed to their capacity for surprise, Hemingway enchanted and thralled the man in the street with his alleged "simplicity" and the literary man with his literary refinement of diction. Fitzgerald, after the years of his youthful legend, did not have the conspicuous qualities to surprise and capture a wide audience. But it was a real lack of critical perception to have undervalued him, because in the novel of manners (whether you call it psychological or a well-made novel does not really matter) he spoke with his own distinct voice and offered a counterpart to the more ambitious and more successful adventure of his two contemporaries. His characters, like those of his more fortunate rivals, have been given a local habitation and a name in the world of fiction; his books assert and preserve an unrepeatable identity.

It is completely off the point to say that his subjects are "frivolous" or to affirm that the degree of his commitment and his capacity for realization are of a minor order. Even if it were so, one has to recall what Marcel Proust wrote almost at the end of his fictional adventure, in the third chapter of *Le Temps retrouvé:* "When it comes to studying the laws of character, one can do this quite as well on a frivolous as a serious subject ... the great moral laws ... vary but little with the intellectual worth of the individual." The really important thing for Proust "was to be found not in the outward appearance of the subject, but in the extent to which this [the artist's] impression had penetrated to a depth where that appearance was of little importance." [20] It was true of Proust, and it is true of Fitzgerald as well. If we keep this observation in mind, we can easily be persuaded that Fitzgerald substantially deserves that "small immortality" to which, in a moment of gentle self-revelation, he had referred as his basic aspiration.

Notes

CHAPTER I

[1] See his letter to John O'Hara, July 18, 1933: "I am half black Irish and half old American stock with the usual exaggerated ancestral pretensions. The black Irish half of the family had the money and looked down upon the Maryland side of the family who had, and really had, that certain series of reticences and obligations that go under the poor old shattered word 'breeding' . . ." *Letters*, p. 503.

[2] The paper was called *Now and Then*; the titles of F.'s contributions were "The Mystery of the Raymond Mortgage," "Reade, Substitute Right Half," "A Debt of Honor," "The Room with the Green Blinds."

[3] He was to explain later "that if you weren't able to function in action you might at least be able to tell about it, because you felt the same intensity— it was a backdoor way out of facing reality." As quoted in Andrew Turnbull, *S.F.* (New York, 1962), p. 36.

[4] He contributed to three of them: *Fie! Fie! Fi-Fi!* (plot and lyrics), 1914–15; *The Evil Eye* (lyrics), 1915–16; *Safety First* (lyrics), 1916–17.

[5] See his letter to his daughter, September 17, 1940, *Letters*, p. 94, and his article "Princeton" (*College Humor*, December 1927), now in *AA*, pp. 70–79.

[6] *FSP*, p. 59; cf. also William Goldhurst, *F.S.F. and His Contemporaries* (New York, 1963), chapter II, for Wilson's influence.

[7] See F.'s article "How to Live on $36,000 a Year" (*SEP*, April 5, 1924), now in *AA*, pp. 87–99.

[8] "When I was your age—he was to write to his daughter, July 7, 1938—I lived with a great dream. The dream grew and I learned how to speak of it and make people listen. Then the dream divided one day when I decided to marry your mother after all, even though I knew she was spoiled and meant no good to me. I was sorry immediately I had married her but, being patient in those days, made the best of it and got to love her in another way. You came along and for a long time we made quite a lot of happiness out of our lives. But I was a man divided—she wanted me to work too much for *her* and not enough for my dream." *Letters*, p. 32.

[9] To show his abasement before Joyce's genius, F. announced that he was going to jump out of the window, and with some puzzlement Joyce had to prevent him. Cf. *FSP*, pp. 132–33.

[10] See his article "How to Live on Practically Nothing a Year" (*SEP*, September 20, 1924), now in *AA*, pp. 100–116. Soon after the publication of *GG*, he had written to Maxwell Perkins: "If it will support me with no more

intervals of trash I'll go on as a novelist. If not, I'm going to quit, come home, go to Hollywood and learn the movie business. I can't reduce our scale of living and I can't stand this financial insecurity." *Letters*, p. 180, also p. 485.

[11] He had met Hemingway in 1925, and even before meeting him he had praised his talent to friends and acquaintances, urging Glenway Wescott, for instance, to write a laudatory essay on him. F. was among the very first to review Hemingway's *In Our Time* (in his essays "How to Waste Material," *The Bookman*, May 1926, now in *AA*, pp. 117–23); he brought Hemingway over to Scribner's when his former publishers, Boni and Live-right, refused to publish *The Torrents of Spring* on account of its parody of Sherwood Anderson, then their best author. In "Handle with Care" (*CU*, p. 79) F. clearly referred to Hemingway when he spoke of his "artistic conscience," but he always disclaimed having imitated his "infectious style." Hemingway, on the other hand, was far too critical of F.'s life and works and never acknowledged his debt. He made fun of F. in *The Torrents of Springs*, criticized *Tender Is the Night*, rebuked him vehemently for his "crack-up" articles, and finally introduced him as a symbol of decadence in "The Snows of Kilimanjaro." After F.'s dignified protest, he took out his name for the book version of the story (see *Letters*, p. 311), but the same allusion seems to be repeated in "Mr. and Mrs. Elliot." In his posthumous book, *A Movable Feast* (New York, 1964), Chapter XVII, Hemingway's report of his first acquaintance with F. gives again an unfair picture both of the man and of the artist. On the subject, see W. Goldhurst, *op. cit.*, Chapter V.

[12] On this rather peaceful period of his life, see Andrew Turnbull's two articles in *The New Yorker*, April 7 and November 17, 1956, and Chapter XIII of his biography, already quoted.

[13] This is how he describes his situation: "I am living very cheaply. Today I am in comparative affluence, but Monday and Tuesday I had two tins of potted meat, three oranges and a box of Uneedas and two cans of beer. For the food that totaled eighteen cents a day—. . . it was funny coming into the hotel and the very deferential clerk not knowing that I was not only thousands, nay tens of thousands in debt, but had less than forty cents cash in the world and probably a deficit at my bank . . . . I washed my two handkerchiefs and my shirt every night, but the pyjama trousers I had to wear all the time . . . My socks . . . served double duty as slippers at night." *CU*, p. 232.

[14] His motivation for going to Hollywood is different this time, cf. *Letters*, p. 548: "Because of this—I mean too many anxieties and too much intro-spection—I'm going to Hollywood next month and extrovert a while. . . ."

[15] After *Three Comrades*, rewritten by the director, F. wrote the film script of *Infidelity*, which was never produced, worked at the script of *The*

Women, then of *Madame Curie* (in both cases he was dismissed after two months), and rewrote the script of *Air Raid.* He finally completed a script of his own story "Babylon Revisited," to be called *The Cosmopolitan,* which was not produced at the time, and was revised for a later production, *The Last Time I Saw Paris,* which bears no resemblance to the original.

[16] See Sheilah Graham and Gerold Frank, *Beloved Infidel* (New York, 1958).

[17] "I had forgotten tomorrow was election eve—he wrote to his picture agent, William Dozier, on November 5, 1940—and I promised to sit up with some sick Republicans. . . . My general plan is to go on with my novel as long as my ill gotten gains hold out." (Quoted in *FSP,* p. 291.) And in *CU,* p. 199, we read: "It is in the thirties that we want friends. In the forties we know that they won't save us any more than love did."

CHAPTER II

[1] See his statements in "Early Success," *CU,* pp. 85–90.

[2] Cf. Henry Dan Piper, "S.F.'s Prep-School Writing," in *The Princeton Univ. Library Chronicle,* XVIII (1955), pp. 1–10; "Reade, Substitute Right Half" is reprinted *ibid.,* pp. 11 ff.

[3] New Brunswick: Rutgers University Press, 1965. Among these titles were: "Football" (1911, poem); "A Luckless Santa Klaus" (1912); "Election Night" (1912); "Pain and the Scientist" (1913, a satiric piece); "A School Dance" (1913); "The Trial of the Duke" (1913)—already a little story on the "very rich."

Literary Magazine from June 1916 to February 1919; the last three are reprinted in *A Book of Princeton Verse, II* (Princeton Univ. Press, 1919), and in *CU.*

[5] Besides these two stories and "The Débutante," the novel incorporated two poems:. "To Cecilia" (*CU,* p. 246), slightly modified and printed as prose (Part II, Chapter III, "When Vanity Kissed Vanity"), and "The Way of Purgation" (*CU,* p. 249), slightly modified and printed without the title at the beginning of Part II, Chapter V.

[6] This was the title of a review by R.V.A.S. in *The New Republic,* XXII (May 12, 1920), p. 362.

[7] "Echoes of the Jazz Age," *CU,* p. 13.

[8] For an analysis of these aspects, see Fernanda Pivano's introduction to the Italian translation of the novel (*Di qua dal Paradiso,* Milan, 1952), now reprinted in *La Balena bianca e altri miti* (Milan, 1961). F. himself had written to E. Wilson, January 10, 1918: "I really believe that no one else could have written so searchingly the story of the youth of our generation. . . ." *Letters,* p. 323, *CU,* p. 252.

[9] *FSP,* p. 70.

[10] " 'But think,' I interrupted with dignity, 'I am the supreme egotist. Consider how brilliantly self-centered my book will be; also I am informed that the time has come for a long rambling, picaresque novel. I shall ramble and be picaresque. I shall be intellectual and echo Compton McKenzie [*sic*]. The chief influence upon my humour will be Booth Tarkington; and, toward the end of the book, I'll be very, very serious indeed—' " etc., on the same line. (From the typescript of *The Romantic Egotist*.)

[11] "As I read over my notes for the chapters, I am astonished to find the immense preponderance of women on all the important pages. Women and mirrors . . . half a life devoted to women and mirrors." "I had better proceed or I'll be giving away my climax in the beginning like H. G. Wells. . . . I will write a novel of second-hand anti-climaxes, if it need be." (From the typescript.)

[12] E. Wilson had urged F. to read Joyce's *Portrait* in a letter, October 7, 1917, describing it as "another of the best novels of the century" (together with *The New Machiavelli* by H. G. Wells); Amory mentions it in his lists of readings.

[13] This preface—dated August 1919—was only typewritten and not printed: it is a humorous account of the composition of the novel, and repeats all the well-known references to its literary models, *Dorian Gray* included.

[14] "I'm sick of a system where the richest man gets the most beautiful girl if he wants her . . . Of course I'm selfish"—says Amory (*TSP*, p. 299), and F. was to repeat with him: "The man with the jingle of money in his pocket who married the girl a year later would always cherish an abiding distrust, an animosity, toward the leisure class—not the conviction of a revolutionist but the smouldering hatred of a peasant. In the years since then I have never been able to stop wondering where my friends' money came from, nor to stop thinking that at one time a sort of *droit de seigneur* might have been exercised to give one of them my girl." (*CU*, p. 77.)

[15] "Grown up to find all Gods dead, all wars fought, all faiths in man shaken"—says Amory, and we think of Mallarmé's "*j'ai lu tous les livres*" or of Pound's *Hugh Selwyn Mauberley*.

[16] In two of his letters F. linked his novel with Oscar Wilde's *Dorian Gray* (*Letters*, p. 277 and p. 469); in the preface above-mentioned he had written that *TSP* was "largely flavored by the great undigested butter-ball of *Dorian Gray*."

[17] For the influence of the English *fin-de-siècle* on these American authors, see Nemi D'Agostino, "La 'Fin de siècle' inglese e il giovane Pound," *English Miscellany*, VI (1955), pp. 135–62, and "William Faulkner," *Studi Americani*, I (1955), pp. 257–308.

[18] *TSP*, p. 302; cf. also p. 285 and p. 286.

[19] Letter to Frances Newman, February 26, 1921, in *Letters*, pp. 468–70.

²⁰ In "The Contemporary Novel," *Fortnightly Review,* XCVI (November 1911), pp. 862–73.

²¹ In "The New Novel," originally called "The Younger Generation," *TLS,* March 19 and April 2, 1914, then in *Notes on Novelists* (New York, 1916), pp. 319–47.

²² H. James, *Letters,* ed. by Percy Lubbock (London, 1920), II, p. 505. For his controversy with H. G. Wells, see *Henry James & H. G. Wells,* ed. by Leon Edel and G. N. Ray (London, 1958), where all relevant material is collected.

²³ James E. Miller, Jr., *The Fictional Technique of F.S.F.* (The Hague, 1957), pp. 1–13 and *passim,* a book to which I am greatly indebted for this part of my analysis.

²⁴ *Letters,* pp. 319–20.

²⁵ R.V.A.S. in *The New Republic,* May 12, 1920, p. 362.

²⁶ In *SEP,* August 6, 1949, pp. 30–31.

²⁷ In her *Autobiography of Alice B. Toklas* (New York, 1933), quoted in A. Kazin (ed.), *F.S.F.: the Man and His Work* (New York, 1951), p. 9.

CHAPTER III

¹ "Have sold three or four cheap stories to American magazines"—he wrote to E. Wilson; "Have written two good short stories and three cheap ones"; "I have written two wonderful stories and got letters of praise from six editors with the addenda that 'our readers, however, would be offended.' " *Letters,* p. 325, pp. 328–29.

² SS, February 1920, then in *FP:* it was based on "The Ordeal," *Nassau Lit.,* June 1915.

³ *SEP,* May 1, 1920, then in *FP.*

⁴ *SEP,* May 29, 1920, then in *FP.* The same device (a fantasy staged in a realistic story) is also found in "Myra Meets His Family" (*SEP,* March 1920, uncollected), in "Rags Martin Jones" and in "Flight and Pursuit": see K. Eble, *F.S.F.* (New York, 1963), p. 55.

⁵ *SEP,* April 24, 1920, then in *TJA.*

⁶ SS, January 1920, then in *TJA.*

⁷ *The Metropolitan Magazine,* October 1920, then in *TJA.* Zelda's ideas were entirely responsible for it, cf. A. Turnbull, *op. cit.,* p. 115.

⁸ *Scribner's Magazine,* June 1920, then in *FP:* F. wrote that "it's a plant, a moral tale and utterly lacks vitality." (Cf. K. Eble, *op. cit.,* p. 60.)

⁹ SS, July 1920, then in *TJA.*

¹⁰ "Each of the three events [in the story] made a great impression upon me. In life they were unrelated, . . . but in my story I have tried, unsuccessfully, I fear, to weave them into a pattern," see Preface to *TJA,* p. viii. He had no reason to fear. They *are* woven into a pattern.

[11] *SEP*, February 21, 1920, then in *FP*.

[12] *SS*, February 1920, then in *FP*.

[13] *SEP*, May 22, 1920, then in *FP*. The story was suggested by Zelda, and it is highly praised by K. Eble, *op. cit.*, p. 56.

[14] *Scribner's Magazine*, May 1920, then in *FP*.

[15] *The Metropolitan Magazine*, February 1921 (with the title: "His Russet Witch"), then in *TJA*.

[16] *The Chicago Sunday Tribune*, December 12, 1920, then in *TJA*.

[17] In the MS there is also an epigraph from Samuel Butler: "Life is a long process of getting tired," which was not used in the printed text.

[18] In the MS the three books bear these titles: "The Pleasant Absurdity of Things," "The Romantic Bitterness of Things," and "The Ironic Tragedy of Things."

[19] In *The Metropolitan Magazine*, LV (March 1922), p. 113; see also *Letters*, p. 152.

[20] Cf. *FSP*, p. 140. Wilson's essay "S. F." had appeared in *The Bookman*, March 1922. See also William Troy, "S. F.—The Authority of Failure" (1945), and J. F. Powers, "Dealers in Diamonds and Rhinestones," both in A. Kazin (ed.), *F.S.F.*

[21] "Gloria—he wrote his daughter years later—was a much more trivial and vulgar person than your mother. I can't really say there was any resemblance except in the beauty and certain terms of expression she used, and also I naturally used many circumstantial events of our early married life. However the emphases were entirely different. We had a much better time than Anthony and Gloria did." As quoted in *FSP*, pp. 124–25. This did not prevent reviewers from interpreting the novel as autobiography.

[22] *CU*, p. 305 and *Letters*, p. 63: on the subject of F.'s moralism, cf. also *ibid.*, pp. 3–4, 16, and 18, among others.

[23] He had "discovered Mencken" as early as 1920 (see *Letters*, p. 144). In a review of Charles G. Norris' *Brass* (November 1921) he had written that "Brigadier General Mencken . . . marshalled the critics in quiescent columns of squads for the campaign against Philistia" (as quoted in J. E. Miller, *op. cit.*, p. 42).

[24] Cf. "The Baltimore Anti-Christ," in *The Bookman*, March 1921.

[25] Cf. James E. Miller, Jr., *op. cit.*, pp. 39–40: his speech was delivered at the Women's City Club in St. Paul, the interview appeared in the *St. Paul Daily News*, December 4, 1921.

[26] Cf. H. L. Mencken, *Prejudices: Second Series* (New York, 1920), pp. 38–41, and J. E. Miller, *op. cit.*, pp. 40–41.

[27] Cf. Nemi D'Agostino, "F.S.F.," in *Studi Americani*, III (Rome, 1957), p. 250. F. had praised Dreiser in a letter to J. B. Cabell, Christmas 1920

(*Letters*, p. 464), and had hinted at *Sister Carrie* in a review of a book by Woodward Boyd in *The New York Evening Post*, October 28, 1922. For other references to *Sister Carrie* see *Letters*, p. 59 ("*Sister Carrie*, almost the first piece of American realism, is damn good . . . ," July 1939), p. 173 (Hurstwood is considered one of "the three best characters in American fiction in the last twenty years," December 20 [?], 1924), and p. 462. In 1922 F. had said that he considered Mencken and Dreiser "the greatest men living in the country today," cf. *FSP*, p. 154.

[28] Another thematic analogy must be noted: in the end, Carrie's success is a form of subtle defeat, and her victory brings only solitude and sadness, dissatisfaction and regret. Her efforts are not crowned by *full* success.

[29] Vivian Shaw, in *The Dial*, April 1922, had described it as "a résumé of *The Education of Henry Adams* filtered through a particularly thick page of *The Smart Set*." J. E. Miller has remarked (*op. cit.*, p. 57) that many ideas of Mencken's found their way into this chapter, and F. himself admitted that in Maury Noble's monologue he had interpolated "some recent ideas of *his* own and (possibly) of others," *Letters*, p. 328.

[30] Letter to John Peale Bishop, February or March 1922, in *Letters*, p. 353.
[31] See, for instance, the inclusion of many boring pages from Gloria's diary: in *TTN* F. included a set of letters written by Nicole, but in this case the inclusion served a specific thematic purpose.

CHAPTER IV

[1] The play was begun in the autumn of 1921 and completed the next spring. It was revised during the summer of 1922 (with the title of *Gabriel's Trombone*) and rewritten completely after it had been refused by some producers. In April 1923, however, Sam Harris decided to produce it, and it opened at the Apollo Theater of Atlantic City, N.J., in November. It was a complete failure and was dropped a week later. Its final title might have been suggested bv a passage of Mencken in his essay "On Being an American," cf. W. Goldhurst, *op. cit.*, p. 88, and Mencken's general influence is apparent in many passages. A reviewer felt justified in writing that "the spirit of the play is an obvious act of deference to Mencken's virulent contempt for the American people," cf. *FSP*, p. 156. In 1922, F. had staged a short play for the St. Paul Junior League, called *The Midnight Flapper*. Cf. *FSP*, pp. 146–48, and *AA*, pp. 93–94.

[2] F. wrote few stories in 1922–23, and in 1924–25 he had to make up for it by composing, chiefly for financial reasons, a good number of them, which often do not come up to his standards. "I really worked hard as hell last winter"—he wrote to Wilson—"but it was all trash and it nearly broke my heart as well as my iron constitution" (*Letters*, p. 341). "I've done about 10 pieces of horrible junk in the last year . . . that I can never repub-

lish or bear to look at—cheap and without the spontaneity of my first work,"
we read in a letter to J. P. Bishop, *ibid.*, p. 356.

[3] *SEP*, February 11 and 18, 1922: uncollected.

[4] *McCall's*, July 1924, then in *ASYM*.

[5] *SEP*, March 15, 1924, then in *ASYM*.

[6] *Woman's Home Companion*, November 1925, uncollected.

[7] *Hearst's International*, May 1923, uncollected.

[8] *The Chicago Sunday Tribune*, June 7, 1925, uncollected.

[9] *SEP*, July 26, 1924; reprinted in pamphlet form, *John Jackson's Arcady.
A Contest Selection*, arranged by Lilian Holmes Strack (Boston: W. H.
Baker, 1928), 8 pp.

[10] The story appeared in *Collier's*, May 27, 1922, and was included in *TJA*.
"This story was inspired by a remark of Mark Twain's to the effect that it
was a pity that the best part of life came at the beginning and the worst
part at the end . . ."—F. wrote, *ibid.*, p. 192.—"Several weeks after completing it, I discovered an almost identical plot in Samuel Butler's 'Notebooks.' "

[11] *SS*, June 1922, then in *TJA*. The background of this story was provided
by F.'s visit to the ranch of his friend Sap Donahoe in Montana (cf. *FSP*,
p. 52), but the idea of a secluded valley might have been derived from
Samuel Johnson's well-known *Rasselas*.

[12] On F.'s early use of symbolism, cf. J. E. Miller, Jr., *op. cit.*, pp. 49–51,
and Marius Bewley, *The Eccentric Design* (London, 1959), p. 259.

[13] *Hearst's International*, February 1925, then in *ASYM*. For a more serious
treatment of a similar theme, see the story "The Adjuster" (1925), in
which the protagonist, however, Luella Hemple, matures through suffering and saves her husband, and the general tone is tragic rather than
comic. Cf. K. Eble, *op. cit.*, p. 105, and W. Goldhurst, *op. cit.*, pp. 197–99.

[14] *The Metropolitan Magazine*, December 1922, then in *ASYM*. F. himself
was to call it later "a sort of first draft of the Gatsby idea," cf. A. Turnbull,
op. cit., p. 133.

[15] *Liberty*, July 5, 1924, then in *ASYM*.

[16] *The American Mercury*, June 1924, then in *ASYM*. On April 15, 1934, F.
was to write to John Jamieson: "It might interest you to know that a story
of mine, called 'Absolution' . . . was intended to be a picture of his
[Gatsby's] early life." *Letters*, p. 509; cf. also *ibid.*, p. 164. Strangely
enough, K. Eble (in *op. cit.*, p. 32) considers it "the most 'naturalistic'
story F. ever wrote." For its Catholic element, cf. Henry Dan Piper, "The
Religious Background of *GG*," in Frederick J. Hoffman (ed.), *GG: A Study*
(New York, 1962), pp. 321–34.

[17] *CU*, p. 310. Writing to Scribner's on October 31, 1933, T. S. Eliot some-

what modified his original statement; he wrote that *GG* had *interested* him more than any American novel he had read since Henry James.

[18] *CU*, pp. 264 and 269; *FSP*, p. 170.

[19] See F.'s own introduction to *GG* (New York: The Modern Library, 1933), p. ix, and *FSP*, p. 164. Originally, the title of the book was to be *Among Ash Heaps and Millionaires*, then *Trimalchio in West Egg* (with the two variants: *Trimalchio* and *On the Road to West Egg*). Two other possibilities were *Gold-hatted Gatsby* and *The High-bouncing Lover*, both suggested by the four lines attributed to Thomas Parke D'Invilliers, which figure in the title page. Cf. *Letters*, p. 169. In the galley proofs, the title was still *Trimalchio*, and Gatsby is identified with this character at the beginning of Chapter VII of the book. Their relationship is analyzed by P. L. Mackendrick in *The Classical Journal*, XLV (1950), pp. 307–14: Mackendrick sees in F. and Petronius two writers of protest and denunciation, and finds similarities of *method*, *aim*, and *experience* in them.

[20] In a MS note the subject matter is clearly divided into nine chapters: "I. Four characters & Landscape. Gatsby suggested. / II. Two more characters. New York. / III. The Party. Gatsby. Summer passes. / IV. The Guests. Wolfshiem [*sic*]. The Past. / V. The Meeting. / VI. More of Gatsby's past. The second party. / VII. The Buchanans. The Playa. The Filling Station. / VIII. The Rest of the Past. Murder of Gatsby. / IX. Wolfshiem. The Funeral (for a total of 48,000 words)."

[21] This symbolic image was suggested to the writer by a tentative jacket for the novel which had been sent to him, and which "he wrote into the book," cf. *Letters*, p. 166.

[22] The information which is here given about Gatsby's past is actually learnt by Nick *after* Gatsby's tragedy (Chapter VIII): this is a clear indication that F. *wanted* as much as possible to avoid describing the actual nature of the relationship between Gatsby and Daisy. The same device had been used by Henry James in *The American*, where Newman and Mme de Cintré are "ignored" by the writer soon after their engagement.

[23] In the galley proofs the episode was slightly different. Tom and Daisy arrive at the party spontaneously, and while Daisy tries openly to "separate" Gatsby from his guests, Tom tries to identify him with them: "He's just like them," he tells Daisy. It is worth noting, also, that part of Gatsby's past was here related in the first person, and not reported by Nick.

[24] In the galley proofs Daisy tells Nick that she wants to run off with Gatsby, and the same information is given by Gatsby, who refuses, however, to "run off" with her. It is not simply that Daisy must break her marriage; she must actually deny its existence. Refusing a bourgeois compromise, Gatsby remains "pure," but puts himself in an impossible situation. For F.'s revisions on the galley proofs, cf. also *Letters*, pp. 171–74.

[25] Cf. Leslie A. Fiedler, "Some Notes on F.S.F.," in *An End to Innocence* (Boston, 1955), pp. 176–83, and in *Love and Death in the American Novel* (New York, 1960). Fiedler sees in *GG* "an eastern drama": F. himself, however, says that it is "a history of the West."

[26] Gatsby's complete lack of taste shows in his way of dressing (he wears for instance "a white flannel suit, silver shirt, and gold-colored tie . . ."), in his cars, in his house, in the display of impossible shirts to Daisy when she visits his house, and in his ill-timed offer of a profitable and "rather confidential" job to Nick, soon after Nick has been asked to bring him and Daisy together.

[27] Cf. Malcolm Cowley, Introduction to *Three Novels by F.S.F.* (New York, 1953), p. xiv, and J. Aldridge, "The Life of Gatsby," in *Twelve Original Essays on Great American Novels*, ed. by Carl Shapiro (Detroit, 1958), pp. 230–31.

[28] Lionel Trilling's preface was prepared for the New Directions edition of *GG* (1945), and then developed into an essay, now in *The Liberal Imagination* (New York, 1950), in A. Kazin (ed.), *op. cit.*, etc. Trilling's interpretation was immediately taken up and discussed by Malcolm Cowley in *The New Yorker* and popularized in many reviews of the book (*Kenyon Review*, *Sewanee Review*, etc.). The "mythic" character of Gatsby is also stressed by William Troy, *op. cit.*

[29] Jacques Barzun's essay, "Myths for Materialists," where his theory was expounded, is discussed at length in Marius Bewley, *op. cit.*, p. 271. Cf. also Richard Chase, *The American Novel and Its Tradition* (New York, 1958); Chase sees in Gatsby the vehicle of a "pastoral" ideal, like Franklin, Natty Bumppo, and Huck Finn, and he stresses his "legendary" character. Forerunners of Gatsby's "divine madness," according to Chase, can be found in Julien Sorel, Don Quixote, and Hamlet (!). Chase seems far closer to the truth when he places *GG* halfway between the *novel* and the *romance*; to stress its "romantic" aspect it is quite unnecessary to go back to Hamlet. On the subject, cf. also Robert Orstein, "F.'s Fable of East and West," *College English*, XVIII (1956), pp. 139–43, and K. Eble, *op. cit.*, pp. 96–97.

[30] *FSP*, p. 171 and *Letters*, p. 358: "I never at any one time saw him [Gatsby] clear myself"—F. had written to John Peale Bishop, August 9, 1925—"for he started as one man I knew and then changed into myself—the amalgam was never complete in my mind."

[31] Cf. his essay "The Art of Fiction," now in *The Future of the Novel*, ed. by Leon Edel (New York, 1956), pp. 15–16.

[32] *Letters*, pp. 341–42 and p. 358. Both Edith Wharton (*CU*, p. 309) and John Peale Bishop thought that Gatsby had been "blurred" by the mystery about his past; both E. Wharton and H. L. Mencken thought that the book

was "no more than a glorified anecdote" (cf. *CU*, p. 309, and W. Goldhurst, *op. cit.*, p. 79).

[33] Cf. *Letters*, pp. 356 and 374; see p. 305 for F.'s waning admiration for Wells and Mackenzie ("The war wrecked him [Mackenzie] as it did Wells and many of that generation," we read for instance in a letter to J. P. Bishop, April 1925), and cf. F.'s essay "How to Waste Material," in *AA*, pp. 117–22, for his waning admiration for Mencken ("His idea had always been ethical rather than aesthetic," p. 118).

[34] He had praised Anatole France in two letters to J. B. Cabell (*Letters*, p. 466 and p. 468) and in a review of Grace Flandrau's *Being Respectable*, in *The Literary Digest*, March 1923, pp. 35–36 (cf. J. E. Miller, *op. cit.*, p. 69). To Galsworthy F. had said that he considered A. France and Conrad the two greatest living writers (cf. *FSP*, p. 132). Stephen Crane was praised at the end of a review of Thomas Boyd's *Through the Wheat*, in *The New York Evening Post*, May 26, 1923—the same review began with a quotation from Conrad's *Youth*. Willa Cather had been praised in an interview in 1924, now in Charles E. Baldwin, *The Men Who Make Our Novels* (New York, 1924), p. 167. For F.'s admiration for Edith Wharton, cf. *FSP*, p. 154, and K. Eble, *op. cit.*, p. 87.

[35] Cf. Wilson's essay in *The Bookman*, March 1922, and Ch. E. Baldwin, *op. cit.*, p. 167. Cf. also *Letters*, p. 163 (where F. speaks of *GG* as "purely creative work" and as "a consciously artistic achievement"), p. 430 (for *GG* being "detached") and p. 480 (where *GG* is described as being written "in protest against my own formless two novels").

[36] J. W. Beach, *The Twentieth Century Novel: Studies in Technique* (New York, 1932), pp. 181–82, and 193 and *passim*. For Henry James's theories, cf. his essay "The Art of Fiction," already quoted, and his Prefaces to the New York Edition of his works, now collected in *The Art of the Novel* (London, 1934), with an extremely useful introduction and index by R. P. Blackmur. On this and related questions, see also Wayne C. Booth's invaluable study *The Rhetoric of Fiction* (Chicago, 1961).

[37] F. M. Ford, *Joseph Conrad: A Personal Remembrance* (Boston, 1924), pp. 136–37, as quoted in J. E. Miller, *op. cit.*, p. 95. Parts of this book are also reprinted in F. J. Hoffman (ed.), *GG: A Study*.

[38] It is significant that *GG* was originally meant to have a Middle West and New York *locale*, and to take place in the 1880's, as is the case with many works by E. Wharton (cf. F. J. Hoffman, *op. cit.*, p. 322). For similarities between *GG* and *A Lost Lady*, see *Letters*, p. 507, and Maxwell Geismar, *The Last of the Provincials* (Boston, 1947), p. 166. For a comparison between F. and E. Wharton, see F. J. Hoffman, in *English Institute Essays* (New York, 1950).

[39] Cf. F.'s introduction to the Modern Library *GG*, p. x. It might be worth noting that Conrad had visited America in 1923 (see *FSP*, p. 158). Refer-

ences to Conrad are particularly frequent in F.'s letters: cf. *Letters*, p. 211 ("Conrad has been, after all, the healthy influence on the techniques of the novel"), p. 246 ("an author's main purpose is 'to make you see'"—as Conrad had written in the preface to *The Nigger of the 'Narcissus'*), p. 301 and p. 362 (a new reference to Conrad's preface, as in p. 309), p. 462 (for F.'s idea of Conrad's pessimism), and p. 482 (May or June 1925: "God! I've learned a lot from him"). Cf. also *CU*, pp. 262 and 288 (a reference to *Lord Jim*). As early as 1923 F. had "discovered" that Conrad was superior to Wells; in *CU*, p. 179, we find an entry which might be easily referred to *GG*:

"Conrad's secret theory examined: He knew that things do transpire about people. Therefore he wrote the truth and transposed it to parallel to give that quality, adding confusion however to his structure. Nevertheless, there is in his scheme a desire to imitate life which is in all the big shots. Have I such an idea in the composition of this book?"

[40] Cf. Joseph Conrad, Preface to *The Nigger of the 'Narcissus'* (1897), reprinted in F. J. Hoffman (ed.), *GG: A Study*, pp. 59–64. In his essay "One Hundred False Starts" (1933), F. was to quote Conrad's second statement, *AA*, p. 136. On Conrad's impressionistic theory, see my essay "Stephen Crane fra naturalismo e impressionismo," in *Annali di Ca' Foscari*, III (Milan, 1964).

[41] As J. W. Beach (*op. cit.*, p. 363) had done for *Lord Jim*, J. E. Miller (*op. cit.*, p. 97) has worked out a diagram of the sequence of events in *GG*, "allowing X to stand for the straight chronological account of the summer of 1922, and A, B, C, D, and E to represent the significant events of Gatsby's past," which runs as follows: X, X, X, XCX, X, XBXCX, X, XCXDX, XEXAX (each group of letters indicates a chapter).

[42] F. disclaimed an influence of Henry James on *GG*, cf. *Letters*, p. 480: in the same passage, however, he makes it clear that he *had* read *The Portrait of a Lady*. He had also read Conrad's essay on James (see his letter to Maxwell Perkins, *circa* June 1, 1925, in *Letters*, p. 187), and already in 1922 he had read *What Maisie Knew*, see *ibid.*, p. 333.

[43] Cf. Henry James, *The Art of the Novel*, p. 14. According to James, a *ficelle* represented "a relation that has nothing to do with the matter . . . but everything to do with the manner" (cf. *ibid.*, p. 342).

CHAPTER V

[1] *The Redbook*, January and February 1926, then in *ASYM*.

[2] There are still echoes of Oscar Wilde in the story. Of Anson Hunter we are told that he drank "whenever and however he liked," but that "it annoyed him if any one else blundered in that regard—about his own lapses he was always humorous." Lord Goring, in *An Ideal Husband*, had stated: "You see, Phipps, fashion is what one wears oneself. What is unfashionable

is what other people wear. . . . Just as vulgarity is simply the conduct of other people." Cf. *The Works of O. Wilde* (London, 1948), p. 507.

³ *SEP*, March 2, 1929, then in *TAR*.

⁴ *SEP*, December 17, 1927, then in *TAR*.

⁵ *SEP*, November 5, 1932, then in *TAR*.

⁶ *SEP*, August 9, 1930: first collected in *Stories*. The story is about the famous marriage of Powell Fowler in Paris in the summer of 1930, cf. *FSP*, p. 324, n. 30.

⁷ Cf. "Echoes of the Jazz Age," in *CU*, p. 22.

⁸ Maxwell Perkins had urged F. to publish them in book form, but he succeeded only in persuading F. to publish eight of them in *TAR*. At one time F. considered making a book out of them (cf. *Stories*, p. 308), which was to be called *My Girl Josephine*: but already in 1929 he wrote that "The Basil Lee stories were a mistake—it was too much good material being shoved into a lousy form," even if he thought them "rather better than the response they had." Cf. *Letters*, p. 495. There is a tendency now to reevaluate these stories, cf. A. Mizener, introduction to *AA* and K. Eble, *op. cit.*, pp. 23–32. ("The stories are as excellent in craftsmanship as any stories Fitzgerald ever wrote.")

⁹ Introduction to *AA*, pp. 3–5.

¹⁰ *SEP*, April 28, 1928, then in *TAR*.

¹¹ *SEP*, July 21, 1928, then in *AA*.

¹² *SEP*, July 28 and September 29, 1928, then in *TAR*.

¹³ *SEP*, December 29, 1928, and January 5, 1929, then in *TAR*.

¹⁴ *SEP*, March 30 and April 27, 1929, then in *AA*. The first of the Basil Lee stories, "That Kind of Party" had been rejected by *SEP*, and remained unpublished; it has been published posthumously in the *Princeton University Library Chronicle* (Fitzgerald number), Summer 1951: in the typescript, however, the names of the characters had been changed. Cf. K. Eble, *op. cit.*, p. 24.

¹⁵ *SEP*, April 5, May 31 and September 6, 1930, then in *TAR*.

¹⁶ Cf. K. Eble, *op. cit.*, pp. 118–19, to which I am indebted for the quotation and the analysis of these two stories.

¹⁷ For an analysis of F.'s second- and third-rate magazine fiction in this period, see K. Eble, *op. cit.*, pp. 119–22. "All of them are long stories . . . expertly plotted. The stories they tell are faithful to the illustrations which accompany them: the handsome, well-dressed man; the clinging or pursuing girl; and, somewhere in the background, a rich father or benign employer." They include such stories as "Millionaire's Girl" (largely written by Zelda), "Jacob's Ladder," "Your Way and Mine" and "Love Boat" (which are two variations on previous stories), "A Penny Spent"

and "Presumption" (on the well-known motive of the young man who wins out through a display of bravado), "The Bowl," "A Freeze-Out" (set in St. Paul), "No Flowers" and "New Types," "The Swimmers" (on the contrast between Europe and America—a typically Jamesian theme), "Sentiment and the Use of Rouge" (an undergraduate war story), "A New Leaf" (again on the contrast between Europe and America), "Hotel Child," "A Change of Class" and "The Rubber Check" (on the motive of social change), "What a Handsome Pair," "On Schedule," "Diagnosis" ("an essay about cracking-up, a kind of unpolished, fictional version of the 'Crack-up'"), "Her Last Case," etc. All of them were uncollected, and Kenneth Eble (who finds only four of them to be "nearly equal to the stories Fitzgerald did select") has been the first to deal with them extensively.

[18] See "My Lost City" (*Esquire,* July 1932) and "Ring" (*The New Republic,* October 1933), both in *CU.* For the relationships between F. and Ring Lardner, cf. W. Goldhurst, *op. cit.,* Chapter IV, pp. 105–54.

[19] *CU,* pp. 19–20. "Echoes of the Jazz Age" had originally appeared in *Scribner's Magazine,* November 1931.

[20] *SEP,* March 3, 1928: first collected in *Stories.* It derived from F.'s six-weeks' experience in Hollywood in 1927.

[21] *The Century,* December 1928, then in *AA.*

[22] Cf. Arthur Mizener, *The Sense of Life in the Modern Novel* (Boston, 1964), pp. 189–90.

[23] *SEP,* January 18, 1930, and February 21, 1931, then in *TAR.*

[24] *SEP,* June 4, 1932, then in *TAR.* F. described it as "based on his experiences in the tornadoes that recently swept part of Alabama," cf. *FSP,* p. 256.

[25] *The American Mercury,* October 1932, then in *TAR.* It had been refused by *The Cosmopolitan* and *The Redbook* (cf. *FSP,* p. 326, n. 66). It was partly based on an actual experience during F.'s second stay in Hollywood in the late months of 1931; cf. K. Eble, *op. cit.,* pp. 125–26, for more details.

[26] *SEP,* June 8, 1929, and October 11, 1930; the first reprinted in *Stories,* the second in *AA.*

[27] See *AA,* p. 161.

CHAPTER VI

[1] Cf. Ortega y Gasset, "Notes on the Novel," in *The Dehumanization of Art* (New York, 1956), pp. 51–97: "The interest of the outer mechanism of the plot is today reduced to a minimum. All the better: the novel must now revolve about the superior interest emanating from the inner mechanism of the personages" (p. 95).

² "I have no facility"—he wrote Maxwell Perkins on March 4, 1934. "After all, Max, I am a plodder . . . everything that I have ever attained has been through a long and persistent struggle." *Letters,* p. 247. For his laborious method of composition, see his own statements in A. Turnbull, *op. cit.,* pp. 259 ff. (". . . three drafts are absolutely necessary. First, the high inspirational points. Second, the cold going over. Third, putting both in their proper perspective." *Ibid.,* p. 260).

³ See Gerald Murphy, "This Was F. S. Fitzgerald," in *Radio TV Scripts,* September 1955, p. 64.

⁴ This material is preserved in six blue cardboard boxes in the Princeton University Manuscript Room. The first contains scattered notes and the MS of the first draft, the second the typescript of the same draft and some MSS, the third and fourth contain the "Rosemary Version" and two typescripts, slightly differing, of the third version, the fifth contains the typescript of the version published serially in *Scribner's Magazine* and most of its proofs, and the sixth F.'s own copy of the book with his revisions. The whole material connected with *TTN* has been now painstakingly studied by Matthew J. Bruccoli in his extremely useful book *The Composition of Tender Is the Night* (University of Pittsburgh Press, 1963). References in my study were originally to the unpublished material; when possible, they have now been referred to Bruccoli's book, for the convenience of the reader.

⁵ Cf. his letter to Maxwell Perkins (August 28, 1925) as quoted in A. Mizener, "A Note on 'The World's Fair,'" *Kenyon Review,* X (fall 1948), p. 701.

⁶ *TTN,* Appendix, pp. 335–36. F. had discussed his material with Hemingway; cf. M. J. Bruccoli, *op. cit.,* p. 19.

⁷ "Will you ask somebody what is done if one American murders another in France," he had written to Perkins (*circa* February 1926). "In a certain sense my plot is not unlike Dreiser's in the American Tragedy." Then Francis himself would have been hunted down and killed. Cf. M. J. Bruccoli, *op. cit.,* p. 27.

⁸ At a certain moment F. reversed the order of the first two chapters, beginning with Francis' arrival on the Riviera, as he would do with Rosemary in the 1934 edition of *TTN.*

⁹ This episode is printed in *Kenyon Review,* pp. 566–78 under the title of "The World's Fair," and is partly reproduced in *TTN,* pp. 338–45 under the title of "Wanda Breasted." Some details of this episode will be used for the Mary Minghetti-Lady Caroline episode in *TTN* (V, 10). In the MS it is made clear that Abe is desperately in love with Dinah, and this is the main reason for his dissipation; in *TTN* there is only a hint at this fact. Cf. M. J. Bruccoli, *op. cit.,* pp. 44–45 and 53, where part of the MS is reproduced.

[10] F.'s "General Plan" is now published for the first time, *ibid.*, pp. 76–78. Bruccoli suggests that F. copied Zola's system in his notes for *L'Assommoir*, as described in Matthew Josephson's *Zola and His Time* (1928), cf. *ibid.*, pp. 86–87.

[11] This variation from the "General Plan" was perhaps due to F.'s own autobiographical experience when he had taken more and more to drinking after his wife's nervous breakdown. In his description of Dick's character, however, F. had stressed his weakness "such as the social-climbing, the drinking, the desperate clinging to one woman, finally the neurosis," and he had charted a "parallel" between the "actual case" and the "case in the novel." Now in M. J. Bruccoli, *op. cit.*, pp. 78–79.

[12] In his notes F. had envisaged the possibility of Nicole's committing either suicide or murder: "Only her transference to him [Dick] saves her—when it is not working she reverts to homicidal mania and tries to kill men." Now *ibid.*, p. 80. F. had originally written ". . . and tries to kill herself"; then he struck out *herself* and substituted *men*. Of Nicole's "homicidal" tendency we have an example in *TTN*, when she tries to kill her family while driving a car. Cf. also *ibid.*, p. 77.

[13] Part of the MS is reproduced in M. J. Bruccoli, *op. cit.*, pp. 144–45 and p. 173.

[14] For a detailed analysis of the differences between the serial version and the book, cf. M. J. Bruccoli, *op. cit.*, pp. 191 and 199–200. Cf. also *Letters*, p. 346.

[15] Cf., among others, C. H. Gratton, *"Tender Is the Night"* (1934), reprinted in A. Kazin, *op. cit.*, pp. 104–7, and Martin Kallich, "F.S.F.: Money or Morals," *The University of Kansas City Review*, XV (summer 1949), pp. 271–80. M. Kallich finds an economic concern in almost all the works of Fitzgerald.

[16] *TTN*, pp. x–xi; *Letters*, p. 281. Cf. also *ibid.*, p. 510 ("The first part, the romantic introduction, was too long and too elaborated largely because of the fact that it had been written over a series of years with varying plans"), and p. 532. For the letter to Cerf, cf. *ibid.*, pp. 340–41.

[17] This well-known note is reproduced in *TTN*, p. xii, *CU*, pp. 180–81. The titles of the five books have been adopted by Malcolm Cowley for his edition of the "final version."

[18] But it is there at work all the time: "My politeness is a trick of the heart," says Dick, and he would later admit that "the change came a long way back—but at first it did not show. The manner remains intact for some time after the morale cracks" (*TTN*, pp. 176 and 304).

[19] The idea of ending his book on a fading away was suggested to F., according to his own admission, by Hemingway (who had adopted it in *A Farewell to Arms*), who had in turn derived it from Conrad; cf. *Letters*,

pp. 362–63 (to John Peale Bishop: "There's a deliberate choice in my avoidance of a dramatic ending—I deliberately did not want it." "I believe it was Ernest Hemingway who developed to me, in conversation, that the dying fall was preferable to the dramatic ending under certain conditions, and I think we both got the germ of the idea from Conrad"). Cf. also *Letters*, p. 310 (where F. speaks of an influence of David Garnett), p. 510 ("the motif of the 'dying fall' was absolutely deliberate and it did not come from any diminution of vitality but from a definite plan. That particular trick is one that Ernest Hemingway and I worked out—probably from Conrad's preface to *The Nigger*—and it has been the greatest 'credo' in my life"), and p. 538. In the light of these observations, Abe North's violent death offers a kind of counterpoint to Dick's fading away: even before he was "beaten to death in a speakeasy" Abe had said that he wanted "to die violently instead of fading away sentimentally" (*TTN*, p. 95).

[20] Cf. Henry James, *The Sacred Fount*, ed. with an introduction by Leon Edel (New York, 1953), and my own introduction to the Italian version of the novel, *La Fonte sacra* (Venice, 1963), for a fuller treatment of the subject. The motive of the transference of vitality, on the other hand, seems to have an autobiographical origin in James as well as in F., and it reappears in quite a number of James's works: from "De Grey: A Romance" (1868) to "Longstaff's Marriage" (1877), from *Watch and Ward* to *Roderick Hudson* and *The Portrait of a Lady*, down to the novels of the "major phase."

[21] *Letters*, p. 346.

[22] *TTN*, pp. 196 and 297. Explicit references to the transference of vitality are to be found, among others, on p. 214 ("waning vitality"), p. 225 ("a lesion of enthusiasm"), p. 240 ("a distinct lesion of vitality"), p. 292, and specifically p. 228 (where Dick says: "I expect some nourishment from people now"). "Taste is no substitute for vitality"—F. was to write—"but in the book it has to do duty for it" (*Letters*, p. 567). Cf. also W. Goldhurst, *op. cit.*, pp. 205–6 and M. J. Bruccoli, *op. cit.*, pp. 80 and 132.

[23] "And being well perhaps I've gone back to my true self—I suppose my grandfather was a crook and I'm a crook by heritage . . . ," says Nicole, and she speaks French with Barban: a typical reversion to her foreign origin. F. had stated in his plan that she was "an aristocrat of half American, half European parentage . . . [an] American with a streak of some foreign blood." Cf. *TTN*, p. 311, and M. J. Bruccoli, *op. cit.*, pp. 76 and 80.

[24] *TTN*, pp. 218–19; "We own you"—Baby Warren had told him—"and you'll admit it sooner or later. It is absurd to keep up the pretense of independence" (*ibid.*, p. 193).

[25] She "is only a catalytic agent," F. was to write to Joseph Hergesheimer, see *Letters*, p. 532.

²⁶ Cf. Karl Jasper, *Über das Tragische* (Munich, 1952). On Dick's "awareness" of his tragic plight, cf. also Eugene White, "The 'Intricate Destiny' of Dick Diver," *Modern Fiction Studies*, VII (spring 1961), pp. 55–62.

²⁷ F. O. Matthiessen, *American Renaissance* (New York, 1951), p. 179.

²⁸ The names of the various characters are obviously significant: Campion may derive from the slang word "camping"; Nicole has a French name which partly justifies her "foreignness" (see note 23, above); Rosemary suggests freshness; Barban is clearly suggestive of "barbarian"; Dick Diver is the man who "dives" headlong into his destiny.

²⁹ *Letters*, p. 363 (to John Peale Bishop, April 7, 1934). In F.'s "Notebooks" we find an entry that might further illustrate the difference he had in mind: "The episodic book (Dos Passos, Romains, etc. [*Gatsby?*]) may be wonderful, but the fact remains that it is episodic, and such definition implies a limitation.... In the true novel you have to stay with the character all the time, and you acquire a sort of second wind about him, a depth of realization."

³⁰ It may be worth noting that according to Walter Rideout (*The Radical Novel in the U.S.*, Cambridge, USA, 1956, pp. 218–19), the most frequent accusation leveled by proletarian literature against the bourgeoisie was concerned with its sexual promiscuity and aberrations.

³¹ "Part III [then Book V]"—wrote F. in a note, *TTN*, p. 354—"is as much as possible seen through Nicole's eyes. All Dick's stories such as are *absolutely necessary* ... must be told without putting in his reactions or feelings. From now on he is mystery man, at least to Nicole with her guessing at mystery." In a letter to Perkins, February 5, 1934, however, F. had written: "In the proof I am pointing up the fact that his [Dick's] intention dominated all this last part but it is not enough and the foreshortening ... does not contain enough of him for the reader to reconstruct his whole personality as viewed as a unit throughout—and the reason for this is my attempt to tell the last part entirely through Nicole's eyes." *Letters*, p. 241. Cf. also M. J. Bruccoli, *op. cit.*, pp. 14 and 132.

³² F. himself had drawn a graph of the action in the last part (now in M. J. Bruccoli, *op. cit.*, p. 131), which shows his visual concept of the "dying fall." Cf. also *Letters*, p. 310.

³³ See *CU*, pp. 312–16 and Chapter VII of this study.

CHAPTER VII

¹ These statements are in a letter to an unknown recipient (March 26, 1940) who had inquired about the novel. For F.'s interest in Marxism while at La Paix, cf. A. Turnbull, *op. cit.*, pp. 226 and 231. For his own references to his "radicalism," cf. *Letters*, pp. 37–38, 47, 102, and 243.

² Cf. *CU*, p. 177: "Just as Stendhal's portrait of a Byronic man made *Le*

Rouge et le Noir, so couldn't my portrait of Ernest as Philippe make the real modern man?"

³ *The Redbook,* October 1934, June and August 1935, November 1941. According to A. Mizener (*FSP,* p. 252) the magazine bought them to help the writer; F. himself (in the letter quoted above) admitted that they had been refused by *SEP.* It is rather surprising to find that he considered Philippe "to some extent completed in the fourth story" and as "one of the best characters I've ever 'drawn,'" and that he wanted, as late as 1938, to publish "a Big collection of stories leading off with *Philippe*—entirely rewritten and pulled together into a 30,000-word novelette." *Letters,* p. 281; cf. also *ibid.,* p. 283, where the original plan is described as "tremendously ambitious."

⁴ Cf. *The Redbook,* June 1935, pp. 20–21. Even if this attempt by F. is seldom mentioned and analyzed, I think it important, for reasons of completeness, to give some quotations and a sketch of the four stories to acquaint the reader with an aspect of F.'s fiction that is often forgotten or ignored. Every great writer has his or her dark moments, and it is a false kind of pity for the critic to pass them over silently, as if they did not exist.

⁵ See, for instance, the beginning of the fourth story, which provides us with a specimen of an involuted and ridiculous language:

"They lay on the sand beside the ford, their bodies drinking in the sun of St. Anthony's summer.

'This is my last bath for a long time,' Philippe said.

'There's where you're wrong,' answered Griselda. 'You're going to sponge off once a week—or you won't be attractive to me.'

'And who are you?' he teased her.

'That's just what I've been wondering,' Griselda answered. 'How about getting married pretty soon?'" *The Redbook,* November 1941.

⁶ *Esquire,* January 1935, then in *TAR.*

⁷ *Esquire,* February 1935, then in *TAR.*

⁸ In this period F. also wrote quite a number of "retrospective" short stories or articles, of little or no aesthetic value, such as "Too Cute for Words" (*SEP,* April 18, 1936), "Three Acts of Music" (*Esquire,* May 1936), "The Ants at Princeton" (*Esquire,* June 1936), "'I Didn't Get Over'" (*Esquire,* October 1936), "'Send Me in, Coach'" (*Esquire,* November 1936). Stories such as "The Intimate Strangers" (*McCall's,* June 1935) or "The Passionate Eskimo" (*Liberty,* June 8, 1935) were purely commercial stories, written for money alone.

⁹ They were first published in *Esquire,* February, March, and April, 1936; reprinted in *CU.*

¹⁰ "—Christ, man, how do you find time in the middle of the general conflagration to worry about all that stuff?" Dos Passos wrote to F. "... We're

living in one of the damnedest tragic moments in history—if you want to go to pieces I think it's absolutely O.K. but I think you ought to write a first rate novel about it (and you probably will) instead of spilling it in little pieces for Arnold Gingrich [the editor of *Esquire*]. . . ." Cf. *CU*, p. 311. "We never quite understand each other," F. had written of Dos Passos (cf. *Letters*, p. 345). The same reproach was contained in a letter by Hemingway, as we can see from F.'s letter to Mrs. William Hamm: "Ernest Hemingway wrote me an irritable letter in which he bawled me out for having been so public about what were essentially private affairs and should be written about in fiction or not at all." *Letters*, p. 545.

¹¹ *Esquire*, December 1934, then in *CU*.

¹² *CU*, p. 79: of particular literary interest are the first (where Edmund Wilson is named as F.'s "intellectual conscience") the third (where there is clear allusion to Hemingway as F.'s "artistic conscience") and the fifth (where F. admits that his "political conscience had scarcely existed for ten years").

¹³ *Ibid.*, pp. 82 and 83. And he went on: "If you were dying of starvation outside my window, I would go out quickly and give you the smile and the voice (if no longer the hand) and stick around till somebody raised a nickel to phone for the ambulance, that is if I thought there would be any copy in it for me."

¹⁴ Cf. Lionel Trilling, "F.S.F.," in A. Kazin (ed.), *op. cit.*, pp. 194 ff.

¹⁵ Many statements contained in these essays might serve as a kind of "ironic" comment on Dick's predicament in the novel: "Of course all life is a process of breaking down, but the blows that do the dramatic side of the work . . . don't show their effect all at once. There is another sort of blow that comes from within—that you don't feel until it's too late to do anything about it . . ."; ". . . it occurred to me suddenly that of all natural forces, vitality is the uncommunicable one . . . one tried to distribute it— but always without success; to further mix metaphors, vitality never 'takes.'" *CU*, pp. 69 and 74.

¹⁶ In A. Kazin (ed.), *op. cit.*, p. 170. According to A. Turnbull, *op. cit.*, p. 270, " 'The Crack-up' was also the work of a lapsed Catholic, for whom confession was a rhythm of the soul." To K. Eble, *op. cit.*, p. 141, "The delicate handling of the narrator as both observer and observed, the movement from awareness to a precise kind of bitterness, and the elegance of the prose are aesthetic values of a high order. Although presented as autobiography, they have the air of highly wrought and intensely felt fiction. They are justifiably famous; taken together, they constitute one of the superb short stories in American literature."

¹⁷ Cf. *AA*, p. ii. Mizener would later describe these writings as "an effort to define an attitude toward living," as "a wry acceptance of everyday

actuality," cf. Introduction to *The Fitzgerald Reader* (New York, 1963), pp. xix and xxv.

[18] *Esquire*, July, August, and September 1936, then in *AA* (except the first).

[19] Cf. *CU*, p. 312, and *Letters*, p. 552. Cf. also *Letters*, p. 551, for a new defense of the "selection" principle, and p. 97 for F.'s strict censure of Thomas Wolfe's fiction. In this case, Wolfe answered F., advocating more or less those principles that H. G. Wells had already used against James: "For your argument is based simply upon one *way* . . . there are a lot of ways . . . *Tristram Shandy* is indubitably a great book . . . it is great because it *boils* and *pours*—for the *unselected* quality of its selection. . . . Well, don't forget, Scott, that a great writer is not only a leaver-outer but also a putter-inner, and that Shakespeare and Cervantes and Dostoevsky were great putter-inners—greater putter-inners, in fact, than taker-outers and will be remembered for what they put in . . ." It is typical that Wolfe expressed in this letter the symptomatic opinion that *TTN* had in it the best work F. had ever done. Cf. *CU*, pp. 313–16.

[20] Cf. Nemi D'Agostino, "F.S.F.," *Studi Americani*, p. 240.

[21] *Esquire*, February 1937, then in *Stories*. "My stories get truer and truer— F. had said—I can't keep the truth out of them." Cf. A. Turnbull, *op. cit.*, p. 259.

[22] *Esquire*, September 1937, then in *Stories*.

[23] *Esquire*, January 1938, then in *Stories*.

[24] *Esquire*, November 1939, then in *AA*.

[25] Cf. *Letters*, p. 96: "Once one is caught up into the material world not one person in ten thousand finds the time to form literary taste, to examine the validity of philosophic concepts for himself, or to form what, for lack of a better phrase, I might call the wise and tragic sense of life."

[26] *Esquire*, July 1941 (posthumous), then in *Stories*.

[27] *Esquire*, December 1939, then in *Stories; Furioso*, Winter 1947 (posthumous), then in *AA*.

[28] The seventeen sketches appeared in the twelve numbers of *Esquire* issued in 1940 and in the first five numbers issued in 1941; they are now reprinted in a separate volume, *The Pat Hobby Stories*, ed. with an introduction by Arnold Gingrich (New York, 1962). According to Gingrich, "much of what he felt about Hollywood and about himself permeated these stories" (*ibid.*, p. ix). F. had planned to revise them, and in a note to Gingrich (September 21, 1939) he had written: "I wish to God you could pay more money. These have all been stories, not sketches or articles, and only unfit for the big time because of their length" (as quoted *ibid.*, p. xi). At other times, however, F. considered them "done to pay the grocer," and in fact he had to turn them in to redeem advances from the magazine.

^⁹ F. had also written two more stories about Hollywood, "Discard" and "The Last Kiss," both published posthumously, the first in *Harper's Bazaar,* January 1948, the second in *Collier's,* April 16, 1949, and both uncollected.

CHAPTER VIII

[1] F. himself had called *TTN* "a woman's book," cf. *Letters,* p. 247.

[2] Cf. J. Dos Passos, "A Note on F.S.F.," in A. Kazin (ed.), *op. cit.,* p. 155.

[3] In the MS notes we read: "Stahr . . . gives up and goes away—with no future that he sees. The plane falls."

[4] This outline is reproduced in *LT,* pp. 138–41.

[5] Cf. *LT,* pp. 140–41: "Now, realizing how much he needs Thalia, things are patched up between them. For a day or two they are ideally happy. They are going to marry, but he must make one more trip East to clinch the victory which he has conciliated in the affairs of the company."

[6] This episode, which F. sketched in detail, is in *LT,* pp. 155–58. Three children find the fallen plane. They come upon some personal objects of the dead, and keep them without saying anything of what they have found. Dan, who makes the suggestion, is a "tough" young boy who "bears, in some form of speech, a faint resemblance to Bradogue," and he "will spend the rest of his life looking for a chance to get something for nothing." Jim, who in the meantime has read the contents of Stahr's briefcase, "has gotten an admiration for the man" and decides to tell the whole story, against the threats of Dan. The two boys can therefore be taken as two "heirs," respectively, of Bradogue and Stahr. Frances, the girl who is with them, has kept the jewel box of an actress and she is described as "faintly corrupted"; she "may possibly go off in a year or so in search of adventure and may turn into anything from a gold digger to a prostitute." While Jim is "all right" and Dan "has been completely corrupted," Frances is left with the "lingering conviction that luxury is over the next valley, therefore giving a bitter and acrid finish to the incident."

[7] That outline and diagram belong to the same stage of elaboration may be inferred from the fact that in both of them the name of Cecilia is still spelt Cecelia, as it was spelt in the first notes.

[8] In this first draft the name of the woman is still Thalia, as it was in the outline and in the notes; it is not yet changed to Kathleen. A rather unsympathetic portrait of Thalia-Kathleen is to be found in two commercial stories of this period, "The Last Kiss" and "Director's Special," which exploited some marginal material of the novel. Sentences from both stories, and from a third ("The Intimate Strangers"), were used in *LT.* It is worth noting here, therefore, that F.'s first conception of Thalia-Kathleen was such as to make her instrumental in compromising Stahr's chances of affirmation.

[9] Chapter A is divided into three episodes in the diagram, reproduced in *LT*, pp. 142–43: "1. The plane. / 2. Nashville. / 3. Up forward. Different. . . . Introduce Cecilia, Stahr, White, Schwartz."

[10] "She was twenty when the events . . . occurred, but she is twenty-five when she tells about the events, and of course many of them appear to her in a different light." *Ibid.*, p. 138.

[11] " 'There would be quite a crash,' Wylie said, 'if steam-roller Brady [Cecilia's father] met steam-roller Smith [Stahr].'

'Is Mr. Smith a competitor of Father's?'

'Not exactly. But if he was a competitor, I know where my money would be.'

'On Father?'

'I'm afraid not.' " *Ibid.*, p. 14.

[12] Cf. *LT*, pp. 134–36, where this longer draft is reproduced.

[13] "Into the warm darkness" might be a verbal echo of Henry James: in *Washington Square*, Catherine Sloper ends her short-lived dream of love "looking out into the warm darkness." Chapter XXXIV.

[14] Chapter B is divided into three episodes in the diagram: "4. Johnny Swanson—Marcus leaving—Brady. / 5. The earthquake. / 6. The back lot. . . . Introduces Brady, Kathleen, Robinson and secretaries. Atmosphere of night—sustain."

[15] Chapters C and D are respectively divided into four and two episodes: "7. The camera man. Stahr's work and health. From something she wrote. / 8. First conference. / 9. Second conference and afterwards. / 10. Commissary and idealism about non-profit pictures. Rushes. Phone call, etc. / 11. Visit to rushes. / 12. Second meeting that night. Wrong girl—glimpse." The two chapters "are equal to guest list and Gatsby's party." *LT*, pp. 142–43.

[16] When Stahr tells Ridingwood that some other director is "finishing his take" in his place and that he is dismissed, this is the end of their brief conversation: " 'How about my coat?' he asked suddenly. 'I left it over a chair on the set.' 'I know you did,' said Stahr. 'Here it is.' " *LT*, p. 52.

[17] Four episodes in the diagram: "13. Cecilia and Stahr and ball. / 14. Malibu seduction. Try to get on lot. Dead middle. / 15. Cecilia and father. / 16. Phone call and wedding. . . . Atmosphere in 15 most important. Hint of Waste Land of the house too late."

[18] This detail is less preposterous than we would think, and it has an autobiographical origin. Sheilah Graham, who supplied F. with many traits for the character of Kathleen, had in fact broken her engagement with an English lord to stay with F. in Hollywood (cf. Sheilah Graham and Gerold Frank, *Beloved Infidel* (New York, 1958), Chapter XVII). It is typical of F., however, that he overdid it.

[19] Four episodes in the diagram: "17. The dam breaks with Brimmer. / 18. The cummerbund—market—(The theatre with Benchley). / 19. The four meet. Renewal. Palomar. / 20. Wylie White in office."

[20] Four episodes in the diagram: "21. Sick in Washington. To quit? / 22. Brady and Stahr—double blackmail. Quarrel with Wylie. / 23. Throws over Cecilia, who tells her father. Stops making pictures. A story conference—rushes and sets. Lies low after cut. / 24. Last fling with Kathleen. Old stars in heat wave at Encino." The episodes at the rushes and on the sets were to contrast markedly with the corresponding episodes in Chapters C and D, where Stahr's efficiency was still unimpaired.

[21] Three episodes in the diagram: "25. Brady gets to Smith. Fleishacker and Cecilia. / 26. Stahr hears plan. Camera man O.K. Stops it—very sick. / 27. Resolve problem. Kathleen at airport; Cecilia to college. . . . The suit and the price."

[22] Three episodes in the diagram: "28. The plane falls. Foretaste of the future in Fleishacker. / 29. Outside the studio. / 30. Johnny Swanson at funeral." For a detailed synopsis of the rest of the story, put together by Edmund Wilson, cf. *LT*, pp. 129–33.

[23] *Ibid.*, p. ix.

[24] Cf. W. Goldhurst, *op. cit.*, p. 207, for whom Dick "may be accurately considered a ruined artist." Of Gatsby himself F. had written that "he had thrown himself into it [his illusion] with a *creative* passion" (my italics).

[25] See *LHUS*, pp. 1039–64. James's *Stories of Writers and Artists* have been collected and edited by F. O. Matthiessen (New York: New Directions, n.d.). James deals with the subject in the VII, XII, and XIV of his Prefaces, collected in *The Art of the Novel*.

[26] *LT*, p. 141. "It is a *constructed* novel like *Gatsby*"—F. was to write his wife—"with passages of poetic prose when it fits the action, but no ruminations or side-shows like *Tender*. Everything must contribute to the dramatic movement." *Letters*, p. 128; cf. also *ibid.*, p. 127.

[27] "He has an overwhelming urge toward the girl, who promises to give life back to him—though he has no idea yet of marriage—she is the heart of hope and freshness. . . . This girl had a life—it was very seldom he met anyone whose life did not depend in some way on him or hope to depend on him." *LT*, pp. 151–52. It is hardly necessary to point out the similarity of Dick's relation to Rosemary in *TTN*.

[28] "It is distinctly *not* about Hollywood," F. had written to Perkins on May 22, 1939, cf. *Letters*, p. 285.

[29] On the subject, see Agostino Lombardo, *Realismo e simbolismo* (Rome, 1957), and *La Ricerca del vero* (Rome, 1961), among others.

[30] J. Dos Passos, "A Note on F.S.F.," in *CU*, p. 339. And he went on: "A

firmly anchored ethical standard is something that American writing has been struggling towards for half a century." In his notes, curiously, F. had written: "Advice to young writers—read Tolstoi and Marx and D. H. Lawrence; and then Tolstoi and Marx and D. H. Lawrence."

[31] Cf. *LT*, p. 141, and *Letters*, pp. 430 and 349. Cf. also *ibid.*, p. 131 ("It is a novel *à la Flaubert* without 'ideas' but only people moved singly and in mass through what I hope are authentic moods"), and p. 79.

[32] *LT*, pp. 147–48. About *TTN* F. had significantly written in a note: "*Tender* is less interesting toward the climax because of the absence of conversation. The eye flies for it and skips essential stuff for they [the readers] don't want their characters dissolved in desiccation and analysis but, like me, in action that results from the previous."

[33] In the diagram, F. actually divided the material in five acts: "Act I (The Plane) STAHR" corresponding to Chapter A; "Act II (The Circus) STAHR and KATHLEEN" corresponding to Chapters B–E; "Act III (The Underworld) THE STRUGGLE" corresponding to Chapters F–G; "Act IV (The Murderers) DEFEAT" corresponding to Chapter H; and "Act V (The End) EPILOGUE" corresponding to Chapter I. *LT*, pp. 142–43.

[34] As a "narrator," for instance, Cecilia often gives away, as it were, her sources: "Prince Agge is my authority for the luncheon in the commissary . . ."; "So I met Robby . . . it was Robby who later told me how Stahr found his love that night." "This is Cecilia taking up the narrative in person," we read on p. 77. It is obvious that these sentences would have been changed or cut out if F. had completed and revised the book.

[35] "The hare limped trembling through the frozen grass" in "The Eve of St. Agnes," cf. *Letters*, p. 29.

[36] Cf. *Letters*, p. 312 (to Hemingway, November 8, 1940): "I never got to tell you how I liked *To Have and Have Not* . . . There is observation and writing in that that the boys will be imitating with a vengeance. . . ." In a previous letter (*ibid.*, p. 309) F. had written to Hemingway: "Save for a few of the dead or dying old men you are the only man writing fiction in America that I look up to very much. There are pieces and paragraphs of your work that I read over and over—in fact, I stopped myself doing it for a year and a half because I was afraid that your particular rhythms were going to creep in on mine by process of infiltration." Cf. also *CU*, p. 79, where F. disclaims having imitated Hemingway's "infectious style" while admitting that "there was an awful pull toward him when I was on a spot." According to W. Goldhurst (*op. cit.*, pp. 210–16) an influence of Hemingway would be clearly perceptible in *GG*, "The Rich Boy," and above all in *TTN*, while the two writers had also thematic interests in common: the motive of the outsider, of the modern woman and of the ruined artist, among others. Goldhurst seems to me to overstate his case.

CHAPTER IX

[1] Cf. for instance the essays by Edmund Wilson (1925 and 1926), by J. C. Mosher (1926) and by P. Rosenfeld (1925), all in A. Kazin (ed.), *op. cit.*

[2] Cf. for instance, among others, the writings of D. W. Harding (1934) and C. H. Gratton (1934) in A. Kazin (ed.), *op. cit.*; of Lawrence Leighton ("An Autopsy and a Prescription," *Hound & Horn*, V (summer 1932), pp. 519–40) and of Matthew Josephson (in *The Younger Novelists*. New York, 1933).

[3] At the death of F., Margaret Marshal wrote that she was "depressed" by his works in an article for *The Nation*, 1941, now in A. Kazin (ed.), *op. cit.*; *The New Republic*, however, published five commemorations and evaluations of F. in the two numbers of February 17 and March 3, 1941; the contributors were J. Dos Passos, J. O'Hara, J. P. Bishop, Budd Schulberg, and Glenway Wescott. The last two essays are in A. Kazin (ed.), *op. cit.*, the last one also in *CU*.

[4] For a list of these partial contributions the reader is referred to the 2d and 3d sections of the "Selected Bibliography" and to Lewis Leary (ed.), *Articles on American Literature* (Durham: Duke University Press, 1954). It is sufficient here to indicate that these essays studied F.'s "tragicomedy," his derivation from Joyce, his "American" motives, his social criticism and his obsession with money and all possible symbolic or realistic aspects of *GG*. Parallels were established with "The Waste Land" and *Great Expectations*, with Frank Norris or John Keats, with Henry James or Edith Wharton. Mythic or mythological archetypes, the East-West polarity, the contrast Europe-America were particularly insisted upon. F. was in turn represented as Keats or as Icarus.

[5] "Tradition and the Individual Talent" (1917), now in *Selected Essays* (London, 1958), p. 15 and *passim*.

[6] "The Novel of Manners in America," *Kenyon Review*, XII (Winter 1950), pp. 1–20; "F. and the Imaginative Possession of American Life," *Sewanee Review*, LIV (Spring 1956), pp. 66–86.

[7] Maxwell Geismar, *The Last of the Provincials* (Boston, 1947): *BD* and *TTN* were set against *GG* and *LT* both for their subject matter and for their method. The first two novels were the result of a confused and overwhelming inspiration, intense but chaotic, while the last two were the result of a careful structural control and of a technical virtuosity. The same dichotomy was suggested by F. himself in a letter to Corey Ford: *TSP* and *GG* were selective, while *BD* and *TTN* "aimed at being full and comprehensive." *Letters*, p. 551.

[8] New York, 1955. The book was severely criticized by Leslie Fiedler in *Partisan Review* (Summer 1955). Leslie Fiedler himself, however, in *An*

End to Innocence (Boston, 1955) and later in *Love and Death in the American Novel* (New York, 1960) considered F.'s fiction as an attempt to give us "the portrait of the artist as a young girl."

⁹ "The Ability to Function. A Reappraisal of F. and Hemingway," in *The New American Library*, no. 13 (New York, 1958), pp. 34–51. Cf. also Nemi D'Agostino, "F.S.F.," in *Studi Americani*.

¹⁰ POSTSCRIPT 1964.—The numerous additions to the body of Fitzgerald criticism that appeared after 1961 confirm most of the points that I have made in the previous pages and represent a logical continuation of the trends discussed here. Most of them deal with F.'s literary achievement and many of them give further evidence of F.'s serious concern with literature, while emphasizing at the same time both the "English" techniques that he used and the American tradition to which he naturally belonged because of the themes he chose to deal with. Late in 1961, Charles Shain stressed F.'s literary and artistic achievement in his perceptive study of his fiction for the Minnesota Pamphlets Series on American Writers. Particular emphasis was given here to the gradual development of his themes and techniques. Shain was particularly good on F.'s early novels and stressed their literary significance; no consideration was given to the Fitzgerald legend, while his reputation as a writer was not only affirmed, but taken as a matter of course. The next year, Andrew Turnbull's new biography threw a great deal of light on F.'s later years, and recreated an image of both man and writer that increased and was bound to increase our consideration of his human struggle to survive and of his conscious and painstaking literary endeavors. Turnbull relied extensively on unpublished materials and letters and was able to show how F.'s artistic awareness grew out of his years of suffering and isolation, regardless of his early association with the Jazz Age. In a sense, Turnbull's biography is complementary to, rather than a substitute for, Mizener's early biography; its main asset is the freshness of approach and the author's personal acquaintance with Fitzgerald, which enabled him to provide us with a lively first-hand impression not only of the man, but of the mature writer. In 1963 Andrew Turnbull edited a comprehensive collection of F.'s letters; if proof was needed, they gave further evidence of the writer's conscious craftsmanship and artistry, of his awareness of the burden of writing, of his cultural sensitivities, of his painstaking concern with literature and the craft of fiction. They reveal a conscious, dedicated artist, aware of his gift but at the same time of the care and nourishment that talent requires. Unfortunately, this is not an annotated edition, and the letters are not given in their chronological order; they are grouped by recipient, starting with the beautiful letters to F.'s daughter. This arrangement tends to emphasize the human side rather than the slow artistic growth of Fitzgerald, the human maturity he achieved through suffering rather than the

artistic maturity he groped for and finally attained through his extensive and perceptive readings, and so forth. In the same year, and in the same way, William Goldhurst's study *Fitzgerald and His Contemporaries* stressed his personal associations with contemporary writers rather than the cultural links he shared with them. There is no general view in this book of the cultural atmosphere in which both F. and his contemporaries worked and no precise examination of the cultural and literary links that existed among them. On the other hand, when he is dealing with a particular writer (Hemingway or Wilson, for instance) Goldhurst seems to be carried away by his subject and to indicate a wealth of influences and cross-relationships that mutually destroy each other. Fitzgerald's role in the Twenties and Thirties is often neglected and no clear grasp is reached of his human and literary position in his times. The book is useful for an understanding of F.'s human side, his full awareness of his concerns and limitations, his unbounded sympathy with his fellow writers. Too often, however, the pleasant anecdote overshadows the meaningful implication or the revealing coincidence of themes and methods. Matthew Bruccoli's *The Composition of Tender Is the Night* (also published in 1963), on the other hand, is a very good example of the painstaking application of scholarly methods to a crucial work in F.'s canon. Bruccoli's examination of the various drafts of the novel is revealing in itself and offers a wealth of material for a documented evaluation of it. One is tempted to say that Bruccoli overdoes his job a little by insisting on the minutest details and the slightest differences among the various drafts. His book gives a final proof of F.'s painstaking method of composition and of his exasperated artistic consciousness, as well as of his crucial difficulties with the overgrowing material that confronted him in his maturity. Every sinew of the preparatory drafts is laid bare. And yet, Bruccoli tends to overlook a little the possible critical implications of his findings. He stops short of the published novel, and one would wish him to apply the various facts that he has brought to light to an aesthetic evaluation of the novel. This was not, of course, his intention, but such a wealth of new material seems to be wasted unless it becomes instrumental to a better appreciation of the work. Also in 1963 Kenneth Eble published his perceptive monograph on the author, which is a little "erratic" but quite useful for a general evaluation of F.'s fiction. Eble seems at his best when dealing with the short stories, and this aspect of his book must be duly emphasized. For the first time F.'s stories are given full consideration both in themselves and in their vital relationships to the novels. Eble does not restrict himself to the collected stories, but also examines the scattered stories published in periodicals, so that his study becomes the most complete of the whole of F.'s fiction. Eble's method of dealing with his material is a little puzzling and somewhat dangerous. Refusing to deal with the works in the chronological order of their composition or publication, he chooses to deal with them according to the fictional order of the experience that they portray (that is, beginning for instance with the Basil stories before *TSP*). In this way, the consistency of F.'s artistic development is rather taken for granted than demonstrated; the examination of the single works is better than the over-all evaluation of them as a whole. In different hands, moreover, this method might easily lead to a new form of critical confusion between what belongs to the man and what pertains to his work. In 1964, to close this brief survey, James E. Miller brought out an enlarged version of his 1957 book on Fitzgerald, dealing more extensively with his later fiction; the main argument of the book is still more relevant to the first novels than to the later ones. Finally, in his latest book (*The Sense of Life in the Modern Novel*, 1964), Arthur Mizener has a valuable appreciation of *LT* in the context of a more general examination of the twentieth-century novel which stresses F.'s belonging to the tradition of the "English" well-made novel. (For the bibliographical references, see the Selected Bibliography.)

[11] *Letters*, pp. 85–6.

[12] Kenneth Eble (*op. cit.*, p. 157) stresses the "Englishness" of F.'s style as well: "the style is in the mainstream of English literary development; it impresses, not because it is intensely original or eccentric, but because it is a graceful, lucid and highly evocative prose almost as easily connected with Dryden as with Joseph Conrad."

[13] *Letters*, p. 572.

[14] Cf. F. J. Hoffman, *The Modern Novel in America* (Chicago, 1951).

[15] "Riches have *never* fascinated me"—F. wrote to Hemingway—"unless combined with the greatest charm or distinction." *Letters*, p. 311.

[16] The two quotations are from *American Prose and Poetry*, ed. by Norman Foerster (Boston, 1947), p. 76, and from *The Main Lines of American Literature*, ed. by R. W. Short and W. S. Scott (New York, 1954), p. 40.

[17] On the motive of frustration, among others, see Leslie Fiedler, *op. cit.*, pp. 175–76 and *passim*. F. himself had written: "I talk with the authority of failure," *CU*, p. 181.

[18] Cf. F. O. Matthiessen, *op. cit., passim*.

[19] William Troy had in fact written: "He has more in common, let us say, with George Eliot, Henry James, and Joseph Conrad than with any of the more prominent members of his own generation." ("The Perfect Life," in *The Nation*, April 17, 1935, as quoted in K. Eble, *op. cit.*, p. 140.)

[20] Cf. Marcel Proust, *The Past Recaptured* (tr. by Frederick A. Blossom), in *Remembrance of Things Past* (New York, 1932), II, p. 1003.

Selected Bibliography

WORKS BY FITZGERALD

Fie! Fie! Fi-Fi! A Musical Comedy in Two Acts Presented by the Princeton University Triangle Club. . . . Plot and Lyrics by F. Scott Fitzgerald. . . . New York: The John Church Co., 1914.

The Evil Eye. A Musical Comedy in Two Acts Presented by the Princeton University Triangle Club. . . . Lyrics by F. Scott Fitzgerald. . . . New York: The John Church Co., 1915.

Safety First. A Musical Comedy in Two Acts Presented by the Princeton University Triangle Club. . . . Lyrics by F. Scott Fitzgerald. . . . New York: The John Church Co., 1916.

This Side of Paradise. New York: Scribner's, 1920.

Flappers and Philosophers. New York: Scribner's, 1920. ("The Offshore Pirate," "The Ice Palace," "Head and Shoulders," "The Cut-Glass Bowl," "Bernice Bobs Her Hair," "Benediction," "Dalyrimple Goes Wrong," "The Four Fists".)

The Beautiful and Damned. New York: Scribner's, 1922.

Tales of the Jazz Age. New York: Scribner's, 1922. ("The Jelly-Bean," "The Camel's Back," "May Day," "Porcelain and Pink," "The Diamond as Big as the Ritz," "The Curious Case of Benjamin Button," "Tarquin of Cheapside," " 'O Russet Witch,' " "The Lees of Happiness," "Mr. Icky," "Jemina".)

The Vegetable, or From President to Postman. New York: Scribner's, 1923.

The Great Gatsby. New York: Scribner's, 1925; with an Introduction by F. Scott Fitzgerald, New York: Modern Library, 1934.

All the Sad Young Men. New York: Scribner's, 1926. ("The Rich Boy," "Winter Dreams," "The Baby Party," "Absolution," "Hot and Cold Blood," "Rag Martin-Jones and the Pr-nce of W-les," "The Adjuster," " 'The Sensible Thing,' " "Gretchen's Forty Winks".)

Tender Is the Night. New York: Scribner's, 1934; With the Author's Final Revisions, ed. by Malcolm Cowley, New York: Scribner's, 1948.

Taps at Reveille. New York: Scribner's, 1935. (Basil: I. "The Scandal Detectives," II. "The Freshest Boy," III. "He Thinks He's Wonderful," IV. "The Captured Shadow," V. "The Perfect Life," Josephine: I. "First Blood," II. "A Nice Quiet Place," III. "A Woman with a Past," "Crazy Sunday," "Two Wrongs," "The Night at Chancellorsville," "The Last of the Belles," "Majesty," "Family in the Wind," "A Short Trip Home," "One Interne," "The Fiend," "Babylon Revisited".)

The Last Tycoon. Edited with an Introduction by Edmund Wilson, New York: Scribner's, 1941.

The Crack-up. Edited by Edmund Wilson, New York: New Directions, 1945. ("Echoes of the Jazz Age," "My Lost City," "Ring," " 'Show Mr. and Mrs. F. to Number . . . ,' " "Auction—Model 1934," "Sleeping and Waking," "The Crack-up," "Early Success," The Notebooks, Letters to Friends, Letters to Frances Scott Fitzgerald, Three Letters about *GG*, A Letter from Dos Passos, A Letter from Th. Wolfe, Essays by Paul Rosenfeld, Glenway Wescott, Dos Passos, "The Hours" by John Peale Bishop.)

The Portable F. Scott Fitzgerald. Selected by Dorothy Parker, with an Introduction by John O'Hara, New York: The Viking Press, 1945. (*GG*, *TTN*, "Absolution," "The Baby Party," "The Rich Boy," "May Day," "The Cut-Glass Bowl," "The Offshore Pirate," "The Freshest Boy," "Crazy Sunday," "Babylon Revisited".)

The Stories. Edited with an Introduction by Malcolm Cowley, New York: Scribner's, 1951. ("The Diamond as Big as the Ritz," "Bernice Bobs Her Hair," "The Ice Palace," "May Day," "Winter Dreams," " 'The Sensible Thing,' " "Absolution," "The Rich Boy," "The Baby Party," "Magnetism," "The Last of the Belles," "The Rough Crossing," "The Bridal Party," "Two Wrongs," "The Scandal Detectives," "The Freshest Boy," "The Captured Shadow," "A Woman with a Past," "Babylon Revisited," "Crazy Sunday," "Family in the Wind," "An Alcoholic Case," "The Long Way Out," "Financing Finnegan," "A Patriotic Short," "Two Old Timers," "Three Hours Between Planes," "The Lost Decade".)

Afternoon of an Author. A Selection of Uncollected Stories and Essays. With an Introduction and Notes by Arthur Mizener, Princeton: Princeton University Library, 1957. ("A Night at the Fair," "Forging Ahead," "Basil and Cleopatra," "Princeton," "Who's Who—and Why," "How to Live on Practically Nothing a Year," "How to Waste Material: A Note on My Generation," "Ten Years in the Advertising Business," "One Hundred False Starts," "Outside the Cabinet-Maker's," "One Trip Abroad," " 'I Didn't Get Over,' " "Afternoon of an Author," "Author's House," "Design in Plaster," Pat Hobby: " 'Boil Some Water—Lots of It,' " "Teamed with Genius," "No Harm Trying," "News of Paris—Fifteen Years Ago".)

The Pat Hobby Stories. With an Introduction by Arnold Gingrich, New York: Scribner's, 1962. ("Pat Hobby's Christmas Wish," "A Man in the Way," " 'Boil Some Water—Lots of It,' " "Teamed with Genius," "Pat Hobby and Orson Welles," "Pat Hobby's Secret," "Pat Hobby, Putative Father," "The Homes of the Stars," "Pat Hobby Does His Bit," "Pat Hobby's Preview," "No Harm Trying," "A Patriotic Short," "On the Trail of Pat Hobby," "Fun in an Artist's Studio," "Two Old-Timers," "Mightier Than the Sword," "Pat Hobby's College Days".)

The Fitzgerald Reader. Edited with an Introduction by Arthur Mizener,

New York: Scribner's, 1963. (*GG*, sixteen stories all previously collected, the three "Crack-Up" articles, selections from *TTN* and *LT*.)

The Letters of F. Scott Fitzgerald. Edited with an Introduction by Andrew Turnbull, New York: Scribner's, 1963.

The Apprentice Fiction of F. Scott Fitzgerald, 1909–1917. Edited with an Introduction by John Kuehl. New Brunswick: Rutgers University Press, 1965. ("The Mystery of the Raymond Mortgage," "Reade, Substitute Right Half," "A Debt of Honor," "The Rooms with the Green Blinds," "A Luckless Santa Claus," "The Trail of the Duke," "Pain and the Scientist," "Shadow Laurels," "The Ordeal," "The Debutante," "The Spire and the Gargoyle," "Tarquin of Cheapside," "Babes in the Woods," "Sentiment—and the Use of Rouge," "The Pierian Springs and the Last Straw," "The Death of My Father").

For a complete list of Fitzgerald's writings published in periodicals, see the Bibliography at the end of Arthur Mizener, *Tthe Far Side of Paradise* (Boston: Houghton Mifflin, 1951), and Henry Dan Piper, "F. Scott Fitzgerald: A Check-List," *The Princeton University Library Chronicle*, XII, no. 4 (summer 1951), pp. 196–208.

BIOGRAPHY AND CRITICISM

1. General

Aldridge, John W. *After the Lost Generation.* New York: McGraw-Hill, 1951.

Beach, Joseph W. *American Fiction, 1920–1940.* New York: Macmillan, 1941.

————. *The Twentieth Century Novel: Studies in Technique.* New York: The Century, 1932.

Bewley, Marius. *The Eccentric Design.* London: Chatto & Windus, 1958.

Bishop, John P. *The Collected Essays.* New York: Scribner's 1948.

Cargill, Oscar. *Intellectual America: Ideas on the March.* New York: Macmillan, 1941.

Chase, Richard. *The American Novel and Its Tradition.* New York: Doubleday, 1958.

Cowley, Malcolm. *Exile's Return.* New York: The Viking Press, 1951.

Fiedler, Leslie A. *An End to Innocence.* Boston: The Beacon Press, 1956.

————. *Love and Death in the American Novel.* New York: Criterion, 1960.

Frohock, Wilbur M. *The Novel of Violence in America: 1920–1950.* Dallas: The University Press, 1950.

Gardiner, Harold (ed.). *Fifty Years of the American Novel.* New York: Scribner's, 1952.

Geismar, Maxwell. *The Last of the Provincials.* Boston: Houghton Mifflin, 1947.

Hoffman, F. J. *The Modern Novel in America.* Chicago: Regnery, 1951.

————. *The Twenties,* New York: The Viking Press, 1955.

Hutchens, J. K. *The American Twenties.* Philadelphia: Lippincott, 1952.

James, Henry. *The Art of the Novel: Critical Prefaces.* New York: Scribner's, 1934.

————. *The Art of Fiction and Other Essays.* New York: Oxford Univ. Press, 1948.

Jones, Howard M. *The Bright Medusa.* Urbana: Univ. Illinois Press, 1952.

Kazin, Alfred. *On Native Grounds.* New York: Hitchcock, 1942.

Lombardo, Agostino. *Realismo e simbolismo.* Roma: Ed. di Storia e Letteratura, 1957.

————. *La Ricerca del vero.* Roma: Ed. di Storia e Letteratura, 1961.

Mizener, Arthur. *The Sense of Life in the Modern Novel.* Boston: Houghton Mifflin, 1964.

O'Connor, William V. *Forms of Modern Fiction.* Minneapolis: Univ. of Minnesota Press, 1948.

Rosati, Salvatore. *Narratori americani contemporanei.* Torino: E.R.I., 1959.

Snell, George D. *The Shapers of American Fiction, 1798–1947.* New York: Dutton, 1947.

Trilling, Lionel. *The Liberal Imagination.* New York: The Viking Press, 1950.

Van Doren, Carl. *Contemporary American Novelists, 1900–1920.* New York: Macmillan, 1940.

Wagenknecht, Edward C. *Cavalcade of the American Novel.* New York: Henry Holt, 1952.

West, Ray B. *The Short Story in America: 1900–1950.* Chicago: Regnery, 1952.

———— and Stallman, R. W. (ed.). *The Art of Modern Fiction.* New York: Reinhart, 1949.

Wilson, Edmund. *A Literary Chronicle 1920–1950.* New York: Doubleday, 1956.

Wright, Austin McGiffert. *The American Short Story in the Twenties.* Chicago: The Univ. of Chicago Press, 1961.

2.   On the Author: Books and Collections of Essays

Bruccoli, Matthew J. *The Composition of Tender Is the Night.* Pittsburgh: Univ. of Pittsburgh Press, 1963.

Bryer, Jackson R. *The Critical Reputation of F. S. Fitzgerald*. New Haven: Archon Books, 1967.

Cross, K. G. W. *S. Fitzgerald*. New York: Barnes and Noble, 1966.

Eble, Kenneth. *F. Scott Fitzgerald*. New York: Twayne Publishers, 1963.

Goldhurst, William. *Fitzgerald and His Contemporaries*. New York: World Publishing Co., 1963.

Graham, Sheilah. *College of One*. New York: Viking, 1967.

Graham, Sheilah and Frank, Gerold. *Beloved Infidel*. New York: Holt, 1958 (Book III).

Hoffman, Frederick J. (ed.). *The Great Gatsby: a Study*. New York: Scribner's, 1962. (Essays by: Edmund Wilson, "F.S.F."; Paul Rosenfeld, "F.S.F."; H. L. Mencken, from "The National Letters"; Joseph Conrad, "Preface to *The Nigger of the 'Narcissus'* "; F. M. Ford, from *Joseph Conrad: A Personal Remembrance*; Edmund Wilson, "The Delegate from Great Neck"; Leo Katcher, "The Man Who Fixed the Series"; F. S. Fitzgerald, "An Introduction to *The Great Gatsby*"; Glenway Wescott, "The Moral of F.S.F."; William Troy, "F.S.F.—the Authority of Failure"; Lionel Trilling, "F.S.F."; Edwin Fussell, "F.'s Brave New World"; Marius Bewley, "F.'s Criticism of America"; Thomas Hanzo, "The Theme and the Narrator of *The Great Gatsby*"; Richard Chase, "*The Great Gatsby*"; Gale H. Carrithers, Jr., "F.'s Triumph"; Henry Dan Piper, "The Religious Background of *The Great Gatsby*"; Letters and Material concerning *The Great Gatsby*.)

Kazin, Alfred (ed.). *F. Scott Fitzgerald. The Man and His Work*. New York: The World Publishing Co., 1951. (Essays by: Arthur Mizener, "F.S.F. 1896–1940"; J. P. Bishop, "F. at Princeton"; R.V.A.S., "*This Side of Paradise*"; Heywood Brown, "Paradise and Princeton"; Edmund Wilson, "The Delegate from Great Neck"; J. C. Mosher, "That Sad Young Man"; Paul Rosenfeld, "F. before *The Great Gatsby*"; Edmund Wilson, "F. before *The Great Gatsby*"; Maxwell Perkins, "A Letter on *The Great Gatsby*"; H. L. Mencken, "*The Great Gatsby*"; T. S. Eliot, "A Letter on *The Great Gatsby*"; John Chamberlain, "*Tender Is the Night*"; D. W. Harding, "Mechanisms of Misery"; C. H. Grattan, "*Tender Is the Night*"; T. S. Matthews, "*Taps at Reveille*"; Budd Schulberg, "F. in Hollywood"; Margaret Marshal, "On Rereading F."; Glenway Wescott, "The Moral of F.S.F."; S. V. Benèt, "*The Last Tycoon*"; Charles Weird, Jr., " 'An Invite with Gilded Edges' "; Malcolm Cowley, "Third Act and Epilogue"; John Dos Passos, "A Note on F.S.F."; Andrews Wanning, "F. and His Brethren"; Mark Schorer, "F.'s Tragic Sense"; Alfred Kazin, "An American Confession"; J. F. Powers, "Dealer in Diamonds and Rhinestones"; William Troy, "F.S.F.—the Authority of Failure"; Lionel Trilling, "F.S.F."; from *TLS*: "Power Without Glory"; Weller Embler, "F.S.F. and the Future".)

Lehan, Richard D. *Fitzgerald and the Craft of Fiction*. Carbondale: Southern Illinois Press, 1966.

Miller, James E., Jr. *The Fictional Technique of Scott Fitzgerald*. The Hague: Martinus Nijhoff, 1957.

————. *F. Scott Fitzgerald—His Art and His Technique*. New York: New York University Press, 1964.

Mizener, Arthur. *The Far Side of Paradise*. Boston: Houghton Mifflin, 1951.

———— (ed.). *F. Scott Fitzgerald: A Collection of Critical Essays*. Englewood Cliffs, N.J.: Prentice-Hall, 1963. (Essays by: Lionel Trilling, "F.S.F."; William Troy, "F.S.F.—the Authority of Failure"; Wright Morris, "The Function of Nostalgia"; John Aldridge, "The Horror and the Vision of Paradise"; Edwin Fussell, "F.'s Brave New World"; Andrews Wanning, "F. and His Brethren"; Malcolm Cowley, "Third Act and Epilogue"; Leslie Fiedler, "Some Notes on F."; Charles E. Shain, *"This Side of Paradise"*; Edmund Wilson, "F.S.F."; James E. Miller, "A Gesture of Indefinite Revolt"; D. O. Stewart, "The Courtship of Miles Standish"; J. H. Ralegh, *"The Great Gatsby"*; Tom Burnam, "A Reexamination of *The Great Gatsby*"; A. E. Dyson, *"The Great Gatsby:* Thirty-Six Years After"; Marius Bewley, "F.'s Criticism of America"; D. W. Harding, "The Mechanisms of Failure"; D. S. Savage, "The Significance of F.S.F."; Arthur Mizener, "The Maturity of F.S.F.".)

Modern Fiction Studies: Fitzgerald Special Number. VIII (spring 1961). (Essays by: John Kuehl, "F.'s Critical Opinions"; Donald A. Yates, "The Road to 'Paradise': F.'s Literary Apprenticeship"; R. F. McDonnell, "Eggs and Eyes in *The Great Gatsby*"; A. E. Dyson, *"The Great Gatsby:* Thirty-Six Years After"; M. J. Bruccoli, *"Tender Is the Night* and the Reviewers"; Eugene White, "The 'Intricate Destiny' of Dick Diver"; John E. Hart, "F.'s Last Tycoon: A Search for Identity"; Kent and Gretchen Kreuter, "The Moralism of the Later F."; M. Beebe and J. R. Bryer, "Criticism of F.: A Selected Checklist".)

Moseley, Edwin M. *F. S. Fitzgerald*. Grand Rapids: Eerdmans, 1967.

Pignata, Piero. *F. S. Fitzgerald*. Torino: Borla, 1967.

Piper, Henry Dan. *F. S. Fitzgerald: A Critical Portrait*. New York: Holt, Rinehart & Winston, 1965.

Shain, Charles E. *F. Scott Fitzgerald*. Minneapolis: Univ. of Minnesota Pamphlets, no. 15, 1961.

Sklar, Robert. *F. S. Fitzgerald: The Last Laocoön*. New York: Oxford University Press, 1967.

Turnbull, Andrew. *Scott Fitzgerald*. New York: Charles Scribner's, 1962.

Note: *Except for special cases, the single essays listed in this section do not appear in the following section.*

3.   On the Author: Separate Essays

Adams, J. D. "F. Scott Fitzgerald," *The American Mercury*, LXI, September 1945, pp. 373–77.

Adams, T. S. "A Noble Issue," *The Gifthorse* (Ohio State Univ.), 1949, pp. 35–43.

Aldridge, John W. "The Life of Gatsby," *Twelve Original Essays on Great American Novels*, ed. by Carl Shapiro. Wayne Univ. Press, 1958, pp. 210–37.

Berryman, John. "F. Scott Fitzgerald," *The Kenyon Review*, VIII, Winter 1946, pp. 103–12.

Bezanson, Walter. "S. Fitzgerald: Bedevilled Prince Charming," *The Young Rebel in American Literature*, ed. by Carl Bode. New York: Preager, 1960, pp. 79–94.

Bewley, Marius. "S. Fitzgerald's Criticism of America," *The Sewanee Review*, LXII, Spring 1954, pp. 223–46.

Bicknel, J. W. "The Waste Land of F. Scott Fitzgerald," *The Virginia Quarterly Review*, XXX, Fall 1954, pp. 556–72.

Burnham, Tom. "The Eyes of Dr. Eckleburg," in *College English*, XIV, October 1952, pp. 7–12.

Cowley, Malcolm. "F. S. Fitzgerald: The Romance of Money," *The Western Review*, XVII, Summer 1953, pp. 245–55.

D'Agostino, Nicola. "F. Scott Fitzgerald," *Studi Americani*, III, Roma, 1957, pp. 239–64.

Decter, Midge. "Fitzgerald at the End," *The Partisan Review*, XXVI, Spring 1959, pp. 303–12.

Friedman, Norman. "*Great Expectations* and *The Great Gatsby*," *Accent*, XIV, Fall 1954, pp. 246–64.

Friedrich, Otto. "F. S. Fitzgerald: Money, Money, Money," *The American Scholar*, XXIX, Summer 1960, pp. 392–405.

Frohock, W. M. "Morals, Manners and S. Fitzgerald," *The Southwest Review*, XL, Summer 1955, pp. 220–28.

Fussell, Edwin S. "Fitzgerald's Brave New World," *Journal of English Literary History*, XIX, December 1952, pp. 291–306.

Giles, Barbara. "The Dream of S. Fitzgerald," *Mainstream*, X, March 1957, pp. 1–12.

Greenleaf, Richard. "The Social Thinking of Scott Fitzgerald," *Science and Society*, XVI, Spring 1952, pp. 97–114.

Guidi, Augusto. "Fitzgerald e *The Great Gatsby*," *Occasioni Americane*, Roma: Ed. Moderne, 1958, pp. 74–85 (1954).

Gurke, Leo and Miriam. "The Essence of S. Fitzgerald," *College English*, V, April 1944, pp. 372–76.

Harvey, W. J. "Theme and Texture in *The Great Gatsby*," *English Studies*, XXXVIII, February 1957, pp. 12–20.

Hindus, Milton. "The Mysterious Eyes of Doctor T. J. Eckleburg," *Boston Univ. Studies in English*, III, Spring 1957, pp. 22–31.

Hoffman, F. H. "Edith Wharton and Scott Fitzgerald," *English Institute Essays*, 1949, New York: Columbia Univ. Press, 1950.

Holmes, Charles S. "Fitzgerald: The American Theme," *The Pacific Spectator*, VI, Spring 1952, pp. 243–52.

Kallich, Martin. "F. S. Fitzgerald: Money or Morals," *The Univ. of Kansas City Review*, XV, Summer 1949, pp. 271–80.

Kuehl, John. "S. Fitzgerald: Romantic and Realist," *Texas Studies in Literature and Language*, I, Fall 1959, pp. 412–26.

Leighton, Lawrence. "An Autopsy and a Description," *Hound and Horn*, V, Summer 1932, pp. 519–40.

Leslie, Shane. "Some Memoirs of F. S. Fitzgerald," *TLS*, October 31 and November 21, 1958.

Mackendrick, Paul. "*The Great Gatsby* and Trimalchio," *The Classical Journal*, XLV, April 1950, pp. 307–15.

Marquand, John P. "*This Side of Paradise*," *The Saturday Review*, XXXII, August 6, 1949, pp. 30–31.

Mizener, Arthur. "Fitzgerald and the Twenties," *The Partisan Review*, XVII, January 1950, pp. 7–38.

——. "The Portable Fitzgerald," *The Kenyon Review*, VIII, September 1946, pp. 343–44.

——. "Scott Fitzgerald and the Imaginative Possession of American Life," *The Sewanee Review*, LIV, January-March 1956, pp. 66–86.

——. "Scott Fitzgerald: Moralist of the Jazz Age," *Harper's Bazaar*, n. 2853, September 1946, pp. 174–78.

——. "The Novel of Manners in America," *The Kenyon Review*, XII, Winter 1950, pp. 1–20.

——. "The F. Scott Fitzgerald Papers," *The Princeton Univ. Library Chronicle*, XII, n. 4, Summer 1951, pp. 190–95.

——. "F. S. Fitzgerald's Tormented Paradise," *Life*, XXX, January 15, 1951, pp. 82–88, 91–98, 101.

——. "F. S. Fitzgerald: A Biography," *The Atlantic Monthly*, CLXXXVII, December 1950, pp. 68–79, January-February 1951, pp. 59–66 and pp. 72–80.

——. "*Gatsby*, 35 Years Later," *The N.Y. Times*, April 24, 1960, pp. 4, 46–47.

Morris, Wright. "The Ability to Function. A Reappraisal of Fitzgerald and Hemingway," *New World Writing*, n. 13. New York: New American Library, 1958, pp. 34–51.

Ornstein, Robert. "Fitzgerald's Fable of East and West," *College English*, XVIII, December 1956, pp. 139–43.

Piper, Henry Dan. "The Lost Decade," *Interim*, II, September 1945, pp. 39–44.

———. "Frank Norris and Scott Fitzgerald," *The Huntington Library Quarterly*, XIX, August 1956, pp. 394–400.

Pivano, Fernanda. Introduction to *Di qua dal Paradiso*. Milan: Mondadori, 1952, pp. 9–68.

———. Preface to *Gli ultimi fuochi [The Last Tycoon]*. Milan: Mondadori, 1959.

Ralegh, John H. "*The Great Gatsby*: Legendary Basis and Allegorical Significances," *The Univ. of Kansas City Review*, XXIV, October 1957, pp. 55–58.

Solomon, Eric. "A Source for *The Great Gatsby*," *Modern Languages Notes*, LXXXIII, March 1958, pp. 186–88.

Stallman, R. W. "Gatsby and the Hole in Time," *Modern Fiction Studies*, I, November 1955, pp. 2–16.

Stanton, Robert. "Symbol and Theme in *Tender Is the Night*," *Modern Fiction Studies*, IV, Summer 1958, pp. 136–42.

Steinberg, A. H. "Fitzgerald's Portrait of a Psychiatrist," *The Univ. of Kansas City Review*, XXI, March 1955, pp. 219–22.

Taylor, Douglas. "*The Great Gatsby*: Style and Myth," *The Univ. of Kansas City Review*, XX, Fall 1953, pp. 30–40.

Taylor, Dwight. "S. Fitzgerald in Hollywood," *Harper's Magazine*, n. 218, March 1959, pp. 67–71.

Thale, Jerome. "The Narrator as Hero," *Twentieth Century Literature*, III, July 1957, pp. 69–73.

Trilling, Lionel. Introduction to *The Great Gatsby*. New York: New Directions, 1945.

Wilson, Edmund. "Imaginary Conversations: Mr. V. W. Brooks and Mr. S. Fitzgerald," *The New Republic*, XXXIII, April 30, 1924, pp. 249–54.

Wilson, R. N. "Fitzgerald as Icarus," *The Antioch Review*, XVII, Winter 1957, pp. 481–92.

Zolla, Elémire. Preface to *L'età del Jazz [The Crack-up]*. Milan: Il Saggiatore, 1960.

For a complete list of articles and essays on F. Scott Fitzgerald, the reader is referred to Jackson R. Bryer, *The Critical Reputation of F. S. Fitzgerald* and to the quarterly lists on American authors in *American Literature*. Selected bibliographies are in most of the books or collections of essays listed above. *The Fitzgerald Newsletter*, ed. by Matthews J. Bruccoli (Columbus: Ohio State Univ. Press, 1958–67), nos. 1–40, is an invaluable source of information for matters related to Fitzgerald and carries in each number a running bibliography.

Index of Names

SELECTED ANN ARBOR PAPERBACKS

works of enduring merit

AA 1   **THE WRITER AND HIS CRAFT**   Roy W. Cowden, ed.
AA 2   **ELIZABETHAN PLAYS AND PLAYERS**   G. B. Harrison
AA 3   **THE INTELLECTUAL MILIEU OF JOHN DRYDEN**   Louis I. Bredvold
AA 6   **RICHARD CRASHAW**   Austin Warren
AA 11   **LITERATURE AND PSYCHOLOGY**   F. L. Lucas
AA 12   **THIS WAS A POET: EMILY DICKINSON**   George Frisbie Whicher
AA 16   **SHAKESPEARE AT WORK, 1592-1603**   G. B. Harrison
AA 26   **RONSARD: PRINCE OF POETS**   Morris Bishop
AA 32   **THE SONG OF ROLAND**   Translated by C. K. Scott Moncrieff
AA 33   **RAGE FOR ORDER**   Austin Warren
AA 36   **NEW BEARINGS IN ENGLISH POETRY**   F. R. Leavis
AA 40   **THE SUBLIME**   Samuel H. Monk
AA 43   **LITERATURE AND REVOLUTION**   Leon Trotsky
AA 46   **THE ART OF LITERATURE**   Arthur Schopenhauer
AA 58   **SEBASTOPOL**   Leo Tolstoi
AA 63   **POEMS FROM THE GREEK ANTHOLOGY**   Translated by Kenneth Rexroth
AA 64   **THE SATYRICON—PETRONIUS**   Translated by William Arrowsmith
AA 68   **AUBREY'S BRIEF LIVES**   John Aubrey
AA 70   **SCENES FROM THE BATHHOUSE And Other Stories of Communist Russia**   M. Zoshchenko
AA 81   **THE LOYALTIES OF ROBINSON JEFFERS**   Radcliffe Squires
AA 82   **MILTON'S KNOWLEDGE OF MUSIC**   Sigmund Spaeth
AA 85   **THE COMPLETE POETRY**   Catullus
AA 87   **THE CLOUD MESSENGER**   Kalidasa
AA 89   **THE INTERIOR DISTANCE**   Georges Poulet
AA 91   **THE BOW AND THE LYRE: The Art of Robert Browning**   Roma A. King, Jr.
AA 101   **CONTEMPORARY FRENCH POETRY**   Alexander Aspel and Donald Justice, ed.
AA 102   **TO THE YOUNG WRITER**   A. L. Bader, ed.
AA 113   **CHEKHOV AND OTHER ESSAYS**   Leon Shestov
AA 116   **GREEK ORATIONS**   W. Robert Connor, ed.
AA 117   **THE STORY OF THE ILIAD**   E. T. Owen
AA 125   **THE STRUCTURE OF COMPLEX WORDS**   William Empson
AA 128   **CAN THESE BONES LIVE**   Edward Dahlberg
AA 132   **PARADISE LOST AND THE SEVENTEENTH CENTURY READER**   B. Rajan
AA 134   **THE WIFE OF HIS YOUTH**   Charles W. Chesnutt
AA 135   **THE SKALDS**   Lee M. Hollander
AA 138   **ELIZABETHAN POETRY**   Hallett Smith
AA 140   **THE RECOGNITION OF EMILY DICKINSON**   Caesar R. Blake and Carlton F. Wells, eds.
AA 141   **SOUND AND FORM IN MODERN POETRY**   Harvey Gross
AA 142   **THE ART OF F. SCOTT FITZGERALD**   Sergio Perosa
AA 143   **THE ULYSSES THEME**   W. B. Stanford
AA 144   **SIR THOMAS BROWNE**   Frank Livingstone Huntley
AA 145   **THE MASTERPIECE**   Emile Zola

For a complete list of Ann Arbor Paperback titles write:
THE UNIVERSITY OF MICHIGAN PRESS / ANN ARBOR